Transformations

D0140892

Transformations

RECOLLECTIVE IMAGINATION AND SEXUAL DIFFERENCE

DRUCILLA CORNELL

ROUTLEDGE • NEW YORK AND LONDON

Published in 1993 by

Routledge
29 West 35th Street
New York, NY 10001

Published in Great Britain by

Routledge
11 New Fetter Lane
London EC4P 4EE

Copyright © 1993 by Routledge, Inc.

Printed in the United States of America on acid free paper.

All rights reserved. No part of this book may be reprinted or reproduced or utilized in any form or by any electronic, mechanical or other means, now known or hereafter invented, including photocopying and recording, or by an information storage or retrieval system, without permission in writing from the publishers.

Library of Congress Cataloging-in-Publication Data

Cornell, Drucilla.
    Transformations : recollective imagination and sexual difference / Drucilla Cornell.
      p. cm.
    Includes bibliographical references and index.
    ISBN 0-415-90746-2 (cl) — ISBN 0-415-90747-0 (pb)
      1. Feminist theory. 2. Feminist criticism. 3. Women—Legal status, laws, etc.   I. Title.
    HQ1190.C69   1993
    305.42'01—dc20   92-38226
                                            CIP

British Library Cataloguing-in-Publication Data also available.

To Ruthe Foster,
for blazing the trail
and
for Dylan Gwaltney,
for our shared world of Xhalia

Contents

Preface   ix

Introduction: The Subject of Transformation   1

1 "Convention" and Critique   12

2 Pragmatism, Recollective Imagination, and Transformative
   Legal Interpretation   23

3 "Disastrologies"   45

4 The Doubly-Prized World: Myth, Allegory, and
   the Feminine   57

5 Sexual Difference, the Feminine, and Equivalency   112

6 Sex-Discrimination Law and Equivalent Rights   147

7 Gender Hierarchy, Equality, and the Possibility
   of Democracy   156

8 What Takes Place in the Dark   170

Notes   195

Bibliography   225

Index   235

Preface

This book was finished during the year I spent at the Institute for Advanced Study at Princeton, New Jersey. I want to thank the Mellon Foundation and the American Council of Learned Societies for their support during my fellowship at the Institute. The Institute provided me with invaluable support for the completion of this book. In particular, I am grateful to Ruthe Foster for her tireless help in preparing and editing the manuscript.

The Monday and Thursday seminars with my colleagues at the Institute prodded me to rethink many of the issues in this book. Michael Walzer played an important role in helping me to clarify the significance of the insights of Continental philosophy for concrete feminist politics. Clifford Geertz provided me with a constant source of intellectual inspiration and stimulation; under his influence I came to understand the insights of anthropology in the context of contemporary questions about the relationship between race and gender. I owe him a profound debt of gratitude for our conversations, from which I learned so much. Joan Scott's intellectual engagement with and critique of the essays in this book were crucial to its completion. Her pathbreaking work in the history of gender has had a significant impact on my own formulation of sexual difference. Joan's support and friendship go beyond any words adequate to thank. I also want to thank Gwen Mikel and Rebecca French for leading me to indispensable anthropological texts and for their endless willingness to engage in conversation and respond to my novice questions about their field of anthropology.

One of the highlights of my year at Princeton was the intellectual engagement with Gananath Obeyesekere. His own analysis and critique of logocentrism crystalized for me the significance of the role of psychoanalysis in feminist theory. His lectures on the work of culture provided me with a new perspective on the relevance of psychoanalytically inspired anthropology in the articulation of how gender and race can only be grasped through an understanding of the role of the unconscious in social and political life.

In the last year, my discussions with Graciela Abelin-Sas continuously enriched and deepened my understanding of transformative possibility. I am grateful for her ceaseless support and encouragement of my own intellectual explorations of the question of feminine sexual difference. Her contribution has tangible expression in many of the essays in this book. As always, I must thank Jacques Derrida for his continuing friendship, loyalty, and intellectual inspiration.

As she has with each of my previous books, Deborah Garfield played a crucial role in shepherding the manuscript through to completion. Her persistent attention to details of source and style has certainly resulted in greater perfection than I could have achieved alone.

My research assistants, Leslie Berman and Sue Yi, students at Benjamin N. Cardozo School of Law, were of immeasurable help during the final stages of manuscript preparation, performing their tasks of reference and citation checking and copy editing the final text with good humor and in record time. Maureen MacGrogan's editorial support and friendship were once again essential in the completion of this manuscript.

Finally, I must thank Gregory DeFreitas for his enduring commitment . . .

The essays in this book have previously been published elsewhere and have been substantially revised for publication here. " 'Convention' and Critique" first appeared in *Cardozo Law Review*, vol. 7 (1986); "Pragmatism, Recollective Imagination, and Transformative Legal Interpretation" was originally published as "Institutionalization of Meaning, Recollective Imagination, and the Potential for Transformative Legal Interpretation," *University of Pennsylvania Law Review*, vol. 136 (1988); "Disastrologies" was prepared as a comment on David Krell's *Postponements* and appeared in *Praxis International*, vol. 9 (1989); a similar version of "The Doubly-Prized World: Myth, Allegory, and the Feminine" was published in *Cornell Law Review*, vol. 75 (1990); "Sexual Difference, the Feminine, and Equivalency," which was originally published with the title "Sexual Difference, the Feminine, and Equivalency: A Critique of Catharine MacKinnon's *Toward a Feminist Theory of the State*, first appeared in *Yale Law Journal*, vol. 100 (1991); an earlier version of "Sex-Discrimination Law and Equivalent Rights" was published in *Dissent*, vol. 38 (1991), and an expanded version was published as "Gender, Sex, and Equivalent Rights" in *Feminists Theorize the Political*, ed. Judith Butler and Joan Scott (New York: Routledge, Chapman and Hall, 1992); "Gender Hierarchy, Equality, and the Possibility of Democracy" was first written for *American Imago*, vol. 48 (1991); and "What Takes Place in the Dark," which was written during my tenure as a Visiting Scholar at the Institute for Advanced Study, also appears in *Differences*, vol. 4.2 (1992).

Since the topic of this book is transformation over time, I thought the dedication should reflect a remembrance of the women who set such strong examples for all of us, and in the hope for those women who will come after us that they will inherit a transformed world. As a result, this book is dedicated to Ruthe Foster, who was committed to feminism long before the second wave of feminism began, and to my niece, Dylan Gwaltney, who continually asks me to remember my own past, and the meaning of my commitment to feminism.

Introduction:
The Subject of Transformation

The essays collected in this book, each in its own way, address the relationship between two interpretations of the phrase "the subject of transformation." The first interpretation reflected in the title of this collection is that the subject of these essays is transformation. By transformation I mean change radical enough to so dramatically restructure any system—political, legal, or social—that the "identity" of the system is itself altered. The second meaning, defined as broadly as possible, turns us to the question of what kind of individuals we would have to become in order to open ourselves to new worlds. The relationship between the meanings of the subject of transformation is demanded by feminism. A feminist perspective focuses on precisely why we can only truly rethink performative possibility if we also confront what kind of subject could be open to the creation of new worlds.

I am contrasting transformation to evolution. In the first essay, " 'Convention' and Critique," this distinction can help us rethink the continuing validity of the separation of "radicals" from more liberal "reformers." For example, Stanley Fish, my interlocutor in " 'Convention' and Critique," recognizes that systems do change. For Fish, all there "is" are social systems. Systems transform themselves and we who are encompassed by systems are transformed with them. Thus, there is no "outside" observer to take note, either positively or negatively, of the desirability of the transformation. For Fish, systems, by definition, maintain their identity even as they evolve; we, as their products, necessarily remain identified with them. Even if a system can be different, there is, ultimately, no difference from the system. Thus, change, for Fish, can only be understood as evolution. This is why Fish argues that critique searing enough to engender the kind of transformation I envision is impossible. The "difference that makes a difference" between change understood as transformation and change reduced to evolution lies in the possibility implied in the word transformation. A system can so alter itself that it not only no longer confirms its identity, but disconfirms it and, indeed, through its very iterability, generates new meanings which can be further pursued and enhanced by the sociosymbolic practice of the political contestants within its milieu.

The second meaning I attribute to the phrase "the subject of transformation" inevitably relates to the first. Focusing on the nature of the individuals capable of opening themselves to new worlds, emphasizes the change required in individual lives, dreams, and aspirations to achieve the autonomy from convention purportedly necessary for critical consciousness and independent moral reasoning. The conception of the critical, moral self has been traditionally identified as the *subject*, as opposed to the actual, empirical individual. The foremost defender of the divide between the moral subject and the empirical self is Immanuel Kant. And the idea that we must strive for autonomy if we are to achieve a critical standpoint in either morality or law continues to play a crucial role in analytic liberal jurisprudence. The most famous example in our time is John Rawls's attempt to give body to the noumenal self or subject by having us engage in the hypothetical experiment of putting ourselves behind the veil of ignorance in order to be able to rationally assess the kind of society justice mandates.[1]

There have been a number of critiques of the traditional conception of the subject—indeed, these critiques are the very hallmark of what has come to be called "postmodernism"—two of which are central to the essays collected in this book.[2] First, there is the revived critique of the Kantian conception of the subject made by the new communitarians, and also forcefully articulated, if in a very different form, by thinkers identified as "postmodern." The new communitarians have argued that Kant's noumenal self or subject is a myth which, in the attempt to realize itself, rejects our interconnectedness and aspires to further separate the moral subject from our actual communities. Instead of embracing the myth of the noumenal self, the communitarians argue that we should cherish our identification with the already-established communities which make us who we are. The "truth" for the new communitarians is that the self is situated. This "truth" means that a certain brand of liberal "individualism" is rejected as false.

I perceive at least an implicit moral dimension in this critique. The commitment to the abstraction from the empirical individual not only violates who we actually are, it makes it difficult, if not impossible, for us to develop laws and other forms of social life that are "true" to the "truth" of the situated self.[3] Further, the communitarians' attempt to spell out the a priori conditions of either morality or justice that would be endorsed by the noumenal subject is condemned, because such an attempt masquerades as philosophy when all it really is is a fancy gloss on the political conventions of the community. For the communitarians, it is better that we face the "truth" about our rootedness in our communities because that recognition can at least help us understand that there is no unshakable foundation to our current political commitments and legal ideals. If these ideals are purportedly mandated by either justice or reason, then there would appear to be no legitimate basis for a political challenge to them.

The problem with the new communitarian critique of the Kantian subject is evidenced in the recent writing of Stanley Fish who, even though he would not refer to himself as a "new communitarian," adopts their understanding of the situated self. To anticipate my discussion in the first essay: Fish agrees with the communitarians that we are always already in a pregiven community which constitutes who we are. For Fish, there can be no distance between the community and the self. We *are* what the community has made us. Fish does not hesitate before the conclusions he believes follow from the insight: critique is impossible and radical transformation is the empty dream of impotent malcontents. Indeed, as he purportedly shows us in "Anti-Professionalism," even when we think we are acting against the standards of our community we are fooled, because we are really only taking our places in the roles allotted to us.[4] Thus, Fish rejects the moral and political aspiration behind the communitarian conception of the subject, while philosophically endorsing a view of the situated self that is similar to theirs. Fish's work is a classic example of how the two senses of transformation I have described are inevitably intertwined with one another. Fish's arguments about critique, the subject, and the possibility of transformation follow from his conception of the significance of a post-Wittgensteinian understanding of the philosophy of language. Perhaps, at least in the sense that it affects how we conceive of possibility and transformation, the philosophical theory endorsed by Fish does have consequences.

The second essay[5] addresses Charles Peirce's analysis of semiotics. Peirce grapples with the central insights of the philosophy of language and explains how innovation and transformation of our form of life and language game are not only possible, but are inevitable given the process by which signs come to signify our reality. Peirce anticipated the "postmodern" critique of the Kantian subject or noumenal self.

For Peirce, the subject can never be self-identical precisely because it is born into language as an other. Peirce also argues, contrary to Fish, that no form of life or language game can shut itself into a totality that would identify the subject completely with any system of shared norms and deny the possibility of transformative change. A slippage always inheres in the iterability of language that in turn, allows for the transmission of meaning over time and, therefore, for the maintenance of a form of life, including the life of the individual. As Judith Butler has explained, "What we might call 'agency' or 'freedom' or 'possibility,' is produced by gaps opened by the regulatory norms in the process of their self-repetition."[6] Peirce would have endorsed this conception of possibility. His unique conception of semiotics offers us a very different version of pragmatism; indeed, it is one clearly allied with "postmodern" social theory. This alliance remains as a challenge to thinkers such as Richard Rorty, who has recently pitted pragmatism against "postmodernism" and, more specifically, against deconstruction.[7]

Peirce also can play a more specific role in challenging the political conclusions drawn by the communitarians and by Fish from their shared insight into what they call the "situated self." Peirce's strength is rooted in his acceptance of the anti-individualist insight of the new communitarians that the self is constituted in a pregiven semiotic field, while still giving a unique account of possibility and explaining how individuals can become open to transformation and to the invitation to create new worlds. Peirce's understanding of the relationship between the individual's constitution within a pregiven semiotic field and the community's commitment to normative ideals that always demand not only interpretation but justification provides for a correct understanding of legal interpretation as what I call "recollective imagination."

The first two essays in this book, then, grapple with how one can and should conceive of the subject of transformation and the role of possibility within the context of the general insights provided by the post-Wittgenstein philosophy of language. The second set of essays in this volume examine how the gender hierarchy, which privileges the masculine and subordinates the feminine, must be addressed if we are to understand the subject of transformation, in both the senses I have discussed. I am arguing that even as we understand how gender hierarchy has imposed a barrier against open-ended democratic experiments, significant, radical social change in the direction of a participatory democracy is still "realistic" in a complex, modern industrial society. First, I argue that in order for women to achieve political, legal, and economic equality, we must dismantle the rigid structures of gender identity and the corresponding categorization of heterosexuality as normal adult sexuality. In both "The Doubly-Prized World"[8] and "Sexual Difference, the Feminine, and Equivalency,"[9] I argue, against Catharine MacKinnon, that such a challenge to the gender hierarchy and the conventional patriarchal, heterosexual organization of sexuality must also involve the affirmation of the feminine within sexual difference. I use the phrase "sexual difference" because gender, even if it operates as a system, divides us into male and female and, thus, is too limited a conception of our lives as sexuate beings. For example, gender does not adequately encompass lesbianism because it subsumes the lesbian under the category "Woman." Certainly, there are many kinds of lived sexuality that are already beyond this limited conception. I also use the phrase because it returns us to the issue of "sex" not as biological body parts, but as sexuality as sexuality is, in turn, central to conceptions of how radical social change can truly take place. Furthermore, I distinguish sexual difference from femininity, as the imposed social constructs that define our gender identity as women within patriarchy. My position is that without the affirmation of feminine sexual difference, we will unconsciously perpetuate the gender hierarchy under which the feminine is *necessarily* devalued. At first glance, it seems paradoxical that the challenge to the gender hierarchy demands the affirmation of the feminine, because that affirmation seems to promote the dichotomous theory it seeks to undermine. But that paradox can be resolved once we see how the repudiation of the feminine is part of the very "logic" of a patriarchical order.

A subsidiary issue which must be addressed and, as a result, becomes central to the argument in "The Doubly-Prized World"[10] is how to affirm the feminine within sexual difference without appealing to essentialist or naturalist theories of who we truly are as women. How, in other words, can we reconcile any appeal to the feminine within sexual difference with the "postmodern" philosophical critique of attempts to "objectively" describe women's nature which implicitly or explicitly reinforce the structures of imposed rigid gender identities. I will argue that we must reexamine the significance to feminism of "deconstruction," which I have renamed the "philosophy of the limit,"[11] to explain why the affirmation of the feminine within sexual difference need not involve an appeal to a self-identical female subject. The philosophy of the limit continually demonstrates the limit of any attempt to self-enclose and, thus, fully capture the "real," including the social reality of the gender hierarchy with its accepted conventions of masculinity and femininity. There is always more that can be written through metaphoric substitution and, particularly, as we will see in the last essay, "What Takes Place in the Dark,"[12] through metonymic displacement. The limit can and should be read as an opening to new meaning, including the dreams of a feminine imaginary which can never be completely foreclosed. This understanding of the limit, particularly in the context of sexual difference, relies on an interpretation of Jacques Derrida's "hymen."[13] Indeed, it is precisely because the feminine, as its lived, can never be reduced to its current definitions that I can advocate an ethical affirmation of the feminine within sexual difference. The philosophical positions which challenge traditional conceptions of identity, including gender identity, are not antithetical to my understanding of the ethical affirmation and thus, re-evaluation of the feminine within sexual difference. Indeed, they serve as its basis. The affirmation of the feminine within sexual difference operates within a performative contradiction that explicitly recognizes that the feminine is precisely what is denied the specificity of a "nature" or a "being" within the masculine symbolic. By recognizing the performative contradiction that we are affirming what is Other to the gender hierarchy and, therefore, *is not now a reality* I answer MacKinnon's charge that any celebration of women's difference only reinforces the oppression.

The political challenge to essentialism and naturalism is necessary if we are to recognize that an appeal to the generic Woman has erased the full significance of national and class differences among women. Such appeals to the generic Woman have been challenged for establishing the hegemony of white women's experience as the experience of all women. The result is that feminism stands accused of silencing women in the name of giving them a voice. Thus, if we are to be just to differences in women's lives, we must conceive of the feminine in a non-essentialist manner. The evocation of the feminine within sexual difference is consistent with the challenge to rigid gender identity and is crucial for an adequate feminist program of legal reform and transformation. We can see the practical feminist significance of the ethical affirmation of the feminine within sexual difference in my own reconstructive program of equivalent rights.

In "Sex-Discrimination Law and Equivalent Rights"[14] I present a program of equivalent rights, which I argue is necessary to translate the re-evaluation of feminine sexual difference into the legal sphere so as to respect rather than eradicate difference. This call for the recognition of equivalent rights must operate within the performative contradiction that the feminine within sexual difference cannot be equally valued in a legal system based on the masculine ideal of the juridical subject. Any attempt to appeal to femininity, as currently defined within the gender hierarchy, will recreate the equality/difference divide that my conception of equivalency seeks to challenge, because these definitions embody the projection of Woman as "not man" and, therefore, as not equal to man. The demand for the recognition of the specificity of the feminine within sexual difference cannot appeal to what exists, to some core of female being, but must, instead, evoke what *cannot* exist under our current conceptualization of the juridical subject through the masculine ideal. I provide a conception of equivalence which recognizes different "sexes" and divergent forms of lived sexuality without reinforcing the stereotypes of femininity and the normalcy of heterosexuality. Further, I justify this conception of equivalency through a revised version of Amartya Sen's understanding of "equality of well-being and capability."[15] Difference and equality only settle into opposing perspectives under conceptions of equality which privilege the right over the good.

A full program of equivalent rights is not only the legal translation of the affirmation of the feminine within sexual difference, it also provides a very different understanding of a feminist theory of the state and of legal transformation than the one offered by MacKinnon. MacKinnon's analysis of gender hierarchy cannot justify a radical revision of what she critiques as the negative theory of the state. On the other hand, a conception of equivalency that recognizes sexual difference, including the difference of lesbians and gay men, can provide the basis for a very different understanding of the state and the legal system. Not only do we need to rethink the conditions for legal transformation for women, we need to examine the way ideas of political change have been influenced by the assumption of the gender hierarchy.

Thus, I will argue that the challenge to the gender hierarchy is not only necessary for the "liberation" of women, it is also crucial for social transformation more generally. I develop the reasons why this is true through an exploration of the ways the myths of women remain with us and glamorize the tragic fate of women under patriarchy. For example, in "Disastrologies"[16] I explore how and why Friedrich Nietzsche's idealized women, the woman who lives outside of the morals of Christianity, must always end badly. I believe the work of Jacques Lacan can help us understand the psychoanalytic bases for the perpetuation of these myths.[17] Lacan offers us a non-naturalistic account of the perpetuation of gender hierarchy which, in turn, can be used to explain the restoration of patriarchy in spite of the innumerable historical movements to end the subordination of women.[18] He allows us to understand gender hierarchy as a system, a system which inevitably legitimates even the most violent forms of oppression of women by giving a seeming "reality" to fantasy projections of femininity.

Lacanian theory is necessary for an adequate understanding of how the projection of stereotypes of gender identity inform our dreams and fantasies, including our dreams of political change. In "Gender Hierarchy, Equality, and the Possibility of Democracy,"[19] I argue that Hannah Arendt, one of the most eloquent defenders of politics as crucial to the very definition of human life, fails to recognize how her understanding of human action and her account of the ancient Greek ideal of the *polis* perpetuate the gender hierarchy with its disparagement of everything identified as feminine. Arendt is only too well aware of the seeming conflict between her conception of politics and the nitty-gritty social reality of modern industrial society, which reduces politics to strategic action. She is pessimistic about realizing her own conception of politics in modernity, and, indeed, her work has been critiqued for its nostalgic longing for a world long since lost. I believe her pessimism should be reinterpreted. Her concepts remain enchained by the very gender hierarchy that blocks all attempts at meaningful change toward a participatory democracy. For example, even her ideal of politics rests on the gender hierarchy in which male-identified public action is glorified and the female, "private" realm of the household is disparaged as the province of need. Further, Arendt's division between the social and the political, a division which is crucial to her thinking, also expresses the privileging of the masculine and the repudiation of the feminine. Without challenging this division, we cannot adequately develop a program of equivalent rights, because such a program demands a recognition of the *social* conditions necessary for women's equality, including women's equality in the public sphere. Arendt's writing, then, is a classic example of how a conception of a transformed political order falters because it does not recognize the way in which it expresses the gender hierarchy.

Derrida conceptualizes democracy as civic friendship so as not to replicate the gender hierarchy in the way that Arendt does.[20] By so doing, he makes a significant contribution to how we can reformulate the idea of political life so that equality for women is not an empty dream or one achievable for only a handful of women who fashion their lives as men. Once we understand the centrality of the gender hierarchy to the restoration of patriarchal, nondemocratic, or only formally democratic social regimes, we can grasp why transformation in the lives of women is necessary if we are to achieve a true participatory democracy. For me, this insight is the truth in the radical feminist saying that the liberation of us all demands the liberation of women.

There is obviously an explicit assumption in the second group of essays that psychoanalysis, and especially the work of Lacan, is crucial for an understanding of the possibilities of political and legal transformation. There are at least two ways in which psychoanalysis is necessary for conceptions of political transformation. First, Lacan exposes the "naturalistic fallacy" behind attempts to justify gender hierarchy as the result of biology. Secondly, Lacan shows us why the gender hierarchy, with its rigid dictates of proper gender and sexual identity, is a cultural construct and, yet, continues to hold sway over both our political aspirations and our personal dreams. Indeed, gender is understood as a cultural imperative imposed by a system that perpetuates itself through our very ascent into what Lacan calls the order of the symbolic.

Once we understand the gender hierarchy as a cultural imperative within an established set of conventional norms, we can grasp why psychoanalysis can play a role in social and political critique and not just in individual self-reflection. Cultural imperatives cannot simply be relegated to the "private" realm of individual fantasy. In the example of Arendt, the unconscious reinstatement of the gender hierarchy profoundly influences her understanding of democracy and political action. Correspondingly, a deeper understanding of how gender influences our assumptions about democracy and legal transformation demands that we rethink and redefine some of our crucial political concepts such as power, equality, and, indeed, the very ideal of liberation itself.

I conclude that we can not adequately address the subject of transformation without confronting the constructed social fantasies that prod us to fear equality, particularly the equality of women and, thus, to restore the patriarchal order. In the last essay, "What Takes Place in the Dark,"[21] I explicitly turn to how the intersection of gender and race demands a psychoanalytic analysis if we are to understand how racism depends on social fantasies that are inseparable from the "coloration" of the projected fantasy figures of Woman. The Lacanian view of the unconscious can help us understand how "blackness" and "whiteness" gain significance within a psycho-sexual dynamic of desire that has historically made the horrifying oppression of African-American women seem the inevitable way of the world. Gender is always already engendered as "colored"; there is no woman first, "black" or "white" later. Psychoanalysis, in my own interpretation of Lacan, can undermine the very universality that has denied that "color" and "race" are constitutive of gender to the degree that we cannot pull "Woman" in her universal form out from underneath racism. I understand that this is an unusual usage of psychoanalysis, which all too often, and justifiably, stands accused of the kind of universalism which erases the difference of the Other, but it is a usage consistent with the psychoanalytic challenge to logocentrism implicit in the recognition of the central role of the unconscious. In "What Takes Place in the Dark" I connect the philosophical challenge to logocentrism with the political fight against both racism and imperialism.

There is a growing recognition within divergent philosophical positions that some account of human psychology must play a role in the development of conceptions of justice, law, and politics, precisely because psychology helps us to examine the question of what is inevitable in the sense of not being subject to change. This shared interest is called for by the need to respond to the oldest argument against radical transformation, which is that radical transformation in the direction of an egalitarian, participatory democracy is against human nature. But it should still seem surprising to enlist psychoanalysis in support of the possibility of transformation, particularly of gender identity. Historically, psychoanalysis has been critiqued for both reflecting and, worse yet, justifying the established patriarchal order. Given the ambiguous role of psychoanalysis, and particularly of Lacan's own theorizing on gender hierarchy, we need to recognize its importance but also expose its limits.

Lacan, in spite of his insight into the social construction of gender hierarchy, devotes his analysis to showing why the system of gender can not be dismantled because it is fundamentally connected to the "era the ego." Our identity as "men" and "women" for Lacan is frozen into the unconscious, if it is not the very basis for the language of the unconscious.

Jacques Derrida has exposed the contradictions within Lacan's analysis of how gender hierarchy is constructed through the symbolic, which, in turn, further promotes rigid gender identity because "men" and "women" enter the world of conventional meaning differently and because that world founds itself on the significance of the phallus. As we will see, Derrida undermines Lacan's political pessimism by showing us why the gender hierarchy, if it is constituted through language, can not protect itself against the slippage of meaning inherent in linguistic structures that, in turn, can not ground themselves in an accurately designated outside referent. Derrida shows us how gender identity can not be reduced to a description of its biological base. As a result, there can always be reinterpretations of gender identity. If such reinterpretations were not possible, we could not reaffirm the feminine within sexual difference other than as the imposed structures of femininity we associate with the patriarchal stereotypes of Woman.

Let me state again that the ethical affirmation of the feminine within sexual difference, *beyond accommodation* to current gender stereotypes, is only possible once we understand why and how rigid identity structures are constantly undermined by the very iterability that allows them to perpetuate their meaning. This ethical affirmation of the feminine within sexual difference does not rest on a "positive" description of Woman within gender hierarchy. My brand of feminism operates within the space kept open for rearticulation by the impossibility of a full account of Woman.

1

"Convention" and Critique

When we think of the world's future, we always mean the destination it will reach if it keeps going in the direction we can see it going in now; it does not occur to us that its path is not a straight line but a curve, constantly changing direction.

Ambition is the death of thought.

It's a good thing I don't allow myself to be influenced!

—Ludwig Wittgenstein[1]

There has been no more virulent antiprofessional than Ludwig Wittgenstein, nor a more searing and profound critic of the philosopher's search for stable forms, unities, and essences to secure us against the contingency, the errancy of language. In his later work, Wittgenstein completely rejected the idea that the goal of the philosophical investigation of language was to identify the form of the identity of words with the form of the entity.[2] The later Wittgenstein of *Philosophical Investigations* was in this sense "antiessentialist" to the core,[3] and argued against the early Wittgenstein of *Tractatus Logico-Philosophicus*.[4]

Yet, if Stanley Fish is right that "anti-professionalism is indefensible because it imagines a form of life—free, independent, acontextual—that cannot be lived,"[5] Wittgenstein's antiprofessionalism would seem to contradict Wittgenstein's own insight into the *sittlich* character of language and the situatedness of the individual subject in a pregiven language game or form of life. Was Wittgenstein actually espousing the ideology of professionalism in spite of his self-proclaimed distrust of it? The question, of course, becomes: Is Fish correct in his assertion that antiprofessionalism rests on a philosophically indefensible view of the subject, and of linguistic meaning?

I will argue, on the contrary, that in spite of Fish's careful recasting of the insights of the later Wittgenstein, Fish makes two mistakes that

Wittgenstein warned us against. First, by arguing that we are somehow enclosed in our form of life or professional context, Fish reintroduces the very idea of the determination of form that Wittgenstein rejected.[6] Fish himself critiqued the idea of determination of form in his earlier debates with Ronald Dworkin[7] and Owen Fiss.[8] In those debates, Fish took his two opponents to task for attempting to predetermine the range of reactivation and redefinition of language.[9] Fish did not deny constraint altogether, but only the attempt to render the constraints determinate, even if only through the metaphor of a "chain enterprise."[10] Unfortunately, as his essay "Anti-Professionalism" makes clear, Fish does not follow this insight to its conclusion. His suggestion that we are the prisoners of a rigidly bounded form of professional life reintroduces another version of the myth of the self-presence of form that Fish otherwise and persistently has urged us to reject.

Second, Fish slides from the recognition that linguistic meaning resides in a form of life to the mistaken conclusion that the preconscious acceptance of convention that makes discourse materially possible *necessarily* enters into the relevant language games and restricts it. Fish mistakenly concludes that the preconscious acceptance of convention that allows us to participate in our form of life forces an agreement among the participants as to the basic question of how to evaluate one's profession and set the standards it sets for professional life. "Critique," in the limited sense that Fish uses the word, is possible, precisely because we live in an open-ended language game in which disagreement is perfectly comprehensible.

The move, within a language game, "I think my colleagues are mistaken when they let their need for tenure influence their choice of research topics" is perfectly coherent. Critique, even as it rises to the level of antiprofessionalism, does not necessarily coincide with the belief in essences or a form of true meaning.

Ironically, to deny critique is to deny that there is a social reality, a horizon which encloses us and liberates us, enabling us to disagree as much as it enables us to agree. The very line between critique and convention is itself blurred. As Wittgenstein reminds us, when we appeal to communitarian standards in order to make sense, we cannot also delimit the entire repertoire of community standards.[11] Fish implicitly recognizes the shifting values in English departments that now allow for the acceptance of doctoral theses on detective novels. He does not, however, appreciate the wider implications of his own insight: To conceptualize the constraints of professionalism is to once again render them determinate.

Both of these mistakes have implications for Fish's critique of the subject. Fish argues that the very idea of the critique of professionalism demands a transcendental subject, "a self or knowing consciousness that is under the sway of no partial vision, and is therefore free (in a very strong sense) first to identify and then to embrace the truth to which a disinterested knowledge inescapably points."[12] I will argue, to the contrary, that the linguistic-philosophic critique of the constitutive subject does not erase the subject without a trace, but forces us to think about the subject, including the self-reflective subject, differently. It makes perfect sense within our form of life to say with Wittgenstein: "It's a good thing I don't allow myself to be influenced!"[13]

One caveat: When I speak of critique I am using the word in the very mundane sense—I am merely arguing that standards used to critique professional life need not replicate the ideology of professionalism. I am not, in this essay, addressing the fundamental question of whether it is possible to critique our philosophical cultural tradition: what Jacques Derrida has called phallogocentrism[14] or Theodor Adorno calls identity-logical thinking.[15] As we will see in the later essays included in this volume, I agree with both Derrida and Adorno that ultimately the practice of critique leads us to confront phallogocentrism. Wittgensteinian "therapy" cannot solve all of our problems precisely because Wittgenstein refused to recognize the full significance of the Other to established systems of meaning, such as the unconscious. However, such "therapy" can provide us with an answer to Fish. Therefore, I avoid the question of whether or how one can move beyond phallologocentrism or identity-logical thinking in this essay not because I think the question is ultimately irrelevant to the issues raised by Fish, but because Fish is not grappling with critique at that level. Fish would dismiss Adorno's and Derrida's insistence on the Other to established forms of life as more of the same bad metaphysics that both thinkers purportedly deconstruct.

Nihilism, for Fish, is another symptom of bad metaphysics; it is the flip side of the foundationalism he attacks in his essay. As I have already suggested, Fish's contribution to the debates on objectivity in interpretation can best be understood as a recasting of the insight of the later Wittgenstein. Fish repeatedly emphasizes the *sittlich* character of linguistic meaning.[16] When one grasps the *sittlich* character of language correctly, the very subjectivism that troubles Dworkin and Fiss vanishes as an illusion. As Fish explained,

> The point is one that I have made before: it is neither the case that interpretation is constrained by what is obviously and unproblemati-

cally "there," nor the case that interpreters, in the absence of such constraints, are free to read into a text whatever they like. . . . Interpreters are constrained by their tacit awareness of what is possible and not possible to do, what is and is not a reasonable thing to say, and what will and will not be heard as evidence, in a given enterprise; and it is within those same constraints that they see and bring others to see the shape of the documents to whose interpretation they are committed.[17]

Yet Fish also understands that the constraints that enable meaning cannot be made determinate, foreclosing the reactivation of definition. We cannot pin down the meaning of a word once and for all, precisely because of the *sittlich* character of language. Derrida has brilliantly shown how the iterability of language implies both sameness and difference. Words as signs are iterable or repeatable by any general user. Derrida accepts Wittgenstein's demonstration of the self-contradictory nature of the idea of a private language. Language communicates because it is public—given meaning within the relevant group of inquirers. The repertoire of community standards is thus independent of any particular empirical subject. The very intersubjective character of language allows for both understanding and communication and for misunderstanding and reactivation of the range of definition.

Described in this way, the intersubjectivity of language—its capacity to function as a vehicle for the repetition of the same by different subjects—is, ironically, at the same time its capacity to be torn away by reader or hearer from what it meant to its issuer, so that it continues to mean something, but not *identically* what it meant to its writer or utterer. Thus, the very *sittlich* character of meaning keeps it from being fully saturated by any particular context. The boundaries of context are always shifting: There is no ideal self-sameness which guarantees exact repetition of meaning.

To deny this is not to reject the *sittlich* character of linguistic meaning nor to argue for unlimited freedom in interpretation. As Wittgenstein wrote, "The wall always has *some determinate (Bestimmte)* degree of elasticity—whether I know it or not."[18] Our immersion in a horizon of historical understanding does constrain us, but it cannot absolutely enforce agreement on the basic questions of life. The attempt to exhaustively determine the form of the constraints fails. The contextual nature of meaning requires that possible new meanings inhere in the very commonness of language. Wittgenstein's (and Derrida's) critique is aimed at the principle of identity, not at the possibility of contextual meaning. To quote Wittgenstein:

"A thing is identical with itself."—There is no finer example of a useless proposition, which yet is connected with a certain play of the imagination. It is as if in imagination we put a thing into its own shape and saw that it fitted.

We might also say: "Every think fits into itself." . . . At the same time we look at a thing and imagine that there was a blank left for it, and that now it fits into it exactly.

Does this spot [*] "fit" into its white surrounding?—*But that is just how it would look* if there had at first been a hole in its place and it then fitted into the hole. . . .

"Every coloured patch fits exactly into its surrounding" is a rather specialized form of the law of identity.[19]

Wittgenstein recognized the contextual nature of meaning but opposed the attempt to rigidly circumscribe it, to render any context a self-identical form. *In other words, meaning is revealed in context but not absolutely determined by it.* Because meaning is not determined by context, disagreement, critique, and the generation of new meanings are always possible.

Fish seemingly understood this difference in his debate with Dworkin. Fish rejected Dworkin's attempt to explicate the determination of the constraints on interpretation through the metaphor or example of a group novel.[20] Fish's central point was that each new writer in the chain can potentially reactivate the range of definition and by so doing shift the understanding of "what direction has already been taken."[21] Dworkin wanted to cement the boundaries and thereby delimit the enterprise as the later writers in the chain come to a project whose form has become ever more clearly delineated. Fish, in response, showed us that the boundaries of the form of the project need not necessarily hold and can always yield to a different interpretation. Context is not just *there*; it must be confirmed or disconfirmed, over and over again. The appeal to the context of the already-developed novel does not provide us with security against innovation and critique.

For all of his insight into Dworkin's failed attempt to define boundaries, Fish himself now falls into the very trap he warns against. In his essay, professional practice becomes a bounded form of life from which escape can only be envisioned by a transcendental consciousness. Fish, of course, denies that such a consciousness exists. As Fish explains, anti-professionalism underwrites a self that is able to see through the mystification of "rhetoric" and achieve an independent clarity of vision; a truth that is perspicuous independently of argument, and which argument tends only to obscure; and a society where pure merit is recognized and the invidious rankings imposed by institutional hierarchies are no more.[22]

And why, according to Fish, must antiprofessionalism appeal to a "transcendental subject" or an "essentialist" view of linguistic meaning? For Fish the inevitable immersion of the individual in her profession is "merely a recognition of the fact that needs and values do not exist independently of socially organized activities but emerge simultaneously with the institutional and conventional structures within which they are intelligible.[23] But Fish's conclusion does not follow from his premises: If our form of life, professional or otherwise, is inevitably unbounded, if there is no context of all contexts to complete experience, then our immersion in socially structured activities does not lead us to conclude that we are helplessly imprisoned in them. The certainties of professional life are only too like the other supposed certainties of life. They can be challenged. As Wittgenstein reminded us in *On Certainty*, logically even the most obvious, mundane perceptions may be thrown into doubt. As he wrote sitting in his room in England,

> Would it not be possible that people came into my room and all declared [that I am not in England]?—even gave me "proofs" of it, so that I suddenly stood there like a madman alone among people who were all normal. . . . Might I not then suffer doubts about what at present seems at the furthest remove from doubt? . . . [M]ight I not be shaken if things such as I don't dream of at present were to happen?[24]

Our certainties are not so firmly anchored that we cannot touch them, nor are our language games ossified into a substratum that completely blocks the formation of new ways of being in the world. Fish directs his fire at Duncan Kennedy and Robert Gordon, two "antiprofessionals," yet, what more are they really asking of us than that we question the certainties of legal education and envision a legal world composed of things which we don't dream of at the present? It is perfectly consistent for Gordon both to recognize that "the legal forms we use set limits on what we can imagine as practical options: Our desires and plans tend to be shaped out of the limited stock of forms available to us,"[25] and yet still to insist that "the institutional space that defines . . . the present shape of things"[26] can be challenged, precisely because the present shape of things is not a rigidly bounded form. Fish's basic mistake (one that Wittgenstein warned us against) is to confuse the assemblage of accepted uses and practices that constitute a form of life—the preconscious quasi-fact which precedes all intentionality and subjectivity—with an enforced agreement between subjects to which language predestines us and from which we cannot escape.[27] The unbounded world of instituted meaning allows us to disagree as well as to agree, to rebel as well as to conform.

Albrecht Wellmer explains the agreement that makes discourse materially possible:

> This given mutuality of a linguistically disclosed world can be interpreted as an agreement in language; only we ought not to think here of "conventions" or of consensus which would be either rational or irrational. The agreement in question is rather constitutive for the possibility of distinguishing between true and false, rational or irrational. . . .[28]

Or as Wittgenstein himself has put it: " 'So you are saying that human agreement decides what is true and what is false?'—It is what human beings *say* that is true and false; and they agree in the *language* they use. That is not agreement in opinions but in form of life.[29] Wittgenstein is not a conventionalist but a challenger to the realist/conventionalist divide. If my niece mistakes a green ball for a red ball I do not say to her, "No dear, the majority of the speakers in our form of life think of that color as green." I simply say—with tact, I like to think—"No, you are wrong. That is a green ball."

The agreement of a form of life need not exclude the possibility of dissent and critique. The individual does not passively find herself in a form of life; she is a participant in it.

> At the moment when the individual gets the idea of the language game—of language as a system of practices in which he participates—the expressive relation between himself and his community becomes problematic. The knowledge that words are also deeds introduces the logical possibility of asking: do the available words represent deeds of a kind that I can perform without shame? . . . The philosophical exercise which brings our commitment to consciousness, compels us, as Stanley Cavell points out, to pass a rational judgement on those commitments, and so to either reaffirm or renounce them.[30]

We are not fated to agree or to act out our social and professional roles like automatons simply because we are immersed in a linguistically constituted horizon. Of course, Fish is right to suggest that there is a pull to the acceptance of constraint in a shared socializing process, professional or otherwise. But what Fish locates is just that, a pull.

Alienation from one's chosen profession or educational background is very much a part of our social reality. Whether or not the critic will be reduced to a role as ironic observer or will instead be hailed as a pioneer for a new way of being in the world depends in part on whether the critical vision takes hold in the form of life. As Wittgenstein reminds us, "If someone is merely ahead of his time, it will catch him up one day."[31]

Yet doesn't my very use of the word automaton imply the idea of a "free, acontextual subject," the view of the subject that Fish critiques? Is Fish correct that the linguistic-philosophic critique of the subject ends by completely undermining critical self-reflection? And indeed, of what exactly does the linguistic-philosophic critique consist? Fish never tells us.

Albrecht Wellmer has succinctly described the Wittgensteinian critique of the intentional, constitutive subject:

> Here it is a question of the philosophical destruction of rationalistic conceptions of the subject and of language; in particular the destruction of the idea that the subject with its experiences and intentions is the source of linguistic meanings. In its place we could speak in Wittgenstein's sense of a critique of the "name theory" of meaning: this theory says that linguistic signs obtain meaning when somebody, a user of signs, allocates a sign to something given—things, classes of things, experiences, classes of experiences, etc., that is, allocates a name to a somehow "given" meaning. . . . Language philosophy's critique of rationalist language theory naturally does not begin with Wittgenstein and it does not end with him; but in a certain sense Wittgenstein was in my opinion its most important exponent in our century. Wittgenstein's philosophizing incorporates a new form of skepticism which calls into question even the certainties of Hume or Descartes; Wittgenstein's skeptical question is "How can I know what I am talking about? How can I know what I mean?" Language philosophy's critique destroys the subject as author and as final judge of his meaning intentions.[32]

Wellmer precisely locates the view of the subject undermined by the Wittgensteinian critique of the name theory of meaning. The very commonness of language renders language essentially independent of an individual's intention to give it meaning. The subject immersed in an already-embodied social reality cannot achieve the self-transparency necessary to keep intent pure. Language is the *Other* to the individual; not her own expression.

But does this mean that critique is an impossibility? Is the subject simply erased or instead reduced to a structural resistance, to an irreducible heterogeneity? Ironically, the very linguistic-philosophic critique of the subject to which Fish appeals turns against his own argument. To be an "I" does have meaning in our form of life. Given the formal recognition of the "I" as distinct from a social role within the legal system (and within other social institutions), the individual becomes an aspect of social reality which cannot so easily be erased. The abstract negation of the "I" denies what it purportedly affirms: the embodiment of social reality in and through language. No one understood the *sittlich* character of social and political life better than Hegel. Yet, for Hegel, the unique aspect of modernity as a form of life is precisely the institutional recognition of the subject separate from social role. The individual who insists that she is something more than the professional role in which she is engaged is not simply asserting with one of the proud traditions of Western democratic revolutions. The move within a language game ("I am right and everyone else is wrong") is perfectly coherent in our form of life. Nor is the assertion that I am right merely the assertion of my opinion.

> The belief that "I am right and everyone else is wrong" prefigures, through its explicit realism, a condition in which others will have come to share my own current practice with regard to the application of normative concepts—to share, in other words, my own values and beliefs. A world in which that condition obtained would be one where "reality" in the positive sense (i.e. that which is fixed by the content of the propositions in the consensual world-view) had come to coalesce with "reality" in the critical sense (i.e. that which is fixed by the content of the totality of propositions that *I* hold true).[33]

We must confirm our agreement or our disagreement with established communitarian values, including the values perpetuated in our profession. A form of life is not a straitjacket that binds our thoughts, unless one reasserts the idea of form as a self-contained identity, the very idea of identity that Wittgenstein deconstructs. We are part of the story we tell, including the story of what it means to be a "professional."

Furthermore, the very assertion that critique is foreclosed by an all-encompassing context, demands an appeal to a stand beyond context that Fish himself denies as an impossibility. Derrida has repeatedly shown us that the structuralist attempt to reduce the subject to contextuality fails.[34] Derrida himself usually speaks of this failure as the effects of subjectivity due to his awareness that the very idea of the subject is bound up with an exclusionary conception of Man. As we will see throughout the rest of these essays, I agree with his philosophical deconstruction of the identification of subject with "Man."

Derrida does not mean by the phrase "the effects of subjectivity" that there is no subjectivity or that subjectivity can be reduced to an effect, in the sense of something objectified "out there." To positively define the "I", as an effect, or even as a site or locale, is to objectify the "I" in accordance with the traditional discourse of the subject which reinstates a subject/object dichotomy with the twist that "I" now becomes an object. This is a reversal that does not truly shift the boundaries of the discourse of the subject. We can call the "I" a "who" rather than a "what" to avoid the objectifying language that reduces the "I" to "a place," an exteriority through which competing constructions of "it" are received or resisted. To reduce the "I" to a "what" denies the full burden of responsibility imposed upon an "I" *who* generates effects and by so doing affects others precisely as a singular "who." The problem with the objectifying language is that it confuses the recognition that the "I" is necessarily extroverted and, therefore, can only be "known" in its exposure to otherness with the reduction of the "I" to a kind of substance, if this time a substance molded by "its" context. Some*one* is only as she is exposed and yet there remains some*one*. Fish's conception of the self is perhaps the most extreme expression of the objectifying tendency that inheres in the abstract negation of the subject. The "I" for Fish is only as it is objectified in its external roles. I will deepen my own analysis of how the "I" becomes indentifiable as a unique someone over time in the next essay when I discuss the relationship between agency, innovative capability, and recollective imagination.

For now I want to stress that if we take seriously the linguistic-philosophic critique of mentalism that Fish endorses, we are not forced to forget the subject, but to think about the subject differently. Fish is right to argue that the Wittgensteinian critique of the name theory of meaning deconstructs subjectivism through the uncovering of the linguistically constituted social reality which precedes all intentionality and subjectivity. But we are not left with a world without selves. Our world, our linguistically disclosed social reality, is rather a world in which "the individual who was constituted by historical and cultural forces [is able] to 'see through' those forces and thus stand to the side of his own convictions and beliefs."[35]

One of those ways of being within a professional environment is to rebel against an unnecessarily limiting way of seeing and experiencing law and lawyering, which can separate lawyers (as well as the other actors in the legal system) from their sense of responsibility to their own values, to argue that there are values that are more important than a successful climb in the law school hierarchy. It is not that acting or playing a part is an inferior form of behavior; it is instead a question of what part one plays. To argue that we are immersed in an already-constituted form of life does not negate our responsibility to it or our rebellion against it. Our form of life may have an alienating, theatrical quality; but we are still the actors and actresses. The antiprofessionals, whom Fish attacks, call on us to question our certainties and to dream again about a different way to pursue our endeavors, whether as law professor, lawyer, or literary critic. And why not dream, and dream again, even if, as Wittgenstein reminds us, "a man's dreams are virtually never realized,"[36] (let alone a woman's). The dream of a different way of being may only be timorous at first. Yet, as Adorno has beautifully written,

> [n]o sunrise, even in mountains, is pompous, triumphal, imperial; each one is faint and timorous, like a hope that all may yet be well, and it is this very unobtrusiveness of the mightiest light that is moving and overpowering.[37]

2

Pragmatism, Recollective Imagination, and Transformative Legal Interpretation

Introduction

This essay explores my understanding of legal interpretation as "recollective imagination." Such a project demands the rethinking of the relationship between the *past*, embodied in the normative conventions which are passed down through legal precedent, and the projection of *future* ideals through which the community seeks to regulate itself. A subsidiary goal of this essay is to redefine pragmatism with a focus on the work of Charles Peirce. Throughout this essay, I will show the relevance of Peirce's conception of pragmatism to my own understanding of legal interpretation as recollective imagination.

Peirce's unique conceptualization of the relationship between the retrospective and prospective aspects of legal interpretation allows him to highlight the importance of the imagination in the enunciation of legal and normative ideals. Therefore, his work helps us to rethink how we should conceive of legal interpretation. It also helps us determine exactly how Critical Legal Studies has contributed to the debate over how we should think about legal interpretation. Peirce can also help us in developing a conception of agency that is consistent with the active role of the judge engaged in the process of what I am calling legal interpretation as recollective imagination. Peirce offers us a convincing account of how we as lawyers, law professors, and judges come to be open to the invitation to create new worlds.

Pragmatism has been adopted by legal scholars, but Peirce's voice has, unfortunately, not been heard. The result is that many neopragmatists reduce the process of interpretation to the evolution of convention or to the strategic overhaul of the legal system in the form of an external future ideal. In *Law's Empire*, Ronald Dworkin has critiqued this version of pragmatism.[1]

According to Dworkin, the pragmatist supposes that members of a community treat their association as only a de facto accident of history and geography. Pragmatism thus ignores the past in favor of visions of the future. The pragmatist does not simply deny principles and rights; rather, she refers to them only as they are strategically useful for the actualization of her own ideal community. Allegiance to her present community is not required if it fails to meet her ideal. She just happens to be a member of this community and no other and nothing follows from that coincidence. For Dworkin, pragmatism requires that judges only look to what they think would be the best future for their community when they ponder a legal decision. Therefore, the pragmatist who operates within our common-law system, with its emphasis on precedent, is a liar, for she appeals to precedent not in the name of the principles it enunciates, but in the name of her own vision. Legal pragmatism, for Dworkin, leaves us with the worst kind of subjectivism in interpretation as each judge attempts to willfully impose her best vision of the future.

My argument in this essay is that Peirce's brand of pragmatism *does* turn us to the future in a very specific sense of the word, but that such a turn does not reduce rights and legal decisions to strategic instruments being manipulated in an attempt to build the best possible community. Indeed, I will suggest that Peirce's understanding of semiotics may well provide the best framework for understanding the seemingly paradoxical role of temporality in legal interpretation. I believe the phrase "recollective imagination" captures that seeming paradox.

The Truth of Indeterminancy and the Process of Recollective Imagination

What Exactly Is the Indeterminacy Thesis

Perhaps no phrase has been more misunderstood by legal scholars than the "indeterminacy thesis" developed by the Conference of Critical Legal Studies.[2] The "indeterminacy thesis," as it has been interpreted by its critics—and sometimes, if rarely, by its proponents—is taken to mean that the critique of the logic of identity, which reflects the idea that there is a self-enclosed form of life to which we can appeal in order to cement meaning, leads us to conclude that there are no shared standards of communicability.[3] But this is a mistaken interpretation of indeterminacy. The concept of indeterminacy is meant to indicate that we do not question by gazing down on institutionalized standards of communicability from a transcendental viewpoint; rather, we question from within our shared context. Yet, as we question, we also inevitably affirm meaning as the "basis" for our understanding of the process of questioning itself. Charles Peirce explained that we can only begin questioning from within a given linguistic context with established interpretations of signs.[4]

Peirce studied more carefully than anyone the institutionalization and internalization of meaning as the habitual structures of thought we take for granted as our representational schema. Yet, Peirce was one of the first thinkers to insist on the "indeterminacy" of any linguistic or semiotic field. If indeterminacy is not the outright denial of shared standards of intelligibility, then what exactly is the "truth" of indeterminacy?

To answer this question, we must explore the truth of indeterminacy on several different levels. For Peirce, the notion that the truth of all reality lies in the realized whole is the central mistake of Hegel's absolute idealism. In the language of semiotics, reality cannot be reduced to the objective norms of our collective ethics, what Hegel called *Sittlichkeit*, or, for that matter, ever be fully captured by a system of signs. The "real," in other words, cannot be reduced to the ideal. There is always an excess that disrupts the full identity of the sign with its object. Peirce explains this as follows: A sign is always in referential relation to some other sign or interpretant. Signs are never simply self-referential or mere representations of an object. In this sense, there can be no full determinacy of any institutionalized system of meaning, including the legal system, because the sign itself always points us to another sign beyond the repetition implicit in self-reference or direct reference to the designated object. As long as the sign is determined in a relation to another sign, there can be no closure of the process of interpretation in the discovery of the truth of the actual. The otherness of thought to being inheres in the insight that we think only within a semiotic field in which reference always involves an appeal to another sign and not directly to the object that it represents. There is a diachronic moment inevitable in any semiotic system which disrupts the full reconciliation of meaning and ethical truth of being. This is what allows Hegel to recollect the past as the reality of the present. The beyond to the system is "there" in the diachrony, which prevents self-enclosure. On one level, then, the "indeterminacy thesis" is the recognition of the otherness to the Hegelian Concept that disrupts totality and opens the chasm between meaning and being. This is also what Peirce has called "Secondness."[5]

The Peircean Critique of Absolute Idealism

The category of Secondness is the key to understanding Peirce's break with Hegel's absolute idealism. Secondness is the real that resists, or what Peirce himself has called the "Outward Clash."[6] Secondness is that against which we struggle and which demands our attention to what is outside ourselves and our representational schema. Peirce's category, Secondness, indicates the "mutual action between two things regardless of any sort of third or medium, and in particular regardless of any law of action."[7] Secondness is dualistic precisely because it involves struggle. The irreducible exteriority of what Adorno called the "suffering physical" is an example of what Peirce would have called Secondness.[8]

To justify his category of Secondness, Peirce does not need to deny the mediation of all human *knowledge* of reality. Secondness is what remains, that which cannot be fully captured by any system of signs. It is, as I noted in the first essay in this book,[9] the Other or the limit to symbolization that is missed by Wittgenstein. Secondness reminds us that there is an irreducible otherness that remains "beyond" to all systems of conscious meaning. For Peirce, all knowledge of reality, on the other hand, is triadic. Human knowledge is enfolded in the habits, rules, signs, and modes of conduct that Peirce designates as thirds.[10]

Thirdness is the category usually associated with Hegel's *Sittlichkeit*, except that the time frame of Peirce's Thirdness turns us toward the future (in a very specific sense) rather than toward the past of what has been actualized. As Peirce explains, "[N]o matter how far specification has gone, it can be carried further; and the general condition covers all that incompletable possibility."[11]

Peirce often used the example of law to demonstrate the significance for interpretation of his category of Thirdness. His example of "giving" demonstrates the triadic structure of Thirdness:

> A *gives* B to C. This does not consist in A's throwing B away and its accidentally hitting C. . . . If that were all, it would not be a genuine triadic relation, but merely one dyadic relation followed by another. There need be no motion of the thing given. Giving is a

transfer of the right of property. Now right is a matter of law, and
law is a matter of thought and meaning.[12]

The condition of generality, or "lawlikeness," pervades all thirds.
The openness to the future inherent in Thirdness yields an essential
indeterminacy that cannot ultimately be theoretically, or even practi-
cally, overcome.

For Peirce, human conduct, precisely because it is general and habitual and embodied in thirds, includes "would be's"[13] and, thus, a future
potential that cannot be reduced to repetition of the past.[14] The very
habitual structure of *sittlich* commitments leaves the habitual "structures" open-ended. To argue, then, that we are immersed in an already-
given historical reality of understanding is not to turn that reality into
a prison which bars us from innovation, for the exact opposite is the
case.

We can now use Peirce's understanding of the essential indeterminacy of Thirdness to uncover the fundamental mistake inherent in
Stanley Fish's "internal realism." Peirce argues that Hegel's central
mistake was to reject the indeterminate possibilities inherent in a concept of the future as undetermined by the past of what has already been
actualized. Fish makes the same mistake by reducing the conditional
generality of Thirdness to a finite set of past and present regularities
that replicate themselves in and through institutional structures.

It is still correct to argue that our habits are encased in the storehouse
of knowledge, which includes the accepted generalities and regularities
that make conduct *sensible*. Even if the conditional generalities of
conduct cannot be reduced to any given set of past regularities, they
are still dependent on them to the degree that they arise out of them.
As Peirce explains,

> How, then, does the Past bear upon conduct? The answer is self-
> evident: whenever we set out to do anything, we "go upon," we
> base our conduct on facts already known, and for these we can only
> draw upon our memory. It is true that we may institute a new
> investigation for the purpose; but its discoveries will only become
> applicable to conduct after they have been made and reduced to a
> memorial maxim. In short, the Past is the storehouse of all our
> knowledge.[15]

Interpretation, then, is retrospective in the sense that we always begin
the process of interpretation from within a pregiven context. The

process is also prospective, because it involves elaboration of the "would be's" inherent in the context itself. Peirce explains that ascertaining the meaning of a norm or proposition involves us in an imaginative enterprise. We conjecture what it would mean if we were to conduct ourselves in accordance with a particular proposition or habit of mind.

> We imagine ourselves in various situations and animated by various motives; and we proceed to trace out the alternative lines of conduct which the conjectures would leave open to us. We are, moreover, led, by the same inward activity, to remark different ways in which our conjectures could be slightly modified. The logical interpretant must, therefore, be in a relatively future tense.[16]

The logical interpretant is the conjecture inherent in a general proposition. We ask ourselves what it would mean *if* we were to guide ourselves and live in the world in accordance with a particular conjecture. The "as if" as a process of understanding is part of our day-to-day law school culture. We practice the "as if" in the hypotheticals we use to teach students the meaning of a particular legal rule or proposition. We ask our students to grasp the meaning of the rule through conjecture. The "as if" is oriented toward the future in that we project the proposition onto a future situation in order to draw out its meaning. This future is implicit in the act of interpretation. As Peirce argues, "[T]he species of future tense of the logical interpretant is that of the conditional mood, the 'would be.' "[17]

We understand the meaning of a right through this same process of conjecture. The meaning of a right as a general proposition is uncovered in the process of conjecture just described. Ronald Dworkin is wrong, then, to suggest that "[l]aw as integrity, is more relentlessly interpretive than . . . pragmatism," although it is important to add here that Dworkin is not speaking of Peirce's work when he defines pragmatism, but of the neopragmatists he associates with the Conference of Critical Legal Studies.[18] The principal aim of Peirce's semiotics is to show that all knowledge is interpretive. The disagreement lies in Peirce's belief that the very process of interpretation demands conjecture and, therefore, the imagined "would be."[19] The insistence on the future as the horizon for the effectuation of meaning is not instrumentalist as Dworkin argues. It does not deny the text in favor of an instrumental vision of the future; nor does it deny that we are always oriented toward the past, precisely because we are in a pregiven context. The future orientation of which I speak has two aspects. First, insofar as all signs only refer to other signs and not directly to reality, there is no past that is simply "there" for us to recollect. As a result—and this is the second aspect—we seek the meaning of an account of our legal history in how it guides us in our future conduct, because we cannot validate its truth as a purely *descriptive* manner. Because the "past" is always offered to us within competing interpretive frameworks, we cannot prefer one framework over the other because one is not a framework at all but a pure account of what "actually was." We must, instead, look to how these accounts can guide us in grappling with the legal problems we are now confronting. The very idea of the meaning of the text itself arises in and through the process of conjecture. Peirce explains as follows: "Pragmatism makes the ultimate intellectual purport of what you please to consist in conceived conditional resolutions . . ."[20] There are, in other words, conceived conditional resolutions that do stabilize meaning. Indeed, a judge's decision can itself be understood as a conditional resolution, which, if it is enforced, will effectively stabilize legal meaning.

This argument should not be confused with the position that would simplistically deny the material weight of the past in favor of the view that a conditional resolution is purely a matter of instrumental construction. We cannot just reach back to the "actually was" as if there were a preinterpretive past that was "just there." We receive the past only through the process of critical interpretation. Peirce shows why the insistence that *meaning* always demands conjecture leads us to conclude not that there is no past, but that the *meaning* of the past cannot be reduced to a pure description:

> It cannot be denied that acritical inferences may refer to the Past in its capacity as past; but according to Pragmaticism, the conclusion of a Reasoning power must refer to the Future. For its meaning refers to conduct, and since it is a reasoned conclusion must refer to deliberate conduct, which is controllable conduct. But the only controllable conduct is Future conduct. As for that part of the Past that lies beyond memory, the Pragmaticist doctrine is that the meaning of its being believed to be in connection with the Past consists in the acceptance as truth of the conception that we ought to conduct ourselves according to it (like the meaning of any other belief). Thus, a belief that Christopher Columbus discovered America really refers to the future.[21]

Peirce's insistence on the category of Secondness indicates the material weight of the past that never can be fully recollected. Given that the past cannot be fully recollected, it also cannot be known other than through interpretation.

The past, in other words, grasps us. We cannot grasp it. Yet it is precisely the "thereness" that we cannot interpret away that makes the past Secondness. The past is there, but not finished. We cannot wrap it up and present it in a determinate conceptual schema as Hegel wanted us to do. Yet even so, no one is denying that there wasn't a body of land that Christopher Columbus ran into *in the past*. (Yes, even the attribution of this act to a man named Christopher Columbus is an interpretive attribution.) When we think about the full meaning of that "reality" we can only do so within an interpretive structure that is oriented to the future, in the sense that what it *means* that Christopher Columbus discovered America can only be resolved if we think about what it *means* for us to guide our conduct by that position. This future orientation does not also mean that there are not conditional resolutions within any given interpretative framework. But these resolutions can only be conditional, since reinterpretation is always a possibility. Yet to argue that reinterpretation is always possible is not necessarily to say that it is always a reality—since no one may call the conditional resolution into question. Past legal precedent, as institutionalized meaning, can be best understood as a body of conditional resolutions.

Conditional resolutions are conditional in that there is no necessary relationship to their logical interpretant and, therefore, they can always be interpreted differently. In the case of law, we can know what the law means only if we open legal precedent, which contains its "would be's" to the questions we are asking because they are put before us in a current case. The very effort to guarantee continuity of the "spirit" of the law demands that we restate the normative message of the legal text. What we pass on, however, cannot be the letter of the law, as if there were a plain meaning that is simply there to be excavated, but instead must be its spirit. In this sense, as already suggested above, the enunciation of the legal principle inherent in the judge's decision implicates the "should be." Continuity in legal interpretation is *always* continuity in principle in Dworkin's sense. A legal verdict is a creative supplement to the texts upon which it relies, which once again brings the meaning of the text to life by telling us how we should guide our conduct in the future.[22] The reconstruction of principle to address the questions with which we are confronted arises not out of a vacuum, but through the potential of the "might have been," which always remains in our reality of historical understanding. The very statement of what the law is, in turn, implicates the "should be," because it depends on justification of a particular interpretation since there can be no pure statement of what the law "is." There can be no acritical reference to the past in the law that does not imply justification. I call this process of legal interpretation "recollective imagination."[23] I will explore the implications of understanding legal interpretation as recollective imagination through the example of Roberto Unger's deviationist doctrine.

The Example of Deviationist Doctrine

In his book on the Conference of Critical Legal Studies Roberto Unger argues that we can understand the spectrum of precedent in contract law through two pairs of principles and counterprinciples: freedom *to* contract and community, and freedom *of* contract and fairness.[24] Unger argues that the sphere of freedom to contract is limited so as not to undermine the effective communal ties in the family.[25] In the interpretation of his work offered here, although Unger certainly does not put it this way, his central point is to give body to the norm of reciprocal symmetry which goes beyond what Hegel himself would have allowed within the sphere of private right.[26] Hegel effectively shows us that contract law applies this established norm as the basis for the relationship between the parties as equal subjects. In Unger's work such a norm not only sanctions contractual relations, it also regulates the range of relations in which the contract should not be upheld, through the translation of the ideal of reciprocity into the counter-principle of fairness. Unger explains as follows: "Fairness means not treating the parties, and not allowing them to treat each other, as pure gamblers unless they really see themselves this way and have the measure of equality that enables each to look at himself."[27] As a result of the commitment to reciprocal symmetry,

> [f]airness also means that inequality between the parties renders a contract suspect and, beyond a certain measure of disparity in power, invalid. In particular, unequal parties will not easily be read into a situation of mere gambling. When the limit of accepted and acceptable risks is reached or when the inequalities in the contractual relation begins to weaken the force of the contract model, the law will try to restore or invent a rough equivalence of performances or of participation in gains and losses. It may do so confusedly and

covertly, but as long as the counterprinciple remains alive it will do
so nevertheless.[28]

By making explicit the underlying value of reciprocal symmetry in
contractual relations and by applying it as a counterprinciple, we can
begin to shift the very parameters of the idea of freedom to contract.

Hegel and Unger disagree over whether reciprocal symmetry is a
counterprinciple to freedom to contract or is, instead, its very basis.[29]
As I have argued, Hegel's own notion of what substantive reciprocity
entails in the legal sphere of abstract right is so limited that it would
have to be refashioned along Unger's lines if it is to continue to be
useful for a modern understanding of contract.[30] For the purpose of
my analysis of how legal interpretation proceeds, this part of their
disagreement is not important. What is relevant is Peirce's understanding of the indeterminancy of any semiotic system of generals to a view
of law as an interpretive praxis which constantly shifts the parameters
of legal discourse itself.

The indeterminacy of the principles of the traditional contract model
allows for the generation of a competing interpretation or, in Unger's
sense, a counterprinciple. The potential for a counterprinciple is there
in the indeterminacy of the present and in the indeterminate presence
of our legal tradition of contract law. Radical lawyering, for Unger, is
the practice of unleashing the potential of the tradition itself.[31] The
theoretical indeterminacy of legal doctrine as a system of signs leaves
open opportunity for active intervention on the part of the individual
lawyer. The reality of our established *sittlich* commitments is not just
there and then reflected in the language of legal argumentation. Instead,
the reality of *Sittlichkeit* is constituted and reconstituted in the very
process of legal argumentation and judicial decision. Our legal reality,
in other words, cannot be separated completely from what we do as
lawyers, judges, and law professors. Nor is there a legal community
that is self-present as a positive fact. The legal community is itself the
embodiment and the expression of those who participate in making
the legal world what it is. Very simply put, our conduct matters.

We can now put Unger's analysis of the development of the counterprinciple of fairness within contract law into a performative understanding of rights. This will further help us understand my conceptualization of legal interpretation as recollective imagination. Rights are
only given meaning within the practice of an established language game
or within a set of pregiven *sittlich* commitments. Unger shows us that
the critical contest in contract law involves the respecification of the

range of application of the principle and the counterprinciple.[32] The rules of the game can be shifted within the terms of the lexicon of the right to contract itself. By shifting the rules of the game, we can also expand the boundaries of our form of life. The central insight of deviationist doctrine is that the meaning of rights is varied over time and space, through the very contest of the participants who attempt to realize their established *sittlich* commitments. In the act of narrating the past, we deviate from it and interpret it differently, precisely because we can never fully recollect the *has been*. Because the discourse is always being reshaped through the interpretation of law, there is no "universal" language of right necessary to rights discourse. Nor do we need to reject the concept of right as the inevitable embodiment of the "possessive" individual. The aim of Unger's own system of rights "is to serve as a counterprogram to the maintenance of re-re-emergence of any scheme of social roles and ranks that can become effectively insulated against the ordinarily available forms of challenge."[33]

To argue that rights discourse is always reshaped through the practice of legal argumentation is not to reduce rights to mere instruments, as Dworkin suggests is the case with the neo-pragmatists, or to deny the relationship of rights to past decisions. Ironically, the understanding of the meaning of rights put forward here is the position consistent with Dworkin's own conception of law as interpretation. We are always in the process of reinterpreting the meaning of the rights given to us in past decisions, through the projection of hypothetical meaning in the future as we conjecture what the right means in the case at hand. What is thought to be consistent with past decisions depends in part—but only in part—on our reinterpretations of the meaning of that past. The result that once seemed to express "consistency with principle" can, in light of new interpretation, appear inconsistent. The expression "as if" in pragmatic discourse indicates the future orientation of conditional generality. The meaning of rights, if rooted in the past, is always open to the future.

Unger, however, seems to take this insight into the future orientation of conditional generality to the incorrect conclusion that we must reject completely the idea that there is an intelligible ethical order objectified in the law. Yet, he also argues that

> deviationist doctrine sees its opportunity in the dependence of a social world upon a legally defined formative context that is in turn hostage to a vision of right. . . . It is the legal-theoretical counterpart to a social theory that sees transformative possibilities built into the

very mechanisms of social stabilization and that refuses to explain the established forms of society, or the sequence of these forms in history, as primarily reflecting practical or psychological imperatives.[34]

There is a difference, frequently obscured in Unger's critique of objectivism, between the argument that a certain vision of rights is imperative and the suggestion that a particular conception of rights is embodied, if imperfectly, in our legal institutions. As I have suggested, the understanding of legal interpretation as an open-ended activity which implicates the "would be" allows us to constantly expand the horizon of established rights discourse. But it is still the case that in law we uncover the "should be" in the *might have been.* If one goes to the opposite extreme and denies all reality to *Sittlichkeit* or to Unger's "mechanisms of social stabilization," deviationist doctrine would itself become an impossibility. Unger does not merely argue that the principles and counterprinciples are "there" in his head; on the contrary, he argues that they are "objective," *there* in the doctrine.[35]

Arguing that the principles and counterprinciples are not purely subjective but are also "there" in the reality of *Sittlichkeit* is not *necessarily* justifying them as defensible. This is the mistake of those who believe that they can answer the indeterminacy thesis simply by an appeal to an institutionalized social reality. The enunciation of what the law "is" implicates the "should be" through the justification of principle. An intelligible moral order may well fail to live up to the normative standards implicit in the projected self-image of the legal order itself. Intelligibility, in other words, is only the first step in legal interpretation. But the very ideal of actualizing potential inherent in Unger's understanding of deviationist doctrine depends on our ability to designate the competing tendencies within our "reality" of historical understanding. In like manner, the idea of deviationist doctrine still appeals to a coherent whole, which can be apprehended in its division into a principle and a counterprinciple. Unger, for example, argues that we can *rationally* grasp the underlying principles of contract.[36]

Hegel reminds us that a modern legal system rests on its implicit appeal to rational justifiability and cognitive accessibility. It is precisely because the self-image of the modern legal order incorporates the appeal to rationality that the failure of rationality is seen as a *failure.* We can, then, disagree with Hegel's assertion that we can apprehend the truth of a fully reconciled actuality and still incorporate his insight that the embodied, rational self-image of a modern legal system facilitates the possibility of immanent critique. The rational self-image depends on what Dworkin calls "consistency in principle," in which contradictory legal principles are synchronized by an appeal to a rational whole.[37] In Hegel, the rational whole is the self-conscious recognition of the " 'I' that is 'We', and the 'We' that is 'I' " in the actualized relations of reciprocal symmetry. Legal principles are rendered consistent with the ideal of reciprocal symmetry or, perhaps more accurately stated, legal principles are grasped correctly in their essence only if they are understood as the embodiment of relations. Peirce's rebellion against absolute knowledge has important consequences for the way we think about the appeal to a rational whole, but it does not demand that we reject such an appeal out of hand.

We can now recast one line of work in the Conference of Critical Legal Studies. The "irrationalist" members of the Conference have criticized the purportedly rational synchronization of "legal liberalism" as fundamentally contradictory.[38] Although the writers of these texts may not agree with me, I read their works as "allegories" which trace the reality of a fall from a projected self-image of the modern legal order. On any reading of this work, the whole is only there negatively as that which is not. Without its negative presence there would be no critical or condemning force, only the precritical demonstration that there are two sides to every issue. To heed the promise of synchronization as a critical force, we need not endorse constructive coherence as if the promise had been realized. We can do it equally well by marking its failure.

The Promise of Synchronization

It is the tension between the promise of synchronization and the failure of its achievement that should open the law to its own transformative potential. I believe the word *synchronization* more accurately describes the aspiration of a modern legal system than does *coherence* which is Dworkin's conception. Coherence locates the problem of legal interpretation in some kind of theory of established meaning, which does not specifically address the institutional, normative role of law, and the possibility of radical transformation. Synchronization, on the other hand, points us to the real problem: How do we develop an institutional analysis which allows us not only to synchronize the competing rights of individuals, but also the conflicts between the individual and the community, and between different groups in society? The goal of a modern legal system is synchronization and not rational coherence. Synchronization recognizes that there are competing rights situations and real conflicts between the individual and the community, which may not be able to yield a "coherent" whole. The conflicts may be mediated and synchronized but not eradicated. In Dworkin, rational coherence depends on the community acting as a single speaker.[39] In reality, a complex, differentiated community can never be reduced to a single voice. Synchronization recognizes the inevitable complexity of the modern state and the imperfection of all our attempted solutions.

Nor is synchronization just balancing. It is "balancing" in and through an appeal to the "conversion principle," for example, Unger's conversion principle of fairness. Without closure, the ideal cannot be justified by an appeal to coherence. Its only justification is that it allows us to synchronize our effectively competing ideals better than any other ideal we have yet to develop. The refusal of closure that inheres in Peirce's rebellion against Hegelianism projects the rationally synchronized whole into the future as a promise that can never be fully realized. But as Derrida reminds us, "[A] promise is not nothing, it is not simply marked by what it lacks to be fulfilled."[40]

The establishment of closure, or even the achievement of rational coherence, can prevent us from searching for the best purported possible justification that Dworkin's community of principle should seek. On the other hand, openness to rethinking the justification for our *sittlich* commitments can lead to challenging the legitimacy of past precedent. To be open to that challenge is to be open to the *nomos*.

The Normative Underpinnings of Community

The process of reassessment through an appeal to the *nomos* cannot be accomplished by one individual. The very idea of critical evaluation demands a transindividual perspective. According to Peirce, when we reflect on our established habits, we do so on the basis of an internal dialogue with ourselves as a projected Other. Peirce explains his communitarian conception of the thought process itself:

> [A] person is not absolutely an individual. His thoughts are what he is "saying to himself," that is, is saying to that other self that is just coming into life in the flow of time. When one reasons, it is that

critical self that one is trying to persuade; and all thought whatsoever is a sign, and is mostly of the nature of language.[41]

If thought is embodied in signs, then the very idea of the internal dialogue demands a set of norms and standards already in place. For Peirce, the historical reality of the community of inquirers is the basis for all knowledge. The community proves itself to be real as it converts its understandings of operative rules into habits.

The community is more than a positive fact for Peirce; it is also an evaluative body. As we reason, we are also evaluating the reasoning process, because this is what it means to reason. Reason, in this sense, is a process of assessment. "Thinking is a kind of action, and reasoning is a kind of deliberate action; and to call an argument illogical, or a proposition false, is a special kind of moral judgment. . . ."[42] Peirce not only recognizes the possibility of dissension, but also argues that the very understanding of reason as assessment breeds critique and divergent opinions. The community of inquirers is guided by norms of dialogic reason and the standards necessary for intersubjective understanding.[43] These norms can in turn be used to assess the actual process of inquiry in any given community. We judge the community by the embodied norms of reasoning.

The Possibility of Developing a Conversion Principle within the Democratic Tradition

Why do we need the critical standard of an *ethical* conception of reason? When we argue for one interpretation of the law in court, we argue for its validity in the sense that this is what the law *should be* if we adhere to the best possible justification of principle. Of course, we seek to persuade the judge, but we seek to persuade the judge on the basis that ours is the valid interpretation. When the judge vindicates one interpretation over another, she does not only claim that in her *opinion* one interpretation is more valid than another; she says this is the legal principle that should be perpetuated. Rightness, in the sense of the claim that this is the interpretation of principle that the community of inquirers should hold to, is implicit in the very structure of legal decision. Thus, it is not only law professors who make this kind of claim. With the judge's decision, the dialogue and the debate end, at least temporarily. But the elaboration of the justification of legal principle which carries within it criteria for the assessment of competing interpretations also leaves open the possibility of reassessment. Essential to this process of reasoning as assessment and reassessment through the recollective imagination of the community is the development of what I would call conversion principles.

By "conversion principle" I mean the act of recollective imagination which not only recalls the past as it remembers the future, but also projects forward as an ideal the very principles it reads into the past. A conversion principle both converts the way we understand the past and converts our current practice of interpretation as we attempt to realize it in the reconstruction of law. Recollective imagination allows us to develop a "conversion principle" from within the democratic constitutional tradition itself. The conversion principle can then serve both as a point of critique and as a regulative ideal.

It would be a mistake to understand a conversion principle as converting the "is" of law into an "ought." As we have seen earlier, the "is" of law contains the "should be" in the enunciation and justification of principle. The critique of positivism insists that law is not simply "there" prior to the act of interpretation. But as we have also seen, the "reality" of law also is not just something in our heads. Laws do come to "exist," both through the process of enforcement and in the act of interpretation. Dworkin shows us that the "existence" of law in a democratic society cannot be separated from its claim to normative authority. As a result, the "existence" of law always demands interpretation and *reconstruction*. The "should be" is connected to the "would be" in that there is no past acting as a dead weight. When the judge defends a legal principle as justified, she also argues that is what the law "should be."

The moment of "fiction" or "literarity" in the act of interpretation is what allows us to tell a "new" story and to project the stories we read into the tradition as constitutive of that tradition, as well as regulative of who we might become. The very ideal of the rule of law itself, then, cannot escape from "the truth" of indeterminacy. The process of categorization in the attempt to put together "like" cases is always imperfect. There is not such thing as pure perpetuation of the law, once we understand that law *is* interpretation.

The iterability of language makes consistency with precedent as exact replication *impossible* and, therefore, interpretation, change, and innovation *inevitable*. Jacques Derrida has brilliantly shown us how the iterability of language implies both sameness and difference.[44] Words as signs are iterable, or repeatable, by any general user.[45] In other words, language is possible precisely because public standards allow intelligibility. Derrida shows us that the intersubjectivity of language—its capacity to function as a vehicle for the repetition of the same by different subjects—is, ironically, a vehicle for innovation. At the same time, as a language functions to repeat the same message by different subjects, it retains its capacity to be turned away by a reader or a bearer from what it meant to its issuer so that it continues to mean something, but not identically what it meant to its writer or utterer.[46]

Linguistic context, then, does not erect barriers against innovation. Instead, it provides for the possibility—indeed the *inevitability*—of innovation. Unless there is an appeal to an ideal selfsameness which guarantees the exact repetition of meaning, the very meaning of the context itself will be constantly shifting. Our tacit sense of the possible always changes as we are offered new interpretations.

An additional point needs to be emphasized: The ideal of the rule of law demands fidelity to principles embodied, even if imperfectly, in past precedent. Of course, once we recognize that the process of recollection of legal principle is never mere exposition, but involves the imagination and the positing of the very ideals to be read into the legal text, we can no longer choose between competing interpretations on the basis of an appeal to what is just "there." All interpretations, as we have seen, entail an inevitable moment of fictionality. As a result we cannot prove the truth of a particular conversion principle. We can only evoke its power and justify its rightness through argumentation. This does not mean that all interpretations are equally effective in the synchronization of competing ideals. It does mean, however, that we can only show that one interpretation is better than another through argument and an appeal to practical effects. To say that there can always be a better interpretation than the one offered is not to say that there necessarily is such an interpretation presently available.

Power, of course, plays a crucial role in designating both who is to decide what is better and on what criteria that decision should be based. But the reality that there are embodied ideals that guide the interpretive process in art or in law imposes at least some limit on what those in power can impose. That such ideals can be constituted against the endless power bargaining of actual individuals is the hope of constitutional government. It is a hope, however, that depends on interpreters of the law for its reality against those who say it is only wishful thinking. Of course, if we *accept* that law is nothing more than power, then there is always the possibility that this is what law will become. This is just a possibility, not a mandate of fate.

This process of elaborating ideals becomes crucial once we understand the inevitable moment of evaluation in legal interpretation. The misunderstanding of the indeterminacy thesis, which argues that indeterminacy denies the power and the hold of institutionalized meaning, has opened the thesis to many attacks which simply insist that there is, indeed, such a thing as institutionalized meaning.[47] In Hegelian language, they appeal to the existence of *sittlichkeit*. Such assertions, while relevant to, but certainly not dispositive of, discussions of how communication and intelligibility arise, do not help us much in the area of legal interpretation unless they explicitly address the problem of normative authority. If one reads carefully, it is evident that—except for a few extreme cases[48]—all sides of the debate *do agree* that there is institutionalized meaning. The real difference between the competing sides of the debate is whether or not it is possible to elaborate standards of "rightness" through an appeal to the potential inherent in embodied ideals within the law, which can in turn be used to judge what has been institutionalized. The "truth" of indeterminacy is that, from within the social reality as we find it, we can always imagine a better world by interpreting the "would be" inherent in the conditional generality of law. Peirce always reminds us of the immanent potential to invite new worlds. Although Peirce recognized indeterminacy, he also projected a hypothetical closure in the community of inquirers.

Unlike Peirce, I do not accept that an ultimate convergence of opinion is either desirable or possible. Convergence in such a strong sense would obscure the diachronic moment of any semiotic field, which marks the transcendence of what is. Emmanuel Levinas has eloquently explained the danger in any attempt to silence once and for all Dworkin's external or internal skeptic: "Does not the coherent discourse, wholly absorbed in the said, owe its coherence to the State, which, violently excludes subversive discourse? Coherence thus dissimulates a transcendence, a movement from the one to the other, a latent diachrony, uncertainty and a fine risk."[49]

The doubt that inheres in the very diversion of any sign in a semiotic field is indeed a "fine risk," one with which we simply have to live. We should not try to speak as a single voice. Banishment has too long been the answer to the one who questions the institutionalized meanings and norms of the community in order to release the *nomos*.[50]

The Subject and Innovative Capability

Who is the "we" to whom the invitation to release the *nomos* can be delivered? In Peirce's early writings he focused on overcoming doubt through the stabilization of belief. In his later work, however, he became increasingly dissatisfied with his own account of habit as it was related to his conception of self-control and of reason.[51] Sam Weber explains the tension that moved Peirce beyond his earlier understanding:

> To establish belief and habit means to establish an interpretation of one's words that will overcome the intrinsic division of those words as signs. Doubt is therefore not—as Peirce himself seeks constantly to convince himself—merely the "absence" of belief, its simple negation: it is a consequence of the divided structure of the sign. Within the individual subject, this takes the form of what Peirce calls "self-reproach." The stronger the habit the less this feeling of self-reproach will be. However, "the more closely this is approached"—that is, the "fixed character" imparted to actual habit—"the less room for self-control there will be; and where no self-control is possible there will be no self-reproach."[52]

I would replace Peirce's self-control with what I call the "natality" that inheres in the demand to ever renew oneself in the very effort to maintain an "I" over time. The subject cannot be foundational in the sense of fully established through autogenesis because of the inevitable intersection with the otherness of a field of signs in which the self is constituted as well as enabled to give content to its "I." By natality I do not mean a capacity, at least not in the sense of an inherent property of the self, but instead the possibility of re-generative interactions that actually do innovate in the sense of effecting change in self-definition. Transformation is demanded of us precisely because there is no self-enclosed subject who can truly cut herself off from the Other. We are constantly being challenged by otherness, including the otherness that marks the boundaries of the self "within," such as the unconscious. The "I" repeats itself through its iterability, but only in a field of otherness in which the "I" is given significance. The very idea of autogenesis, then, is a myth. My conception of natality accepts that autogenesis is a myth, at the same that it emphasizes how the self is continuously "birthed" again through time and its encounters with others. What we think of as agency is precisely the engagement of the self with its own iterability, which is never just given but always confirmed or disconfirmed in the process of signing for oneself. It is the very process that allows us to underwrite a statement such as "I am Drucilla Cornell" again and again over time. The self is implicated in the process of recollective imagination for which we sign, "Yes, this is me, my life," as it also both develops and constantly changes.

Agency is this specific sense of possibility for an "I" that is both defined and recreated through recollective imagination. The recollection of oneself is always an act which imagines through the remembrance of its own claims of selfhood what can never be fully recollected, but only forever reimagined and re-told. The iteraribility of language allows us to regenerate ourselves through the continuing process of re-definition. In psychoanalytic terms, the self re-collects itself through a series of hypothetical fantasies that allow for ever-changing self-definitions.

The Difference between Innovative Capability and Kantian Autonomy

There is a distinction, then, between this view of natality and a more traditional Kantian understanding of the role of autonomy. In Kant, the subject of reason, the transcendental subject, is the "I," which commands the empirical subject of desire.[53] Reason, in Kant, is pitted against desire, in part because desire itself is relegated to an empirical "property" of the concrete "me." The concrete "me" of empirical desire is a reality. One does not so much change that "me" as control it. What I am suggesting is that Peirce's understanding of the self as "habit" or, as I have reinterpreted it, as the natality that allows for innovation, means that there is no empirical "me" that is simply there. In the Hegelian conception, desire is itself social and contextual and, therefore, open to reinterpretation. Desire is not a "property of the empirical self" but an intersubjective relation itself defined and rede-fined in the field of signs.

Let me give an example which will emphasize the significance of the distinction I am trying to make. Think of a man whose sexual "desire" has been thoroughly shaped by the cultural stereotypes presented to him in pornographic literature. His dilemma is that his desire is out of touch with his own conception of what a relationship between men and women should be like. Under the Kantian schema, he should try to control the desiring "me" through the reasoning "I." Under the Peircean schema offered here, the same man will be *pulled* to transform his desires through the challenge to his habitual practice of desire inherent in his own conception of the ideal and in his contact with those he desires. He will not so much force himself to change as he will be forced to change. Yet he can also assess the changes in himself through the projection of hypothetical fantasies about himself, who he has been, and who he wants to become. He can *assess* as well as *accept* his habitual structure of desire as it inevitably breaks down in his contact with others. It is this process of assessment that allows him to intervene in what is happening to him. Of course, all change is not necessarily desirable. Even so, reasoning and thinking in Peirce are connected to the ability to accept and to enhance change. Thinking in Peirce is related to "musement," that openness to new worlds which prods us to wonder about what we once took for granted. Reasoning is more akin to musing over what we once accepted as we let ourselves be invited to new worlds than it is to the assertion of control over the desiring self. Thinking in this sense demands our openness to otherness and our willingness to accept the invitation.

This appeal to an "I" that is continually defined and re-created through recollective imagination does not implicate a transcendental subject. Although, as I suggested in the last chapter,[54] it does mark a residually transcendent subject, an "I" that is irreducible and thus remains other to its context. Such an understanding preserves what is valued in the idealist conception of autonomy, without endorsing a subject that can pull itself together and away from otherness. The ideal of autonomy has always been justified by the need for critical assessment of communal standards. We need the ability to say "no" as well as to say "yes" to our community. Peirce recognized that the traditional interpretations of the Kantian understanding of autonomy rested on the myth of a subject that could constitute itself as a transcendental subject.[55] Not only is the Kantian subject a myth, it may be a description of a self whose habits are so encrusted that the illusion of his separateness prevents the acceptance of the invitation which prods us to think.

By habit, iterability, and change, this conception of the self as the natality that proceeds through recollective imagination does not deny that the self is a stabilized sign immersed within a field of habits and a pregiven linguistic context. Indeed, such a view insists that it is the immersion in a pregiven context that marks the self as an interaction with otherness. This stability is always breaking down, because of the diachronic nature of any semiotic field and because of the reality that we are always facing new circumstances. The very idea of repetition we associate with habit implies difference and modification. Weber shows us that it is more correct to describe the self as this process of modification or innovation than as the locus of habit:

That "self" consists in all the factors contributing to habit change, to "a modification of consciousness" that entails modification of behavior. If it necessarily involves repetition it is in the sense assigned by Derrida to "iteration," which "alters." As Peirce writes, "it naturally follows that repetitions of the actions that produce the changes increase the changes."[56]

It would, then, be a mistake to interpret the view of the self as natality as a return to the individualism that denies the precedence of the community to the self-conscious subject. Indeed, the Peircean view of the subject is radically antiindividualist. It is because of the precedence of the field of signs to the self that the subject cannot achieve self-enclosure and, in that sense, identify herself as a fully present substantive reality. Who "we" are is the intersection with otherness. As a result, we are constantly pulled to modify our habits. As I have already argued, natality is not so much a property of the self as it is a potential inherent in our inevitable relation to otherness and the very iterability that designates each one of us as a self. Moreover, this description of the self as natality can also be understood as a good to which we aspire. Rather than seek control through closure, we should instead open ourselves to the invitation that otherness constantly provides. The very image of the subject who strives for closure and control, rather than accept the invitation of otherness, is Odysseus as he ties himself to the mast before daring to listen to the sirens.[57] He is willing to hear them only once he has created a situation where he cannot respond. Of course, to tie oneself up is also a response. However, it is a response that resists rather than accepts the invitation. Those of us who are participants in the legal system have to be reminded of our responsibility it we refuse rather than heed the invitation.

To quote Robert Cover: "Legal meaning is a challenging enrichment of social life, a potential restraint on arbitrary power and violence. We ought to stop circumscribing the *nomos*; we ought to invite new worlds."[58] Charles Peirce's pragmatism, which I defend, does precisely that: it stops circumscribing the *nomos* and invites us to new worlds.

3

"Disastrologies"[1]

In the writings of the principal male philosophers in the last century, Woman has evolved from abstraction to metaphor to allegory. I am writing as a woman describing the significance of that development for the way we think about "heterosexual" love. As a springboard, I decided to address David Krell's *Postponements*, because it is a brave book. Unlike Nietzsche (whose speculations on feminine love as martyrdom in *Beyond Good and Evil* lead him to conclude: "But why insist on such painful things? Assuming that one need not do so"),[2] Krell insists that we face the painful things when it comes to understanding the relationships among femininity, sensual love—I would add here "heterosexual" love—and tragic death, usually the woman's. Krell tells us that Nietzsche intended to write a play in which Woman would stand in as the figure of sensuality and death. It is important to note that the play was not to address the relationship of death and pestilence to the feminine as if the feminine were somehow an independent phenomenon. Rather, in the play, at least according to Krell's description of Nietzsche's plans, which I believe is accurate, Woman stands in as the very figure of death and sensuality.

The play, in other words, was to confront Woman as metaphor, and yet it was precisely the confrontation with the feminine as metaphor that Nietzsche ultimately postponed. Before we answer the question of why this postponement was necessary—assuming we ever can—we must note an irony in what I have just said. I am suggesting that Nietzsche's use of Woman as the metaphor for the eroticism of death and pestilence replicates, in spite of his intention, some of the worst aspects of the metaphysical tradition. There is no such metaphor without metaphysics. Yet, this being said, we still need to ask ourselves a further question: What was so frightening that it could not be verbalized in Nietzsche's own prefiguring of Woman? As Krell himself puts it, speaking of Nietzsche, it was "as though confrontation of sensuality and death in the figure of woman had to be postponed for essential reasons, reasons that resisted even Nietzsche's incomparable gifts of language and intelligence."

What, then, are the essential reasons and why are they essential? In *Postponements*, Krell carefully turns the question around. What we do know is that the "postponements" which obsess Krell are not only Nietzsche's. Indeed, what makes Krell's text so interesting to me is that Nietzsche is standing in as a figure of masculinity. At stake in Krell's *Postponements* is not so much Nietzsche's play but the relationship of femininity, feminism, and heterosexuality, and in turn the possibility of grand passion that is other to the deadly dynamic of sadomasochism.

Krell implicitly recognizes what he has put at stake through his explorations of Nietzsche's plans for the play and the reasons for his deferral in executing them. This perhaps explains why he tells us, toward the end of the text, that he does not want Nietzsche's postponements to be his own. Krell does not want to give up his hope for a love that is neither the lackluster lassitude of tired and cynical collusion in "normal" marriage nor the Pollyanna optimism of Hegelian reconciliation. He hopes for something *more*. Krell indicates that there is a connection between this hope and the need to come to terms with Nietzsche's masculine duplicity. (I want to note here that I use the words "masculine" and "feminine" deliberately to avoid the simplistic identification of a particular set of properties and characteristics with actual men and women. When I speak of "Woman" as metaphor, I am not speaking of women. Indeed, the dazzling images of Woman with which we are presented in Western culture all too easily blind us to actual women.)

What exactly is Nietzsche's duplicity which can no longer be skirted? How and why does it stand in for masculine duplicity more generally? As we read *Postponements*, it becomes increasingly difficult to ascertain precisely what it is about the relationships among femininity, sensuality, and death which Nietzsche postpones and which Krell wants us to face. And why must we face it? Just for the sake of facing duplicity? Or is it in the name of the "elsewhere" where we might at last find the mother of tragedy whom, Krell tells us, Nietzsche was so desperately seeking? Hélène Cixous has dreamt of the elsewhere which Nietzsche, at least in his most "feminine" moments, strove to reveal in his praise of and indeed identification with the affirming Woman:

> [A] "place" of intransigence and of passion. A place of lucidity where no one takes what is a pretense for life. Desire is clearly there like a stroke of fire, it shoots the night through with something. Lightning! that way! I don't have it wrong. Life is right here.[3]

The question of the "elsewhere," of the mother of tragedy, haunts Krell's *Postponements*. If we are to find a way out of this haunting problem, we need to know exactly what we are seeking to escape from. Krell leaves us with a series of questions rather than with answers, but also with at least a glimmer of what he thinks he must do if Nietzsche's postponements are not to be his own.

> Yet may one also look elsewhere? To the ineluctable necessity of displacement, doubling and blurring of the lines in Nietzsche's own writing? To satyr-play as postponements of the tragedy, but a postponement that is in pursuit, relentlessly? Theseus chasing the Ariadne thread. The under hero, and not the god, useless as Zagreus, Dionysos in pieces who loses the thread, never gets out, is lost or was ultimately more dedicated to groping his way through the labyrinth than to escaping or fleeing in the face of it. No matter what is eating away at him, or was, or who. Corrina, Pana, Calina. All the pleats and plaits of Ariadne. Not to be skirted. All the duplicity.[4]

Krell is honest enough to admit that for him, Woman *is* still the labyrinth. At least he is not running away; certainly his refusal to run is in and of itself significant. I do not want to take anything away from it or pretend that it is trivial. Yet, speaking as the labyrinth, as a woman, if never Woman—for after all we are always more to ourselves than a metaphor—it is perhaps no coincidence that I am *forced* to confront the duplicity which leaves Nietzsche endlessly in pursuit of the mother of tragedy. Feminine difference may be unreachable within our current system of representation of Woman, but even so women cannot completely avoid answering in their own lives the enigma of the feminine. In Nietzsche's notes, Ariadne responds with gratitude to Dionysos's metaphor of her: "Oh, Ariadne you yourself are the labyrinth, one doesn't get out of you again. Dionysios, you flatter me; you are divine."[5]

Yet, in the end, the so-called flattery was the justification for fleeing the scene to live in peace with the ideal, present now only as a beautiful memory which can no longer threaten with the "real" of possibility.

In the plaint of Ariadne, we confront what Krell himself calls, "the deadly nostalgia of masculinity,"[6] even if we do not yet know why the nostalgia is so deadly for actual women. Even to speak in this way is to court the danger of appearing as the castrating, moralizing woman Nietzsche so despised. It is to sound like an embittered feminist, who identifies with the suffering of the victim rather than with the *jouissance* of the lover, the very feminist who warns the women of great souls, the affirming women, against their own grandeur. For we know the kind of woman Nietzsche identified with, he refers to her constantly. She is the one who gives herself without reserve. She is able not to return to herself, never settling down, going everywhere to the Other. She does not flee extremes. She is the one who refuses her castration.

The castrating woman, Nietzsche's despised feminist, nevertheless seems to have a legitimate point in her constant moralizing. There is such terrible anguish expressed in Ariadne's plaint. Ariadne is possessed by her love and therefore dispossessed of herself; she is left only with her despair. Krell responds to her suffering, and to the masculine complacency which would disregard her anguish. He openly disagrees with Giles Deleuze's claim that Nietzsche successfully integrates Ariadne into the philosophy of Dionysos. Ariadne represents for Deleuze the complete expulsion of negativity. And yet, as Krell remarks, "If Ariadne is pure affirmation what has she to complain about?"[7] For Krell, Ariadne's travail is not wholly affirmative. It would be insensitivity bordering on misogyny to think so. As Krell explains, "[I]n his eagerness to salvage affirmation from negation and nihilism, Deleuze is blithe about, and even blind to, Ariadne's suffering. He is death to her keen."[8]

Ariadne's martyrdom, which results from her very abundance, becomes her passion and introduces Christian negativity into the soul of the noncastrating women. For Krell, it is not at all evident that we can—as Deleuze would have it—separate the feminine power of affirmation from the martyrdom of despair. Nietzsche expresses his own ambivalence toward the despair he associates with one version of a feminine view of love in a passage from *Beyond Good and Evil*, a passage Krell cites:

> Woman would like to believe that Love can do everything; that is her proper faith. Alas, knowers of the heart will surmise how powerless, dull-witted, helpless, presumptuous, blundering—how much more—how much more likely to destroy than to rescue—even the best, most profound Love is! It is possible that behind the sacred fable and disguise of the life of Jesus is one of the most painful cases of martyrdom arising from Knowledge about love lies concealed; the martyrdom of the most innocent and yearning heart, which was never satisfied by any human love, which demanded love, to be loved, and nothing else; a heart that turned on those who refused to love in return, turned into hardness, sadness and frightful rage; the history of a poor wretch who was never sated, never satisfied in

love, who had to invent an inferno to which he could dispatch those who refused to love him—and who, finally, having learned about human love, had to invent a God who is all love, pure potentiality—for-love—a God who has mercy on human love because it is so flimsy, so incompetent. Whoever feels this way, whoever knows such things about love seeks death.[9]

Suicide, the ultimate expression of feminine martyrdom, hardly seems an affirmation in Nietzsche's sense of the word. It is not so easy, then, as Nietzsche himself seems to recognize in his Pana notes, to redeem "[t]he woman in women." Or, as Krell would put it, to separate the castrating woman from the affirming Woman Nietzsche so admired. The woman who loves so passionately goes down, but is this really a going over? The imagery of the Woman's pain Nietzsche uses demands her own end. "In flowing tears pours out all your suffering, your suffering from abundance and from the cluster's urge to go the vintner and the vintner's knife."[10] Wine becomes whine. *Jouissance* turns into anguish. In his dreams of Pana, Nietzsche expresses his deep ambivalence toward the pining woman whose abundance has brought her down. Is it not better that she die than that she court the danger of becoming the castrating woman she has previously refused to be? Indeed, Nietzsche allows himself to imagine killing Pana off. Better death than the sorrow that leads to bitterness. How far are we here, truly, from the diary of the seducer who admits that when he is confronted with the pain that he finds so unattractive in the woman he has most recently left, he would, if he were a god, turn her into a man?

Does Nietzsche have it right, then, that if sensual love for men is a kind of "possessiveness," it is for women, including the affirming Woman, "adoration of a suffering and veiled godhead."[11] We need to ask: Does the affirming Woman really seek suffering in the *worship*—given that adoration is just another way of saying worship—of the veiled godhead or does she instead blasphemize through her insistence on happiness? Indeed, we can understand the plaint itself as a continuing expression of the refusal of the unhappiness of castration. The common sense of the castrating woman who espouses the ideology of lesser expectations results in the "wisdom" of resignation and the mock dignity of denial, and not in the browbeating anguish of Ariadne's mourning. The affirming Woman embraces "disastrologies" rather than cut herself off. She wails because she still does not accept the lukewarm discontentment of the castrated woman as her fate. Despair is not resignation.

If Nietzsche does not have it right, can we say with Derrida that when Nietzsche speaks of the affirming Woman, "he writes with the hand of woman"?[12] The Derridean reading of Nietzsche with which Krell himself begins his *Postponements* is extremely generous. There are at least two ways of reading *Spurs*. The first reading, which we see in the feminist critique of *Spurs*, insists that Derrida makes the mistake I am attributing to Nietzsche, the mistake of turning Woman into metaphor, and hence the identification of Woman as truth. The second, and I think clearly correct, reading is that Woman is not a metaphor in Derrida; instead, Woman *and* truth both mark the invitation to otherness which remains beyond representation. Derrida finds in Nietzsche the destabilization of the Ça—Lacan's term for the erection of gender identity in the unconscious. This destabilization protects the dream of a new choreography "beyond" the familiar steps of both homosexuality and heterosexuality and by so doing "redeems the woman in women," without just relocating her proper place. In the Nietzschean portrayal of the feminine *as* death and pestilence there is not nearly as much destabilization as Derrida finds in his texts—which is not to say that one cannot find it at all.

Derrida, unlike Nietzsche, consistently reads feminine difference as allegory. The feminine marks both the difference that cannot be stated and the trace of the beyond that cannot be erased. To read the myth of the feminine allegorically is to guard the "elsewhere" as the absence that has not been and might yet be. It is to affirm the dream of "other love." In Nietzsche's metaphorization of Woman, on the other hand, she is not only represented, as Derrida carefully avoids, she is represented as the difference that must go under in the name of her own affirmation. Nietzsche's metaphor of Woman as the figure of death does not ultimately celebrate her difference; rather, it risks her obliteration. This is the moment of misogyny that Krell detects not only in Deleuze but also in Nietzsche. To protect the feminine difference which cannot be represented within the masculine order of the symbolic is to live with an invitation which can never be closed off. The irony in Nietzsche is that in the name of heeding her invitation he ultimately refuses the radical call of otherness through his postponements and therefore assuages his own anxiety. To turn Woman into a metaphor of pestilence and death is to try to locate her once again. Perhaps there is some basis for Nietzsche's fear that he was the castrated woman.

We have still not reached the duplicity which inheres in Nietzsche's own ambiguous attitude toward feminine passion. Why must the affirming woman with whom Nietzsche identifies himself end so badly, not only in Nietzsche's works, but in myth (think of Dido) and of course in life? Why does the feminine refusal of castration seem to end in an early, tragic death, often by suicide?

At this point we are returned to the deadly nostalgia of masculinity, a nostalgia which cannot be separated from the erection of the Ça, the myth of femininity, and the pull of the ideal that Pana, Calina and Ariadne stand in for in Nietzsche's texts. Lacan hammers home one point: The Phallic Mother is the pull to otherness which can never be adequately represented. As an invitation to *jouissance*, she pulls men toward her. As the beyond, as the gaping hole, the abyss, she is not only an invitation; she is a threat to the masculine-identified subject who confuses independence with castration. Nietzsche clearly wants to accept the invitation, but he himself wavers before his own anxiety. The "place" of the mother of tragedy is where *jouissance* bursts forth without constraint, Bataille's eroticism of white heat. The Phallic Mother is the source of longing, the mark of the absence that is transcendence. In Lacan, however, there is no going back to Her once the subject has entered the symbolic and assumed his castration. Woman does not exist in Lacan, because Woman only "is" as the unrepresentable absence which lingers in desire. Cut off from her, she is present in the nostalgia for the place she has never been. Woman is the lie to Hegel's *Erinnerung*. We cannot recollect what we have lost. Nostalgia for her can never be fulfilled. There can be no reconciliation. Yet the nostalgia remains, precisely because of the lack which becomes the subject's desire.

In sensual love, however, there is the illusion that the Phallic Mother is there again. As *jouissance*, yes, but also as the invitation into the abyss that seemingly threatens all identity. Perhaps there is no better account of the threat to identity presented by the invitation of otherness than the one offered by Adorno and Horkheimer in the *Dialectic of the Enlightenment*. Odysseus wants to accept that invitation offered by the sirens, but only so long as he is in control. So he ties himself up in knots. His confusion is to think that he is in control, when he is just tied up in knots. *Jouissance* is both exhilarating and terrifying. To throw off the ropes and to listen to the sirens, to accept the invitation of otherness, is to be pulled along into uncharted territory, territory that the subject cannot chart. Hence the identification of woman as the labyrinth and the production of unbearable anxiety which seeks to reassert control through resistance. The stronger the pull of the Other, the closer to ecstasy, the more intense the anxiety. As Lacan reminds us over and over again, when men flee the woman of desire who evokes the ideal, they are running away from the Phallic Mother they seek. Because she, of course, is never there and cannot be there she must be ever sought again. Don Juan chases after the ideal that is the forever-lost Mother.

What, then, is the fundamental duplicity inherent in masculine desire? We can put it very simply: It is the inability to live with what one seeks. We also have a clue to Krell's puzzlement as to why all the magnificent heroines Nietzsche gives us must be deserted in sensual love and end so badly. They are abandoned precisely because they evoke the call to otherness that undermines the certainty of the subject. Desire creates its own loss because the anxiety generated by the pull of the ideal can only be borne if the other loses her otherness and is now internalized as memory. The pattern in Western literature, in which Woman is exalted as the one true love only once she is dead, inheres in Lacan's description of masculine desire. In death she has found her proper place, and can be recollected as the subject's very own love, rather than as an invitation to that which is always beyond him.

We can now also see the connection between the dynamic of masculine desire and the urge to turn Woman into the metaphor of pestilence and death and to stabilize her as myth. As Derrida brilliantly shows us in *La Carte postale*, Lacan himself cannot resist the urge to turn the feminine into the truth of the rigid erection of the Ça. The feminine becomes the very representation of the inevitability of castration. Only by so doing can he quell his own castration anxiety before the Phallic Mother. For Lacan, the truth of the purloined letter lies "where Freud spells it out: in the mother's lack of a penis in which the nature of the Phallus is revealed."[13]

In *Glas, La Carte postale*, and *Spurs*, Derrida exposes the lie of Lacan's identification of the "Feminine" as the truth of castration. The lack, the inevitable absence of the Phallic Mother, is precisely what cannot be given a proper place, indeed She disrupts the very notion of a proper place.

The fallacy of the phallus is that it attempts to erect itself as its own truth. The Feminine as the Other which remain(s) beyond any system of representation cannot be erased. The Mother remains, but not as the truth of castration. The truth of castration cannot successfully erect itself so as to defend effectively against the pull of otherness. The truth is neither the *hole* nor the *whole*, the truth is only an invitation. In *Glas* Derrida refuses castration in the name of the Other in himself.

If I write two texts at once you will not be able to castrate me. If I delinearize, I erect. But at the same time I divide my act and my desire. I mark(s) the division, and I am always escaping you, I simulate increasingly and take my pleasure now, here. I remark(s) myself, thus, I play at coming.[14]

The refusal of castration should not be understood as turning away from the reality that castration exists; such a rejection would deny the violation of woman which has occurred in order to secure her place. What is denied is the "there is," always reinstated in the myth of the Feminine, which refuses the remain(s) of the rigid system of gender identity.

When Derrida remembers the Mother, then, he does not just recollect her. She remain(s) the other beyond his effort at interiorization. The Mother's distance from man is temporal: she both comes before and remain(s) after. The distance of the Mother opens up the diachronic experience of time which triggers memory and calls us to mourning. In Derrida, as in Lacan, the Feminine is the lie to *Erinnerung*, but not as a substitute erection of truth.

The subject of *Glas* mourns for himself as he mourns for the one who has made him what he is, the one who comes before him, the one whose passing leaves its mark. The subject, in other words, is there for himself only in and through the dialogue with the Other, who is never fully present but calls him to mourning by her very absence. Yet the subject only comes to himself by sending itself to her. Subjectivity is not constituted in the present, nor does the subject exist as a presence in and of itself. Instead, the subject only comes to himself in the act of remembrance of the Other, which marks the limit both of memory and of interiorization. We know the Other as the other through the mourning for the absence that can never be overcome.

The subject who refuses his castration, then, is the subject of mourning, who knows himself as a relation to an Other, who cannot be repossessed. Mourning rejects the illusion inherent in nostalgia that we can come home to the Other. The striving for reconciliation turns into the violence of resistance and denial and ultimately into the rejection of women in the name of Woman. It is only once we have given up on the striving for reconciliation that we can love. That is the lesson of *La Carte postale* and of course, of *Glas*, the wake for Hegelianism. Love is the hope that the acceptance of exile from the Phallic Mother makes possible.

It is not only, then, that mourning is necessary for love; it is instead that love is itself a kind of mourning. Hegel had it exactly wrong. Love is not possible because truth has been actualized. Instead love is necessary because truth can only "be" as an invitation which remain(s) beyond our attempt to possess it. Love demands that we give up the dream of turning the Other into a home for ourselves. The Other remains the *unheimlich*, or as Derrida has put it, "the thing remains an other whose law demands the impossible."[15]

All we can give to the Other, and again I quote Derrida, is to send to her "with life and desire, something like my signature."[16] If it is not the case that Woman is death, the acceptance of the invitation of otherness demands the relinquishment of self-certainty, which we can easily identify as the experience of dying to ourselves. The lovers in *La Carte postale* know themselves only by sending themselves "off" to the one who is the Other. This act of sending oneself off cancels the certainty of identity associated with living as a subject securely encased in individuality.

> "I am destroying my own life I said to him (lui) in the English car."
> If I address myself, as it is said always to someone else, and otherwise (right here again) I can no longer address myself by myself. Only to myself, you will say, finally sending me all those cards, sending me Socrates and Plato just as they send themselves to each other. No, not even, *to return*, it does not come back to me. I even lose the identity of the, as they say, sender, the emitter. And yet, no one better than I will have known how, or rather will have loved to destine, uniquely. This is the disaster on the basis of which I love you, uniquely. You toward whom at this very moment, even forgetting your name, I address myself. A Bientôt, à Toujours.[17]

Have we now just returned, if in a different form, to the Nietzschean metaphor of feminine eroticism as death? Not at all. It is the frantic rejection of the self-relinquishment inherent in love that brings forth the association of woman as *death*. But it is not the Woman who sucks the lover in with the untold force of gravity; it is the love. The pressure to give oneself up is *internal*, not external, to the very act of loving. In this sense, love is a "disaster" for the subject; the "story" of love, a series of "diastrologies."[18] But love would be impossible without the acceptance of the inevitable traversal of the self by the Other, and it is precisely this openness to "disaster" that disrupts the endless repetition of Lacan's tragic-comedy in which the masculine subject inevitably flees the one he loves. In this sense, Bataille is right to remind us of the inevitable association of eroticism with death and with the transgression of the barriers of the self. The Other traverses me, pulls me forward. The subject of mourning does not say "I am" but only "I follow." The truth of the fort-da, Derrida's postal principle, is that the Other is never just here for me, She is always "there."

The recognition that the distance of the Other is not within the control of the subject should not be confused with the subjective parody of the postal principle employed by the masculine subject who desperately seeks to enforce distance by sending the Other away so he can at last return to himself. The Other remains in spite of the attempts to brush her off. The effort to preserve her distance only further entangles the self in the ropes which cut him off from her and choke his own desire. The lover of *La Carte postale* throws the ropes away, surrendering himself completely to the one who has called, hoping only to arrive—if not to come—together with the Other in the "elsewhere," so it is no longer necessary to read and be read.

> But I will arrive, I will arrive at the point where you will no longer read me. Not only by becoming more illegible than ever (Its beginning, its beginning) but by doing things such that you no longer recall that I am writing to you that you no longer encounter, as if by chance, the "do not read me." That you do not read me. That you do not read me, this is all, so long, *Ciao*, neither seen nor heard, I am totally elsewhere. I will arrive there, you try to.[19]

The distance of the Other inheres in the waiting for the beloved to come, since her very otherness prevents the lover from taking her into himself. The lover in *La Carte Postale* does not want distance, he wants the Other of his fascination who is in the distance. The distance of which Derrida speaks is not, then, self-imposed distancing of the castrated subject, it is instead the distance of the auratic gaze which sees the Other over there, looking back. The lover must wait for Her response. She comes before.

Since the Other cannot be reduced to an external object or my own meaning, but instead constitutes who I am as I wait for her response to me, the self is lost to Her; "I love you remain me."[20] I also can never fully re-collect myself. As Derrida reminds us, we cannot overcome this fundamental uncertainty.

> Who is writing? To whom? And to send to desire, to dispatch what? To what address? Without any desire to surprise and thereby to grab

attention by means of obscurity, I owe it to whatever remains of my honesty to say finally that I do not know.[21]

We can never know. Not for sure. To love, as Derrida tells us "puts in relation without discretion to tragedy. It forbids that you regulate distances, keeping them or losing them."[22] Masculine nostalgia is ultimately deadly because it attempts to skirt the relation to tragedy inherent in love and ends only in thwarting love. The elsewhere of other love of which Cixous dreams, Nietzsche's land of the mother of tragedy, is not a location but a possibility given to us as subjects of mourning. If thinking demands we live in anxiety, love demands we accept the relation to tragedy. By postponing the tragedy, we only postpone love. The tragic heroine is ironically the result of the masculine refusal of the relation to tragedy which inheres in the inviting love of the Other. Krell's hope lies in the mourning which undoubtedly brought forth his text. I share his hope and his determination to continue to dream. I leave him with a short poem by Samuel Menache:

> At the edge
> Of a world
> Beyond my eyes
> Beautiful
> I know Exile
> Is always
> Green with hope—
> The river
> We cannot cross
> Flows forever.[23]

4

The Doubly-Prized World:
Myth, Allegory, and the Feminine

> Who in his heart doubts either that the facts of feminine clothering are there all the time or that the feminine fiction, stranger than the facts, is there also at the same time, only a little to the rere? Or that one may be separated from the other? Or that both may then be contemplated simultaneously. Or that each may be taken up and considered in turn apart from the other.
>
> —James Joyce[1]

Introduction

My purpose in this essay is to give an account of the "feminine fiction, stranger than the facts" that is there "at the same time, only a little to the rere." I will then elaborate the relationship between the metaphoric significance of the feminine within sexual difference, the experience of actual women, and the dream of a new choreography of sexual difference. Feminine sexual difference should neither be identified with the experience of any given historical group of women, nor philosophically denied and politically rejected as a regrettable return to essentialism belied by the play of difference. Indeed, through my own deconstructive reading of Jacques Lacan, I will argue that the feminine can never be identified with any set of cultural designators. This reading of the feminine allows us to affirm the feminine within sexual difference, without essentialist or naturalist theories of Woman; such theories are ethnically and politically problematical because they deny that class, national, and racial differences are themselves constitutive of the conventional meanings given to the gender designation "Woman" within any particular context characterized by gender hierarchy.

I also want to note that there are ethical and political dangers in the "inessentialist"[2] position, if it is interpreted as denying "feminine" reality and rejecting the need to affirm the feminine within sexual difference. Why, indeed, would we, as feminists, want to join the chorus of those who would deny feminine "reality," even if we also want to emphasize how that reality is always shifting—by definition never fully there? Thus, I put the word "reality" in quotation marks deliberately. It is precisely the status of feminine reality as "stranger than the facts" and "a little to the rere" which must be accounted for if we are to move beyond the central dilemma confronting feminist theory. That dilemma can be summarized as follows: If there is to be feminism at all, as a political movement that adequately challenges the gender hierarchy which necessarily repudiates the value of the feminine sexual difference, we must rely on a feminine voice and a feminine "reality" that can be identified as such and in some way correlated with the lives of actual women. Yet, as I have already suggested, all accounts of specifically feminine sexual difference seems to reset the trap of rigid gender identities, deny the real differences between woman (white women have certainly been reminded of this danger by women of color), and reflect the history of oppression and discrimination rather than an ideal to which we ought to aspire. In order to solve this dilemma, we will have to understand the metaphoric significance of the feminine within sexual difference, but as metaphor not as accurate description. As we will see, this metaphoric understanding of the feminine does not reduce the feminine to a set of characterizations shared by all women—an understanding that has been correctly critiqued for erasing the significance of class, national, and racial difference.

Emily Brontë once wrote in her journal, "this world is hopeless without the world I doubly prize." Without the dream of the doubly-prized world, the failings of this world, particularly as they are experienced by Brontë as a woman, are unbearable. For purposes of feminist theory, I suggest that we must give a new twist to Brontë's lines to give an account of the feminine. The world doubly prized is the world "stranger than the facts" that opens us to the possibility of a new choreography of sexual difference, through an allegorical account of the feminine as beyond any of our current stereotypes of Woman. We also need to retell the myths of the feminine through the refiguration of the feminine within sexual difference in order to challenge the devaluation of the feminine by the gender hierarchy in which the masculine is privileged. Both myth and allegory are necessary, indeed unavoidable, in feminist theory if we are to seek a new economy of desire, beyond the logic of phallogocentrism, which has marked the very discourse of liberation, including that of feminism. As Trinh T. Minh-ha has explained, "In every diverse fashion . . . laying claim to the specificity of women's sexuality and the rights pertaining to it is a step we have to go through in order to make ourselves heard; in order to beat the master at his own game."[3] Beating the master at his own game, however, demands that we rethink the game itself. As we will see, the identification of liberation with imagined phallic power reinscribes the logic of phallogocentrism in the very expression of the desire to overthrow it.

Once we understand the relationship between myth and allegory in accounts of the feminine, we can also unfold the role of the utopian, or redemptive perspective of the "not yet." This perspective exposes our current system of gender representation as "fallen." Within feminist theory, feminine sexual difference has often stood in as the figure that gives body to redemptive perspectives. How should we hope to become? Where do we find the new economy of desire? In the writing of feminine desire. But we have to be clear that the writing of feminine desire need not appeal to the generic Woman. Given the racism of American culture, would not the generic Woman necessarily be envisioned as white?

The writing of feminine sexual difference should then be separated from descriptions of the way women supposedly "are." Yet the ethical dimension, which is implicit in the writing, for example, of Carol Gilligan, is irreducible to a mere descriptive account of the way women are or have been. Of course, it is crucially important to break the silence that has kept "herstory," in all its variations, from being heard. But we also need to recognize explicitly the "should be" inherent in accounts of feminine sexual difference insofar as the feminine is prized as not only a different, but a better, way of being human. My goal is to suggest ethical feminism as an alternative to both liberal and radical feminism. Ethical feminism explicitly recognizes the "should be" in representations of the feminine. It emphasizes the role of the imagination, not description, in creating solidarity between women. Correspondingly, ethical feminism rests its claim for the intelligibility and coherence of "herstory" not on what women "are," but on the remembrance of the "not yet" which is recollected in both allegory and myth.

I begin this essay with a critique of countervailing narrations to the one I will offer, which traces feminine sexual difference to its roots in the unique bodily experience of women. There have been competing conceptions of how femininity as the expression of the female body shapes women's identities and maintains feminine difference as divergent from the experience of masculine subjectivity. Michèle Montrelay, for example, describes how the shadow of a primary female identity, and a separate libidinal economy, are created through the girl's primordial experience of internal genital organs.[4] This uniquely female libidinal economy lingers even after it is restructured and reorganized by the little girl's entry into the symbolic order. Although both sexes enter the realm of what Jacques Lacan calls the symbolic, the feminine unconscious differs from the masculine because the dynamic of repression differs. The little girl's identity continues to be marked by the shadow of her primordial experience. Julia Kristeva also provides a complex account of how a woman's experience of her body provides the basis for a different way of being human.[5] For Kristeva, it is the experience of mothering that differentiates women from men. Motherhood connects us to the Other in a way that undermines the masculine notion of the self as a "possessive individual" and correspondingly gives us another normative understanding of the relation of self to the other. Within American jurisprudence, Robin West developed a narration similar to Kristeva's without the same recourse to psychoanalytic theory.[6] I will combine my critique of Kristeva with a discussion of West's writing.

West's "Phenomenology" of the Feminine

West develops a conception of women's hedonic experience which is correlated with women's reproductive capacities and which separates the female identity from the male. For West, the central goal of feminist theory is to develop a "phenomenology"[7] of woman's difference which will expose woman's experience. Only within the context of a "phenomenology" of women's experience can feminists critique the values of the current legal system as male-dominated. As West explains,

> This abandonment by feminist legal theorists of the phenomenological realm of pleasure and desire is a function of legalism, not true feminism. It reflects the extent to which we have embraced the ideals of legalism—whether we regard those ideals as substantive equality, liberal tolerance, privacy or individual autonomy—rather than the methodology of feminism—careful attention to phenomenological narrative. It reflects the extent to which we have allowed liberal and radical norms drawn from non-feminist traditions to become the

criteria by which we judge the narratives of our lives that emerge from consciousness-raising, *instead of the other way around.*[8]

West gives us several examples of how the experience of women goes unnoticed by the law.[9] Within the legal sphere, the identification of the human with the male keeps our claims from being heard, let alone justified. This lack of attention perpetuates tremendous suffering in the lives of actual women by denying their experience.

> Just as women's work is not recognized or compensated by the market culture, women's injuries are often not recognized or compensated *as injuries* by the legal culture. The dismissal of women's gender-specific suffering comes in various forms, but the outcome is always the same: women's suffering for one reason or another is outside the scope of legal redress. Thus, women's distinctive gender-specific injuries are now or have in the recent past been variously dismissed as trivial (sexual harassment on the street); consensual (sex harassment on the job); humorous (non-violent marital rape); participatory, subconsciously wanted, or self-induced (father/daughter incest); natural or biological, and therefore inevitable (childbirth); sporadic, and conceptually continuous with gender-neutral pain (rape, viewed as a crime of violence); deserved or private (domestic violence); non-existent (pornography); incomprehensible (unpleasant and unwanted consensual sex) or legally predetermined (marital rape, in states with the marital exemption).[10]

For West, the central mistake of liberal feminism is its attempt to justify women's injuries as legally redressable by translating them into a framework which inevitably only further distorts the "real" experience of women.[11] West argues that the norms of the legal system itself—such as autonomy—make such translation impossible because these norms reflect male, rather than female, experience.[12] We get legal redress in our current system only by denying, or at least distorting, the truth of female "reality." As West explains, a reconstructive feminist jurisprudence must face this dilemma directly; otherwise, legal reform will only perpetuate the silencing of women's voices: "Reconstructive feminist jurisprudence, I believe, should try to explain or reconstruct the reforms necessary to the safety and improvement of women's lives in direct language that is true to our own experience and our own subjective lives."[13]

For West, this process of translating the harms suffered by women into legally established rights should reflect women's fundamental experience of our bodies based on our reproductive capacity.[14] As a result of our unique bodily structure, we relate to the world differently from the way men do. According to West, we value intimacy rather than individuation because of our connection to birthing and child rearing. Our bodies also make us vulnerable to invasion. For example, we are susceptible to rape and unwanted pregnancies. For West, the right to abortion is the right to defend against bodily invasion.[15] Only on the basis of such a justification will the right reflect the experience of women. If our legal system is to overcome its masculine bias, we must introduce into the law women's experience of bodily vulnerability, self-defense, and the values of intimacy and love. But we can only understand the legal system as masculine if we first grasp the basis of the unique relationship to the world which women share simply because we are women. West's account of women's bodies is the "foundation" for both her critical and her reconstructive projects.

> Underlying and underscoring the poor fit between the proxies for subjective well-being endorsed by liberals and radicals—choice and power—and women's subjective, hedonic lives is the simple fact that women's lives—*because of our biological, reproductive role*—are drastically at odds with this fundamental vision of human life. Women's lives are *not* autonomous, they are profoundly relational. This is at least the biological reflection, if not the biological cause, of virtually all aspects, hedonic and otherwise, of our "difference." Women, and *only* women, and *most* women, transcend *physically* the differentiation or individuation of biological self from the rest of human life trumpeted as the norm by the entire Kantian tradition. When a woman is pregnant her biological life embraces the embryonic life of another. When she later nurtures children, her needs will embrace their needs. The experience of being human, for women, differentially from men, includes the counter-autonomous experience of a shared physical identity between woman and fetus, as well as the counter-autonomous experience of the emotional and psychological bond between mother and infant.[16]

There is a tension in West's work as to the causality of the biological in the formation of female identity. At times, West indicates that it is because of our biology that women are and have been different from men. Biology, in other words, causes women to have a particular psychic structure. Our reproductive capacities shape our psychic identity—women value intimacy and connection rather than autonomy and separation.[17] Yet, West also recognizes that women may experience their biology in the way she describes because it is given expression and lived in a particular system of gender representation.[18] Thus, the system of gender representation, rather than the underlying biological "facts," engenders feminine identity. Correspondingly, the system of gender representation, and not biology, provides the basis for women's shared experience.

> More generally, as Dinnerstein, Chodorow, French, and Gilligan all insist, maternal biology does not *mandate* existential value: men *can* connect to other human life. Men can nurture life. Men can mother. Obviously, men can care, and love, and support, and affirm life. Just as obviously, however, most men don't. One reason that they don't, of course, is male privilege. Another reason, though, may be the blinders of our masculinist utopian visionary. Surely one of the most important insights of feminism has been that biology is indeed destiny when we are unaware of the extent to which biology is narrowly our fate, but that *biology is destiny only to the extent of our ignorance.*[19]

Yet, in spite of her recognition of the limits of biologically determined explanations of feminine difference, West continues to maintain that there are connections among women's identity, experience, and biology.[20] Indeed, she defends the need to root feminist theory as a theory of female *nature,* which requires an account of how biology functions in the acquisition of a female identity. Without a theory of female *nature,* West believes it is impossible to develop a "phenomenology" of women's unique and shared experience.[21] Furthermore, without such a "phenomenology," West argues there is no basis for a feminism founded in the unique experience of women. For feminism to exist, we must have a naturalist or essentialist view of who woman truly is, for only this view provides a "female reality" that all women can, at least potentially, understand as their own. Women, in other words, are differentiated from one another, but, as *women,* we share a common biological structure, which in turn affects our psychic identity. Individual identity remains, in this sense, a female identity. Therefore, shared experience is possible because of a female nature.

Yet it is precisely essentialist and naturalist accounts of the feminine that have been philosophically rejected as inconsistent with "postmodern" philosophy.[22] It is not a coincidence that many of the works that are often labeled "postmodern" grew out of the critique of Husserl's phenomenology. West's own project, however, is based on neither

French nor German phenomenology. West wants to root the feminine in a natural account of women's reproductive capacity. West finds the ultimate reality of Woman in her biological structure. By so doing, she collapses women's essence into her nature. In Husserl, on the other hand, "essences" are irreducible to the "factual" or to the natural. Husserlian phenomenology is instead concerned with essences that are eidetically abstracted pure phenomena. Yet, as we will see, West's insistence on a feminine "reality" that is just "there" as women's nature would still fall prey to the postmodern deconstruction of the philosophical basis of phenomenology.

The Feminist Dilemma Restated

Jacques Derrida's deconstruction[23] of Husserl's metaphor of the interweaving of the "preexpressive" noema with the "expressive" power of language[24] is relevant here. Derrida, with others, has deconstructed the rigid divide between *Sinn* and *Bedeutung,* which can be roughly translated as *reference* and *meaning.* Derrida shows that reference involves a context of pre-given meaning, which makes pure revelation impossible because we cannot wipe out the metaphoric aspect of language.[25] Although Husserl recognizes the productivity of language as expression through metaphor, and its inevitable "use" in the relation of preexpressive noema, he continually seeks a mirror writing that would ultimately cancel out his own inevitable use of metaphor to "describe" the relation between the "two states," so as to let us uncover the essence the things form. To quote Derrida:

> Thus, the preexpressive noema, the prelinguistic sense, must be imprinted in the expressive noema, must find its conceptual mark in the content of meaning. Expression, in order to limit itself to transporting a constituted sense to the exterior, and by the same token to bring this sense to conceptual generality without altering it, in order to express what is already thought (one almost would have to say written), and in order to redouble faithfully—expression then must permit itself to be imprinted by sense at the same time as it expresses sense. The expressive noema must offer itself, and this is the new image of its unproductivity as a blank page or virgin tablet; or at least as a palimpsest given over to its pure receptivity. Once the inscription of the sense in it renders it legible, the logical order of conceptuality will be constituted as such.[26]

For Derrida, this attempt to achieve mirror writing, which ultimately erases its own metaphors and with metaphor the performative power of language, is the very definition of metaphysical language which could be true to the things themselves. As we will see, Derrida believes that such a language is impossible. But for Husserl, it is necessary for the revelation of *essence* as a conceptually generalizable form. Crucial to Husserl's project is the "purification" of the concepts of form and essence from the metaphysical tradition which had "corrupted" them. But, as Derrida explains, this "purifying" critique continually gets bogged down by the very productivity of language in which it must be carried out and explained which then undercuts its own claim to "cut" through to the "essence" of the form of things themselves. This is why Derrida states "[f]orm 'is' its ellipsis,"[27] because the interrelationship between the two strata cannot be described other than through expression which involves metaphors. It would only be possible to achieve phenomenology's stated goal of revealing the form of the things themselves, if expressing is to do nothing more than transport a constituted sense to the exterior, and by so doing merely re-issue a noematic sense by providing access to conceptual form. But just as Husserl is trying to explain how this purification is to take place, he gets strung up in the expression of the interlacing of the two strata, the preexpressive and linguistic expression:

> The *interweaving* (*Verwebung*) of language, the interweaving of that which is purely language in language with the other threads of experience constitutes a cloth. The word *Verwebung* refers to this metaphorical zone. The "strata" are "woven," their intercomplication is such that the warp cannot be distinguished from the woof. If the stratum of the logos were simply *founded*, one could extract it and bring to light its underlying stratum of nonexpressive acts and contents. But since this superstructure acts back upon the *Unterschicht* in an essential and decisive manner, one is indeed obliged, from the very outset of the description, to associate a properly *textual* metaphor with the geological metaphor; for cloth means text. *Verweben* here means *texere*. The discursive is related to the nondiscursive, the linguistic "stratum" is intermixed with the prelinguistic "stratum" according to the regulated system of a kind of *text*.[28]

Thus, Derrida shows us in his deconstruction of Husserl's problematic that the interweaving of *Sinn* and *Bedeutung* is regulated by its textuality and *mode* of expression, which is not to say that there is no distinction, but only that the distinction is itself dependent upon textuality.

We can now begin to understand what Derrida means—and does not mean—by his famous statement "there is nothing outside of the text." He does not mean that deconstruction suspends reference as if such a suspension would be possible. Indeed, Derrida recognizes that language necessarily implies reference. If we can say that without *Bedeutung* there would be no *Sinn,* we could also say that without the postulation of reference there would be no *Bedeutung.* We will return to the relationship of this postulation of reference to undecidability which, within the context of Husserl's philosophy, indicates the impossibility of purifying form, so as to know, through eidetic abstraction, the essence of things themselves. We will also see how undecidability plays a necessary role in the reconceptualization of feminism as ethical feminism. For now, I simply want to emphasize that deconstruction's insistence that the real world is "there" as textual effect, does not mean that there is no "real" world to which we refer. The "real world" can not be erased precisely because it is "here" as textual "effect." Deconstruction reminds us, in other words, of how the real world "is"; it does not deny its pull on us, even as it insists that it is a pull which, in turn, implies the possibility of resistance. This reminder of how the real world "is" as textual effect does reinstate a transcendental aspect in Derrida's thought, which is why Derrida himself is careful to remind us that deconstruction is neither antifoundationalist nor foundationalist. But the transcendental moment is itself called into question as the relationship between *Sinn* and *Bedeutung* is continuously problematized.

> To say, in effect, that the description of the infrastructure (of sense) has been guided secretly by the superstructural possibility of meaning, is not to contest, against Husserl, the duality of the strata and the unity of a certain transition which relates them one to the other. It is neither to wish to reduce one stratum to the other nor to judge it impossible completely to recast sense in meaning. It is neither to reconstruct the experience (of sense) as a *language,* above all if one takes this to be a *discourse,* a verbal fabric, nor to produce a critique of language on the basis of the ineffable riches of sense. It is simply to ask questions about *another relationship* between what are called, problematically, *sense* and *meaning.*[29]

Deconstruction, then, undermines the attempt to establish language as a pure medium that simply accepts sense and brings it to conceptual form. The discourse of phenomenology cannot free itself from the productivity of *Einbildung,* because of its own use of images, figures, etc.

West herself does not speak directly to the issue of the status she wants to give to her phenomenology.[30] But to the degree that she wants to get back, beyond language, to the *very essence of form of Woman,* she is ensnared in the phenomenologists' dilemma. An essentialist theory of Woman would have to reveal Woman for what she truly is, beyond the trappings of culture and the "false consciousness" of patriarchy. This attempt demands that we "purify" language so that it is only a medium which would allow the "true" form of woman to at last be self-evident. West misunderstands the degree to which her own essentialist project necessarily replicates the attempt to cleanse language of its productivity. It is in this sense that the deconstruction of the rigid divide between *Sinn* and *Bedeutung*[31] is relevant to recent feminist debates over the question of essentialism. Essentialism, in the strong sense, demands a particular view of language. Even West's belief that women lie implies something like an appeal to a known interiority in which "our experience" is safely enclosed.[32] If one takes West's phenomenology literally, then consciousness raising would be the end of this lying. Consciousness raising would bring "our experience" into the exterior, giving it conceptual form through expression. I believe that West herself has a more expansive concept of consciousness raising than making explicit what was already there. But I also want to suggest that to the degree that she continues to advocate essentialism, she is in danger of limiting the role of consciousness raising.

To better understand what is at stake in the essentialist/antiessentialist debate as it has been developed in feminist theory, we are again returned to Derrida's analysis of philosophical language as necessarily involving the aspiration to effectively erase the metaphors in which it is enclosed. The goal is to achieve a pure conceptual knowledge through the constant cleansing of language so as to allow an accurate representation of the thing it seeks to know. This aspiration inevitably involves a suspicion of metaphor as the "contamination" of mirror writing. Yet, as we have seen in Husserl, metaphor is inevitable to the description of the metaphysical project itself. To quote Derrida:

> Metaphor, therefore, is determined by philosophy as a provisional loss of meaning, an economy of the proper without irreparable damage, a certainly inevitable detour, but also a history with its sights set on, and within the horizon of, the circular reappropriation

of the literal, proper meaning. This is why the philosophical evaluation of metaphor always has been ambiguous: metaphor is dangerous and foreign as concerns *intuition* (vision or contact), *concept*
(the grasping or proper presence of the signified), and *consciousness*
(proximity or self-presence; but it is in complicity with what it
endangers, is necessary to it in the extent to which the de-tour is a return guided by the function of resemblance (*mimēsis* or *homoisōis*),
under the law of the same. The opposition of intuition, the concept,
and consciousness at this point no longer has any pertinence. These
three values belong to the order and to the movement of meaning.
Like metaphor.[33]

Derrida shows us that there is no reassuring opposition of the metaphoric and the proper while simultaneously demonstrating that it is
through metaphor that we assign what is "proper" to a given thing.
As we have seen, Derrida deconstructs the possibility of reaching the
essence of the form of the thing itself through eidetic abstraction. But
there is still the aspiration in philosophy to know the "essence" of the
real so that one can decisively separate the real and the literal from
fantasy, illusion, and fiction. Let us for the moment define the "literal"
rendering of the real as that which most clearly respects the properties
of things. If we cannot escape language, or render it a pure medium, we
are forced to attribute properties through the "de-tour" of metaphor.
Figuration through metaphor is a tool that must be eventually thrown
away if it is to achieve its function of taking us to the "literal." This
fundamental ambivalence inheres in the relationship Derrida describes
between metaphor and philosophy. Put very simply, philosophy needs
metaphor to reach the real and yet metaphor always takes us away
from "it" by performing on "it." Metaphorical transference, in other
words, is a mechanism by which we attempt to reach the literal,
understood as the necessary or essential properties of things. But ultimately we must discard it as a mechanism, if we are to achieve "mirror
writing," and therefore know the essence of the things themselves. To
quote Derrida's description of the conditions "necessary" for metaphoric transportation:

> The transported significations are those of attributed properties, not
> those of the thing itself, as subject or substance. Which causes
> metaphor to remain mediate and abstract. For metaphor to be possi-
> ble, it is necessary, without involving the thing itself in a play of
> substitutions, that one be able to replace properties for one another,
> and that these properties belong to the same essence of the same

thing, or that they be extracted from different essences. The necessary condition of these extractions and exchanges is that the essence of a concrete subject be capable of several properties, and then that a particular permutation between the essence and what is proper to (and inseparable from) it be possible within the medium of quasi-synonymy. That is what Aristotle calls the antikategorēisthai: the predicate of the essence and the predicate of the proper can be exchanged without the statement becoming false.[34]

Essence and property are not identical. The point is that without "direct" access to the essence of the thing, we reach that essence only through the metaphorical transference of properties. Metaphor, however, must then ultimately be re-collected if Husserl is to achieve his goal of reducing expression so that it merely reissues noematic sense. But if this cannot be done, and it cannot be done if the trail of metaphor never comes to an end, then we are left with a *prescriptive* transference through metaphor of the properties supposedly essential to the thing. It is in this *prescriptive* moment in metaphorical transference, that is supposedly erased in the myth, that we can ultimately re-collect metaphor. In other words, there is the myth that I am not speaking of what is *proper* to the thing as it should be, I am only indicating what it truly is in its essence. Otherwise, we are left with the prescription of properties that cannot erase its normative underpinnings. We prescribe these properties as the essence of the thing because that is how we know the thing, or more precisely how we think the thing should be, because if we cannot simply give the thing its proper name through pure expression, we are always *prescribing* its properties. It is this moment of prescription in metaphorical transference, which assigns the proper, that makes Derrida himself suspicious of metaphor.

I want to return now to the way in which the appeal to the essence of Woman, since it is not possible in any pure sense, leads to reification of so-called properties of femininity and with it the proper place of women. What gets called the essence of Woman is precisely this metaphorical transport of the so-called proper. Therefore, what one is really doing when one states the essence of woman is reinstating her in her proper place. But the proper place, so defined through West's essential properties of what women can be, ends by shutting them in once again in that *proper* place. In this unique sense, the appeal to the essence of Woman, since it cannot be separated completely from the *prescription* of properties to her, reinforces the stereotypes that limit our possibilities, including the possibilities inherent in the metaphoric expression of the significance of feminine sexual difference. I want to emphasize how, to the degree it claims to have reached the "essence" of Woman, West's essentialism misses its prescriptive reinstatement of the proper.[35] This essence, as we have seen, carries within it our "should be," in the sense that women are better because of their essence or nature.

There appear in the literature two ethical presentations—one stronger and one weaker, sometimes without a clear line of demarcation between them—of the view that the female voice should count as an expression of feminine difference. The first is that women's voices should count because all voices should count. The second is more explicitly rooted in the feminine as a different way of being human. Women's experience should count because it is ethically superior and, therefore, can provide us with a standard for judging this world. To paraphrase the argument: We, unlike men, know what it means to care and to love others. As a result, if we bring our voice into the public realm, the ethical and political reality of all of our lives will be changed. West embraces as her own the stronger rather than the weaker version of the story that tells of the *value* of taking into account female difference. For West, the rejection of the relevance of love as fundamental in public life is a reflection of masculine values. Moreover, this exclusion has severely crippled even the most radical of masculine political visions.

> Indeed, I can't imagine any project more crucial right now, to the survival of this species than the clear articulation of the importance of love to a well-led public life. We not only need to show that these values are missing from public life and not rewarded in private life, but we also need to show how our community would improve if they were valued.[36]

When West makes statements about the ethical significance of our difference, she is very close to Aristotelian naturalism—indeed, closer to Aristotelian naturalism than she is to Husserl's phenomenology—although no "modern" Aristotelian would embrace her conception of love as necessary to public life. Women *are* X. A *good* woman is true to what she is. This description of the true woman carries within its own properties. We know what a *good* woman is because we know what a woman is and, therefore, what it means to be "true" to our own nature. To be "good" is to live up to the aspiration that this truth lays out for us, at least if we take seriously the Aristotelian form of argumentation.

West wants to ground woman's difference in her nature; yet, in spite of herself, she limits consciousness raising to revelation. "True consensus" in other words, is ultimately possible among women even if we currently disagree because we can *use* consciousness raising to take us back to our nature. Once we know what our true nature is, we can also assess whether our nature is "better" than men's, by comparing the properties that inhere in our "true" nature to theirs. The prescriptive moment in this argument demands the ascription of properties to women. It is this relationship of prescription to ascription that allows ethical statements to achieve the objectivity that West seeks. In spite of her affirmation of the creative power of consciousness raising and her sensitivity to the danger of accusing any woman of the distinction between her own sexuality and the "true" nature of woman, she cannot avoid—at least as long as she wants to embrace naturalism—telling us of the proper place for Woman.

The sense in which I am writing of prescription is exactly of the kind that makes Catharine MacKinnon suspicious of any writing of the feminine that affirms feminine difference as "it" has been defined within the current gender hierarchy. In the name of an appeal to essence we are only reinstating the vision of what is proper to us in patriarchical society. This is why MacKinnon insists that any affirmation of the feminine involves limiting our possibilities. MacKinnon insists that we must reject any notion of Woman's proper place. To reify this proper place as nature is worse yet because for MacKinnon our "nature" has always been defined by man.

To summarize, the deconstructive project resists the reinstatement of a theory of female nature as a philosophically misguided bolstering of rigid gender identity within the dichotomous structure of the logos. Deconstruction also demonstrates that there is no essence of Woman that can be eidetically abstracted from the linguistic representations of Woman. The referent Woman is dependent upon the systems of representation in which she is given meaning and these systems of representation, in turn, are also constituted by racial, national, and class difference, in the very image of what is projected as Woman.

Moreover, essentialist and naturalist theories of the feminine have been ethically and politically condemned for providing a new justification for the old stereotypes, even if those stereotypes are now supposedly being used to *affirm* the feminine. The price we pay for the affirmation of the feminine, so the argument goes, even if it could be philosophically defended, is too high. This view that the price is too high is the basis for the sophisticated version of liberal feminism which would insist that the only way for women to achieve legal recognition of their equal status to men is, at the very least, to deny the legal relevance of their difference to the degree that it exists. Women are individuals, and as individuals they should be recognized as legal persons and not be reduced to their specific gender identity. There is, in other words, no shared female identity. There are only individuals who happen to be women.

But, of course, the feminist response is that this strategy joins forces with the dominant discourses so as to again deny women legal redress. Worse yet, to the degree liberal feminism accepts masculine norms, it undermines the possibility of recognition of the unnoticed suffering of women. West seems to have a powerful argument that without an account that affirms the unique experience of women *as women* we participate in our silencing. For West, we are not just individuals. We are women and we cannot escape our destiny as genderized human beings by maintaining the illusion that women and men are just "people."

Moreover, as we have seen, the challenge to "individualism" in West is not made in the name of protecting the reality of a shared female experience, although this is obviously the central goal. Female difference should be valued not just because it is "there" but because it indicates a better way to live. For West, a crucial aspect of feminist theory is to affirm the feminine.

Note that I use the words "*affirm* the feminine," for, as already indicated, West does not merely claim that women's suffering exists. She also claims that there is "value" in this experience and that major social institutions, like law, should not deny this value by privileging the "masculine" as the norm. For West, to "prize" the feminine we must have a phenomenological account that shows us why this way of being in the world is better and how this experience is rooted in female nature.

If, however, we reject West's explicit return to naturalist or essentialist theories of woman's difference, as I believe we must, the question remains whether we can still *affirm* the feminine. Even if they are not the same, both theories rely on the postulation of the essence of Woman that we can know as her Truth. It is precisely the idea that we can discover the truth of women in reality that I am challenging both methodologically and ethically. And yet, if we refuse this affirmation, how can we answer the accusation that we are indeed participating in the traditional repression and the disparagement of the feminine, at the same time that we are also undercutting the basis for a "phenomenological" account of female experience upon which West and other radical feminists rely as *their basis* for a critical take on what is?

One response to this charge is to focus on how the feminine as a psychoanalytic category is produced so that it also serves as a disruptive force of the very gender system in which it is given meaning. The "feminine" is not celebrated just because it is the feminine, but because it stands in for the heterogeneity that undermines the logic of identity. As Barbara Johnson reminds us, when we write of women everything is out of place, and it is precisely this displacement of gender difference, that potentially inheres in the writing of women, that is celebrated.

This position has appeal because it does not claim to show what women's nature or essence actually is. Instead, all that is demonstrated is how the feminine is produced with a particular system of gender representation so as to be disruptive of gender identity and hierarchy. The "feminine" is a critical heuristic device within the dichotomous system of gender identity in which the masculine is privileged as the norm. Yet inherent in this position is the risk that the "not yet" of a new choreography of sexual difference will be presented as an actual "reality" now, rather than as a promise that remains to be fulfilled. Even as we want to recognize that the play of feminine sexual difference is not captured by the stereotypes of any gender hierarchy, we also do not want to deny the tragedy of women's suffering. The explosive power of feminine jurisprudence can only too easily be cut off by the reality of a legal system that denies the feminine within sexual difference in the name of the masculine; however, it can also be cut off by undermining the actual experience of suffering that exists now, in the name of a possibility that "exists"—but as a dream not as an actuality.[37]

We need to ask: Is it just the critical heuristic force of heterogeneity that is valued in the feminine or is there something "valuable" in the feminine that cannot be reduced to the affirmation, in general, of difference? If, on the other hand, we affirm the feminine for its own sake, how can we do so without relying on essentialist or naturalist conceptions of what women are? In order to even begin to answer these questions, we must rethink the philosophical underpinnings of the very understanding of sexual difference. We will begin this exploration within the psychoanalytic framework which opens up a nonbiological view of the feminine. We will then turn to a reconsideration of how deconstruction has worked within the psychoanalytic account of the feminine to expose it as allegory. Let me begin by discussing how and why Kristeva's account of mothering diverges from that offered by West.

The Difference Between West and Kristeva

The central difference between West and Kristeva is that Kristeva relies on a psychoanalytic framework that explicitly rejects West's biologism. Indeed, Kristeva's psychoanalytic insight works against her own representation of the female body and of mothering as the "basis" for female difference.[38] To understand Kristeva, we must put her account of mothering into the context of Jacques Lacan's psychoanalytic theory.[39] Lacan's central insight has been to correct the biological readings of Freud's account of gender differentiation through the castration complex.[40] According to Lacan, the genesis of linguistic consciousness occurs when the infant recognizes itself as having an identity separate from the mother. The primordial moment of separation is experienced by the infant as both loss and as acquisition of identity. The pain of loss results in a primary representation that buries the memory of the relationship to the mother within the unconscious and catapults the infant into the symbolic realm to fulfill its desire for the Other. Once projected into language, however, this primary identification with the mother is projected only as lack. The Phallic Mother and what she represents cannot be spoken in language, which is why Kristeva emphasizes that we can only reach Her through the semiotic, not through the symbolic. Thus, Kristeva insists that the feminine, when "identified" as the Phallic Mother, embodies the dream of an undistorted relation to the Other that lies at the foundation of social life, but that cannot be adequately represented. From this view of Woman, or the feminine, "[i]t follows that feminist practice can only be negative, at odds with what already exists so that we may say 'that's not it' and 'that's still not it.' "[41]

So far, in this account, it would seem that both sexes are castrated by their exile from the Phallic Mother. Despite this facially gender-neutral account, however, Lacan goes further and appropriates signification in general to the masculine.[42] Although Lacanians maintain the difference between the penis and the phallus—the phallus represents the lack of both sexes—it remains the case that, because the penis is visible and can represent the lack, the penis can stand in for the would-be-neutral phallus. The phallus as the transcendental signifier, then, cannot be totally separated from its representation as the anatomical counterpart, the penis. Woman, as a result, is identified only by her lack of the phallus. She is different *from* the phallus. She can know herself only as this difference, as this lack. As lack, she cannot speak of herself directly. As Lacan remarks, "[T]here is no woman, but excluded from the value of words."[43] She *is* only as a hole in the system of linguistic representation. She is that which cannot be represented in the realm of the symbolic. This is the basis for Lacan's infamous assertion that Woman does not exist,[44] which is one way of saying that the Phallic Mother and women's repressed relationship to Her cannot be represented.

Lacan's assertion, however, is also a way of insisting that women cannot tell of the experience of Woman, because it is exactly this universal experience which is beyond representation. Lacanianism, in other words, seems to undermine all attempts on the part of feminists or antifeminists to tell us what Woman is. She is the beyond. The impossible within the Lacanian Real. At the same time, Woman or the feminine, is "there" in her absence, as the impossible, as the lack that marks the ultimate object of desire in all defined subjects. To say that She is unknowable is not, then, to argue that Her lack does not operate. Indeed, Woman as lack, as the impossible, the unreachable projection of an inexpressible desire, is constitutive of genderized subjectivity. Even so, Woman does not exist as a "reality," present to the subject, but as a loss.

Lacan explains some of the great myths of the quest in which masculine identity seeks to ground itself as a quest for Her. The feminine becomes the Holy Grail. Within the Lacanian framework, the myths of Woman are about this quest to ground masculine subjectivity. As a result, these myths cannot serve as clues to unlocking Her mystery. They tell us about masculine subjectivity, not about Woman.

As women, we are cut off from the myths that could give the feminine meaning and, therefore, in Lacan's sense, we are silenced before the mystery of the ground of our own identity. The feminine is only given meaning in the symbolic order that belies Her existence as "real." The feminine "is" imaginary, represented only in the contents of masculine fantasy. Thus, women cannot knowingly engage the feminine in order to advance an affirmation of their own "sex." They are, instead, appropriated by the imaginary feminine as it informs male fantasy. But the "truth" of this fantasy is rooted in a primordial desire for the Other that cannot be destroyed and continues to threaten the order of the symbolic. In this sense, the feminine as the impossible in the Real remains a subversive force in Lacanian psychoanalysis.

Kristeva accepts this basic Lacanian framework. Her Lacanianism, at first glance, seems to belie her own attempt to make mothering a basis for an explanation of feminine difference.[45] Lacan denies that the feminine or the Phallic Mother as a fantasy figure is closer to women than to men, even if the two sexes are not cut off from her in the same way. Kristeva, on the other hand, attempts to draw a close connection between Woman and women.[46] Kristeva argues that through pregnancy, women experience an *other* within themselves: "redoubling up of the body, separation and coexistence of the self and of an other, of nature and consciousness, of physiology and speech."[47] Thus, women can overcome the destructive dualities created by the separation from the Mother by relating as mothers themselves. Women's reproductive capacity carries with it the potential to overcome, to some degree, the "effects" of the castration that both genders suffer in their separation from the Phallic Mother. In this way women are differentiated from men in their relationship to the feminine fantasy figure of Woman. By mothering, women can learn to relate in a non-dominating way that is inaccessible to the masculine subject, at least to the degree that he accepts his castration. However, it must be emphasized that because Kristeva associates the semiotic with the feminine, not with actual empirical women, she always leaves open the possibility that men, too, can reach beyond their own gender identity to reconnect with the repressed Mother. Despite this recognition that the semiotic is not the unique province of women, women are still different from men in their relationship to their castration, because they themselves can eventually mother. In this way, mothering potentially creates a difference between the genders in their internalization of the separation from the Phallic Mother.

Kristeva's account of the feminine, unlike West's, does not rest solely on biology. Kristeva's account gives us room to explain why men, as well as women, can care and love. There are not the "two" realities, one male and female, that West inevitably establishes. West accepts the story of masculine "separation" from the Mother as the foundation for male identity, and, therefore, she cannot explain how a man could get beyond this identity. Kristeva's psychoanalytic framework, on the other hand, shows how men too can escape entrapment in gender identity, because, on a theoretical plane, both the masculine and the feminine positions are accessible to each—albeit not in exactly the same way.

West's difficulty stems from her reliance on object-relations theory, which draws a direct connection between the social relations of mother-based childrearing and gender identity.[48] Psychic structure, in other words, is understood as engendered by social relations. The result is the reduction of psychic structure to social reality. But the recent American version of this theory also presumes certain basic characteristics of families. This very presupposition denies how race and national difference may alter those characteristics, and correspondingly, at least in this version of object-relations theory, how the psychic qualities that supposedly develop because of this presumed commonality may also vary. In this version of object-relations theory, the feminine position is not even theoretically available to males as it is in the psychoanalytic framework. West's two "realities," one male, one female, lie at the basis of her analysis of the writers in the Conference of Critical Legal Studies.[49]

In West's view, men, lacking reproductive capacity, do not connect to others in the primordial way that women do. The male subject may, therefore, live out the fundamental contradiction elaborated in Critical Legal Studies. West summarizes the "fundamental contradiction," as it has been expressed in the work of Duncan Kennedy, as an accurate expression of masculine subjectivity:

> According to Kennedy, we value *both* autonomy and connection, and fear *both* annihilation by the other and alienation from him, and all for good reason. The other is both necessary to our continued existence and a threat to that continued existence. While it is true that the dominant liberal story of autonomy and annihilation serves to perpetuate the status quo, it does not follow from that fact that the subjective desires for freedom and security which those liberal values reify are entirely *false*. Rather, Kennedy argues, collectivity is both essential to our identity and an obstacle to it. We have contradictory desires and values because our essential human condition—physical separation from the collectivity which is necessary to our identity—is itself contradictory.[50]

But this reality is not the same for women, according to West, although she recognizes that women, too, may fear intimacy as an invasion against their personhood. West believes that men, more than women, internalize their separation from others as the very basis for their identity.

The Lacanian Account of Masculine Subjectivity and the Basis for Female Solidarity

The Lacanian account turns West's story on its head. Although both genders are cut off from the repressed mother, and, theoretically, have access to the position of the other, only men, to the degree they become traditional, heterosexual men, are fundamentally "connected" to one another in the order of the symbolic. Without this connection, there would be no ground for masculine identity.

At first glance, this may seem a strange argument because of the association of connection with a particular normative practice of intimacy. But within Lacanianism, connection has a technical meaning. Masculine identity is not about separation from, but subordination to, the reign of the symbolic which is the foundation of social order. The order of the symbolic, in turn, provides the basis for the "boys club." The myth of the autonomous man protects against the painful recognition that the brothers find their masculinity only through their subordination to the Law of the Father and that it is this shared reality of the Law that maintains their sense of belonging to their identities as men. Women are *the other* to this club, marking its boundaries and defining its membership. David Mamet once described men as the puppy dogs of the universe. The Lacanian account of gender difference helps us to explain why they are "puppy dogs." It also helps to explain why the rhetoric of castration is repeated in so many descriptions of imperialist domination. To be subjected is to be refused status as a man. It is to be excluded from the illusionary set. A good example of this is bell hooks's moving analysis of the way the rebellion of Afro-American men has been expressed in the language of phallogenocentrism. In her discussion of Soul on Ice, she reminds us how Eldridge Cleaver's vision of liberation was informed by his desire to put himself in the position of the castrator. His masculinity was demonstrated by raping the women of the imperialist, the symbolic Father. By so doing, he imagines himself in the position of the Father. Sexual difference defined within the gender hierarchy engenders a shared, social, masculine "reality" which, as hooks reminds us, creates a kind of identification between black men and their white male oppressors.[51] This social "reality," however, is not as West sees it through the window of object relations. Within the Lacanian framework, the legal norms described by West may represent an aspiration shared by men to achieve autonomy, but they do not reflect the actual social "reality" created by sexual difference, for that "reality" is one of subordination to the Law of the Father.[52]

Within this framework, if there is a basis for the solidarity of women, it is the shared experience of exile and, more profoundly, of mourning for the feminine that is shut out of the realm of the symbolic except as represented in male fantasy. Women cannot easily find themselves in the representations of feminine sexual difference that appear in masculine fantasy, because these fantasies represent the male loss of the Mother.

Perhaps the most elegant expression of the communion of mourning that "unites" women is found in the novels of Marguerite Duras. Marie Stretter weeps continually: "She looks . . . imprisoned in a kind of suffering. But . . . a very old suffering . . . too old to make her sad any more. . . . And yet she cries. . . ."[53] But her tears are not hers alone. There is no love that can fill this void. The mourning is not for the man who does not come but for the feminine that is shut out.

Duras portrays the tragedy imposed upon women by the lack of the feminine within sexual difference in the opening pages of *The Vice-Consul*[54] and in *India Song*.[55] In *India Song,* a young Laotian peasant woman is sent away by her mother because there is no place for her at home now that she is pregnant. She can neither save herself, nor her child, in a world where the feminine has no place. In her dreams, she is returned to the Mother. But her dreams cannot be realized. Her only escape from incessant longing is madness. She embraces the lack of the feminine that is her only identity. "She's always been trying to lose herself, really ever since her life began. . . ."[56]

Instead of seeking female identity, Duras turns the reader to mourning and to the subversive power of the holes in discourse that point beyond the order of the symbolic. In order to write of Woman, we need

> a hole-word, whose center would have been hollowed out into a hole, the kind of hole in which all other words would have been buried. . . . Enormous, endless, an empty gong, it would have held back anyone who had wanted to leave, it would have convinced them of the impossible, it would have made them deaf to any other word save that one, in one fell swoop it would have defined the future and the moment themselves. By its absence, this word ruins all the others, it contaminates them, it is also the dead dog on the beach at high noon, this hole of flesh.[57]

We mourn for the Phallic Mother that never has been and yet reminds us of the "not yet" in which feminine sexual difference would not be reduced to male fantasy, including the fantasy that the female lover is merely the Mother replacement. The woman in Duras's *The Malady of Death*[58] grows impatient with the man's identification of her as the lost Mother. The woman who is figured as the feminine in *The Malady of Death* is absent in her slumbering and eternally fleeing the full presence that would allow her to be his fantasy:

Perhaps you'd look for her outside your room, on the beaches, outside cafés, in the streets. But you wouldn't be able to find her, because in the light of day you can't recognize anyone. You wouldn't recognize her. All you know of her is her sleeping body beneath her shut or half-shut eyes.[59]

Kristeva, unlike Duras, does not endure the unique relationship of women to the Phallic Mother as a communion of mourning for the lost ground of female identity. This is Duras's "unavowable community."[60] Like Cixous and Irigaray,[61] Kristeva emphasizes that through our access to the semiotic, women can move toward the lost Mother. The maternal is not just the actual experience of pregnancy and reproductive capacity, but the possibility of reconnection with the repressed maternal which can be more easily achieved by women than by men because of women's potential for mothering. Kristeva, Cixous, and Irigaray emphasize the connection with the Mother, rather than our exile from Her in a world in which the feminine is rejected. As Cixous muses,

In woman there is always, more or less, something of "the Mother" repairing and feeding, resisting separation, a force that does not let itself be cut off but that runs codes ragged. . . . Text, my body: traversed by lilting flows; listen to me, it is not a captivating, clinging "mother"; it is the equivoice that, touching you, affects you, pushes you away from your breast to come to language, that summons your strength; it is the rhyth-me that laughs you; the one intimately addressed who makes all metaphors, all body(?)—bodies(?)—possible and desirable, who is no more describable than god, soul, or the Other; the part of you that puts space between yourself and pushes you to inscribe your woman's style in language. Voice: milk that could go on forever. Found again. The lost mother/bitter-lost. Eternity: is voice mixed with milk.[62]

The "not yet" is already here in this potential for resurrection of the repressed maternal, even if only as mythical refiguration.

Although not impossible, it is difficult to base feminist practice on Duras's own allegory of the feminine. This difficulty undoubtedly explains why West and Kristeva have both turned to mothering and women's reproductive capacity as the basis for a feminine practice of writing—and in West's case for a feminist politics—rooted in the way women are or potentially can be.

The Critique of West and Kristeva

There are, however, several difficulties with relying on the bodily experience of mothering as a basis for feminist theory. Of course, not all women mother. Therefore, some would not have this experience of difference. But more important, West's and Kristeva's reliance on motherhood identifies the feminine with the Mother. Duras's allegories, on the other hand, underscore the *separation* of the feminine from the Mother.

Montrelay's analysis of the young girl's primordial relation to her own body—represented in the symbolic—is more helpful because it roots feminine identity in female sexuality rather than in mothering.[63] Women may choose not to become mothers, and feminists have certainly insisted that women need not become mothers to become "real" women. If the actual experience of mothering provides for the "ideal" of a different way of relating, then women who choose not to mother will never become real women. Feminism defined in this way would not rely on the experience of women, but on that of women as mothers.

Even if we recognize that the maternal is being used as a metaphor for the feminine, and not as the actual experience of mothering, we still have the problem of the perpetuation of the identification of Woman as Mother. The maternal as a metaphor in Cixous and Irigaray evokes the lost paradise of intimacy, not only with the Phallic Mother, but more generally with the world around us.[64] The maternal is but one metaphor for the feminine. I do not argue that the maternal as a metaphor is unimportant, but rather that feminine sexual difference should not be limited to the patriarchal definition of the maternal as a reproductive function.

The next problem is the danger of reifying the historical experience of a group of women into a "second nature" that is then attributed to all women. We do not have to accept MacKinnon's bleak description of our different voice as the expression of complicity in subordination[65] to suggest that women's difference as it has been described in history cannot, in and of itself, serve as the ideal, precisely because it has been contaminated by the "reality" of patriarchy. There is a serious danger in simply turning the "is" of our difference, even if it were found to be true, into an "ought."

The third problem in relying on women's experience of mothering and reproductive potential as the basis of feminist theory is that women themselves disagree as to what that experience "is" and what it ultimately means for a female identity. Mothering is not a unitary experience. What it means to mother is clearly influenced by racial, national, class, and other differences. Not only do we potentially trap ourselves in an experience that may represent a contaminated ideal, we must also attempt to determine exactly what the actual experience of women is, as an empirical matter and as a subjectively felt "reality," when there is clearly no consensus among us. Without consensus, we are confronted with the actual dilemma of how to uncover shared experience. West herself recognizes that in a fragmented society like our own any attempt to root feminine experience in women's consensus of our reality will be problematic:

> As Adrienne Rich has eloquently argued, one of women's most disabling problems is that women *lie*. For a multitude of reasons, we lie to ourselves and to others. And, one thing women lie about more than any other, perhaps, is the quality and quantity of our own hedonic lives. . . . This lying has hurt us. We lie so often we don't know when we are doing it. We lie so often we lack the sense of internal identity necessary to the identification of a proposition's truth or falsity. We lie so often that we lack a self who lies. We just *are* lies; we inhabit falsehood. Our lives are themselves lies.[66]

I suggest that we place West's concern about the presumed female propensity to lie into the problematic offered by Lyotard's writing on the differend.[67] The differend is that which has been shut out of traditional legal discourse and the social conventions of meaning. The suffering of women can be understood as the differend. The harm to women literally disappears because it cannot be represented as a harm within the law. It is not so much, then, that we are lying as that we cannot discover the "truth" of our experience in the current system of gender representation. The "truth" of our own experience awaits the discourse in which it can be expressed. As women, in a very profound sense, we are creating our experience as we write differently. Within law, this attempt to give expression to the *differend* is necessary to avoid the danger of analogizing women's experience to that of men in order to find redress within the legal system. We cannot give expression to the *differend* simply by turning woman into "a litigant," if such transformation demands that women's suffering be translated into the prevailing norms of the system which cannot adequately express the suffering of women, if it can be expressed at all. Feminist jurisprudence demands a new idiom. The legal system must be forced to hear women without translating their suffering into a harm already recognized as such within the prevailing system. If women cannot express their reality within the legal system, their reality disappears. As Lyotard explains,

> In the differend, something "asks" to be put into phrases, and suffers from the wrong of not being able to be put into phrases right away. This is when the human beings who thought they could use language as an instrument of communication learn through the feeling of pain which accompanies silence (and of pleasure which accompanies the invention of a new idiom), that they are summoned by language, not to augment to their profit the quantity of information communicable through existing idioms, but to recognize that what remains to be phrased exceeds what they can presently phrase, and that they must be allowed to institute idioms which do not yet exist.[68]

We depend on the performative power of language, particularly of poetic signification, to bring our feminine "reality" into view. As we will see, this need to expand the current discourse in order to "discover" our "reality" explains the necessity for the retelling of the myths of the feminine.[69] These myths function within metaphors which, as metaphors, have a surplus of meaning that allows us to both expand and create a new feminine "reality" from within the old.

In law, a shift in the representation of feminine "reality" can have important political and legal implications. Modes of behavior that were formally thought to be outside the parameters of the legal system can be seen as harms to women. We can expand the scope of litigation to turn women from silenced victims into plaintiffs who now find the words with which to speak.

> The plaintiff lodges his or her complaint before the tribunal, the accused argues in such a way as to show the inanity of the accusation. Litigation takes place. I would like to call a *differend* [*différend*] the case where the plaintiff is divested of the means to argue and become for that reason a victim.[70]

For example, the debate over what kind of male behavior constitutes sexual harassment inevitably turns on how the legal system "sees" women or, more precisely, allows them to be seen. If women are seen as "asking for it" when they dress to enhance their attractiveness, then it would make sense to allow evidence of a woman's dress in a sexual harassment case. After all, how would the poor man know that she did not want his advances? Evidentiary standards and procedures define relevancy. I am suggesting that what is relevant will turn, not just on the interpretation of those procedures and standards, but on how one "sees" women and sexual relations. As a result, the redefinition of the legal wrong, as well as the harm to women, will involve the process of changing the representation of feminine sexual difference.

The criticisms of West that I have advanced thus far do not necessarily undermine her "phenomenology," at least in a weak sense, as a narrative account that attempts to confirm the experience of women. West wants to show harms to women that have remained invisible within our current legal system, particularly in areas like wife battering and sexual harassment. West believes that we are forced to rely on some account of the "objective" reality of all women, irreducible to women's subjective perceptions. As we have seen, this objective "reality" is rooted in West's account of female nature. It does not rest on a consensus between women as to what that "reality" is. West's account of female nature is the basis for her "phenomenology." We can meet her aspirations, however, by trying to show that gender representation harms women by defining and enforcing "reality" in a way that makes legal redress difficult, if not impossible. In other words, we do not need to point to an "objective" reality rooted in the nature of all women in order to overcome the dilemma created by lack of consensus. We can point, instead, to a particular view of women within a particular system of legal definition.

Susan Estrich, for example, has very successfully demonstrated that the "consent" defense in rape harms women by making it very difficult for them to successfully press charges in court.[71] More important, because of the consent defense, the harm in rape becomes the harm of nonconsensual sex rather than the violation of the women's bodily integrity and of her soul. The consent defense, in other words, misconstrues the harm in rape and, by so doing, prevents the full suffering of rape victims from being "seen." It is one thing to be subjected to nonconsensual sex, it is quite another to be fundamentally violated by a terrifying assault that strips the woman of even the pretense that she is a subject and is recognized as such.

We are then confronted, as Estrich reminds us,[72] with the further difficulty of the meaning of consent, because it is the conventional wisdom that when women say no, they mean yes. The reality of rape is in this way shaped by the legal system in which it is interpreted.

If women find it difficult and humiliating to press their claims in situations like rape, then men *are* given license by the law to violate women. Law has the power to make itself true. A normative reality is created by who is or is not found guilty of rape and why. The justification "boys will be boys" is only too well known and truly horrifying, particularly as used recently in situations of date rape.[73] But there is also meaning to the statement that they are being boys. Gender is a system that gives meaning and that establishes identity and shared reality. None of us are free to just be beyond gender. It matters, however, whether we focus on how gender hierarchy is produced and reinforced by the legal system so as to harm women, or whether we instead rely on a theory of female nature that attempts to identify what Woman is as the basis of an account of the feminine. Women of color have frequently argued that such attempts are inherently suspect because they identify the "essence" of women with white women.[74]

By looking at how gender hierarchy is produced and represented in the law, we can provide for a version of West's "phenomenology" and avoid relying on the consensus of women's felt experience as the basis for expanding legal definitions. We can, at the same time, destabilize the system of gender hierarchy in the name of a new choreography of sexual difference that is beyond mere replication of what is.

This need to protect the possibility of a new choreography of sexual difference takes me to my next objection to West's and Kristeva's account of mothering as the basis for what is different in the feminine. Freud and Lacan teach us that there are no such "things" as men and women in any theoretically pure sense.[75] As split subjects we are all defined as both masculine and feminine, because there can be no pure referent outside of the system of gender representation that designates our "sex." The Lacanian story reveals the feminine inherent in the masculine desire for the imaginary relation to the Phallic Mother. The Lacanian story also demonstrates that women, as well as men, are masculine in so far as they enter the symbolic.[76] Genderized subjectivity, as a system, is produced imperfectly. Gender identity is bounded by historical circumstances. Such constraint can never, in a theoretical sense, be total. As a result, there cannot be the sharply divided, totally genderized, "realities" West describes. I do not want to reject entirely West's account of the differences between men and women in their experiences of acquiring an identity through the internalization of a genderized social reality. I do, however, want to argue that this experience is not, and cannot be, the whole story. If it were, we would have two worlds, one male, one female, and never the twain would meet. Without in any way denying how deeply imprinted our gender identify is, it is still possible to change, and, more specifically, it is possible for men to change by allowing themselves to "accept" the feminine in themselves.

The Deconstructive Allegory of Woman

The second approach to the revolutionary power of the feminine also returns us to Derrida's deconstructive reading of Lacan. Derrida shows us how Lacan cuts off the revolutionary implications of his own statement "Woman does not exist." In *Glas,*[77] *La Carte postale,*[78] *Spurs,*[79] and *Choreographies*[80] Derrida exposes the lie of Lacan's identification of the "feminine" as the *truth* of castration, as the "hole" that can only be filled in, never understood or represented, and certainly not by women themselves, who are excluded from the value of words. The lack, the inevitable absence of the Phallic Mother, is precisely what cannot be given a proper place. Indeed, Woman disrupts the very notion of a proper place, even the Lacanian "designation" of her as the lack of the phallus. The fallacy of the phallus is that it attempts to erect itself as its own truth. To quote Derrida:

> By determining the place of the lack, the topos of that which is lacking from its place, and in constituting it as a fixed center, Lacan is indeed proposing, at the same time as a truth-discourse, a discourse on the truth of the purloined letter as the truth of *The Purloined Letter.* . . . The link of Femininity and Truth is the ultimate signified of this deciphering. . . . Femininity is the Truth (of) castration, is the best figure of castration, because in the logic of the signifier it has always already been castrated; and Femininity "leaves" something in circulating (here the letter), something detached from itself in order to have it brought back to itself, because she has "never had it: whence truth comes out of the well, but only half-way."[81]

Derrida shows us that within Lacan's own analysis the feminine is the Other that remains beyond any system. Yet, because he desires to analyze, Lacan locates her again. But if one takes Lacan at his word there can be no definitive locale for Woman.[82] She cannot, as a result, be contained by any system of gender identification, including the one offered by Lacan. The feminine expresses the play of difference that cannot be wiped out. Yet, Lacan wants to contain the feminine by proclaiming her truth. Derrida, on the other hand, reads the feminine allegorically, through his deconstruction of Lacan's insistence that he can turn Woman into another truth that he can know. Lacan, in other words, creates, in spite of himself, the place of Woman as opposition, in the sense that she is defined as the lack of the phallus. He thinks that he has gotten to the bottom of her. Single-handedly, he claims to know Her.

In other words, Lacan indulges in "essentializing fetishes." He does so because of his conviction that he has grasped the truth of Woman as the fact of the lack of the phallus, a *fact* that is just "there." Derrida deconstructs Lacan's insistent separation of the Truth of Woman as castration from the fictions that surround and inhabit her. Lacan is determined to show us that "truth inhabits fiction." Derrida explains that for Lacan

> "[t]ruth inhabits fiction" cannot be understood in the somewhat perverse sense of a fiction more powerful than the truth which inhabits it, the truth that fiction inscribes within itself. In truth, the truth inhabits fiction as the master of the house, as the law of the house, as the economy of fiction.[83]

Derrida, on the other hand, reverses the order of the Lacanian relationship of Truth to fiction, particularly as Lacan's more general statements about the relationship of Truth and fiction inform his proclaiming of the Truth of "Woman." However, Derrida's understanding of the relationship between Truth and fiction does not deny reference to women or even to Woman as Woman is embodied in any given social context.

As we have seen earlier, the deconstruction of the rigid divide between *Sinn* and *Bedeutung,* which also emphasizes the inevitable figural or metaphorical casting of the real itself, is not meant to deny reference. But since this misreading of deconstruction is common among its political foes, I return to it again. To quote Derrida:

> To say for example, "deconstruction suspends reference," that deconstruction is a way of enclosing oneself in the sign, in the "signifier," is an enormous naiveté stated in that form. . . . Not only is there reference for a text, but never was it proposed that we erase effects of reference or referents. Merely that we re-think these effects of reference. I would indeed say that the referent is textual. The referent is in the text. Yet that does not exempt us from having to describe very rigorously the necessity of those referents.[84]

Translated into the sphere of feminist politics, Derrida's text recognizes the need to "describe" the referent Woman as it has been played with on the historical stage and as it has trapped, oppressed, and subordinated actual women. But he is also saying that such "descriptions" are never pure explanations, as if Woman could be separated from the texts in which she has been told. Our oppression is not a fiction, nor is it all a reality, a site, indeed a prison from which escape is impossible. If escape were impossible, it would also be impossible to avoid replicating the very structure of rigid gender identity which has imprisoned women and made the dance of the maverick feminist so difficult to keep up. Yet, these fictions as representations are still there for us. Indeed, it is only through these metaphors, representations, and fictions that we attempt to reach Woman. We cannot separate the Truth of Woman from the fictions in which she is represented and through which she portrays herself. In this sense, she becomes veiled. Therefore, we cannot not know once and for all who or what She is, because the fictions in which we confront Her always carry within the possibility of multiple interpretations, and there is no outside referent, such as nature or biology, in which this process of interpretation comes to an end. As a result, we cannot "discover" the ground of *feminine identity* which would allow us to grasp her Truth once and for all. Yet, Woman is not just reduced to lack because the metaphors of Her produce an always-shifting "reality." If there is a danger in Duras's extraordinary allegories of the feminine, it is in the seeming implicit acceptance of the truth of the feminine as lack of the phallus. Thus, the *only* "basis" for female solidarity is the unavowable community of mourning.

Derrida, on the other hand, wants to affirm the power to dance differently. He bows to the maverick feminist, determined to escape the confines of the given stereotypes of the feminine. Correctly understood, the feminine also opens the space in which the productive power of the metaphors of the feminine can operate to enhance and expand our "reality." We are not fated to simply repeat the same old dance, we can *be* out of step. The feminine is not engraved in stone.

> Perhaps woman does not have a history, not so much because of any notion of the "Eternal Feminine" but because all alone she can resist and step back from a certain history (precisely in order to dance) in which revolution, or at least the "concept" of revolution, is generally inscribed. That history is one of continuous progress, despite the revolutionary break—oriented in the case of the women's movement towards the re-appropriation of woman's own essence, her own specific difference, oriented in short towards a notion of a "truth." Your "maverick feminist" showed herself ready to break with the most authorized, the most dogmatic form of consensus, one that claims (and this is the most serious aspect of it) to speak out in the name of revolution and history. Perhaps she was thinking of a completely other history: a history of paradoxical laws and

non-dialectical discontinuities, a history of absolutely heterogeneous pockets, irreducible particularities, of unheard of and incalculable sexual differences; a history of women who have—centuries ago— "gone further" by stepping back with their lone dance, or who are today inventing sexual idioms at a distance from the main forum of feminist activity with a kind of reserve that does not necessarily prevent them from subscribing to the movement, and even, occasionally, from becoming a militant for it.[85]

This emphasis on the possibility of moving beyond the identification of the feminine as opposition is inherently ethical and political in Derrida. The need to push beyond the limit of the "reality" of Woman defined as lack of the phallus, the insistence that Woman cannot be separated from the metaphors in which she is presented and in which she veils herself, does not mean that there "is" no reality to women's oppression. Derrida completely understands the importance of bringing the dance of the maverick feminist in line with the "revolution" that seeks to end the practical "reality" of women's subordination:

The most serious part of the difficulty is the necessity to bring the dance and its tempo into tune with the "revolution." The lack of place for [*l'atopie*] or the madness of the dance—this bit of luck can also compromise the political chances of feminism and serve as an alibi for deserting organized, patient, laborious "feminist" struggles when brought into contact with all the forms of resistance that a dance movement cannot dispel, even though the dance is not synonymous with either powerlessness or fragility. I will not insist on this point, but you can surely see the kind of impossible and necessary compromise that I am alluding to: an incessant, daily negotiation—individual or not—sometimes microscopic, sometimes punctuated by a poker-like gamble; always deprived of insurance, whether it be in private life or within institutions. Each man and each woman must commit his or her own singularity, the untranslatable factor of his or her life and death.[86]

As Derrida reminds us, there is always more to the story of Woman than meets the eye, including Lacan's eye and his identification of Woman with castration. To quote Derrida:

The feminine distance abstracts truth from itself in a *suspension* of the relation with castration. This relation is suspended much as one might tauten or stretch a canvas, or a relation, which nevertheless remains—suspended—in indecision. . . . It is with castration that this relation is suspended, not with the truth of castration—in which woman does believe anyway—and not with the truth inasmuch as it might be castration. Nor is it the relation with truth-castration that is suspended, for that is precisely a man's affair. That is the masculine *concern,* the *concern* of the male who has never come of age, who is never sufficiently skeptical or dissimulating. In such an affair the male, in his credulousness and naivety (which is always sexual, pretending even at times to masterful expertise), castrates himself and from the secretion of his act fashions the snare of truth-castration.[87]

The reinstatement of rigid gender identity in the symbolic is replicated in Lacan's own account of Woman. In this sense, Lacan, like other men who think they know Woman, participate in their own castration by imprisoning themselves in a system of gender representation that cuts off their own desire for Her and replaces it with the illusion that they have grasped Her in their fantasies. But what they know is only the content of those fantasies, not Woman. Even as the idealized Mother (*mère*), she is more (*mehr*). Lacan cannot hold her down:

> Woman (truth) will not be pinned down. In truth woman, truth will not be pinned down. That which will not be pinned down by truth is, in truth—*feminine.* This should not, however, be hastily mistaken for a woman's *femininity,* for female *sexuality,* or for any other of those essentializing fetishes which still tantalize the dogmatic philosopher, the impotent artist or the inexperienced seducer who has not yet escaped his foolish hopes of capture.[88]

Spurs is often mistakenly read as just another attempt to identify Woman with Truth. Derrida, however, understands that because he writes within the problematic he cannot simply dislocate himself from it:

> The truth value (that is, Woman as the major allegory of truth in Western discourse) and its correlative, Femininity (the essence or Truth of Woman), are there to assuage such hermeneutic anxiety. They are the places that one should acknowledge, at least that is if one interested in doing so; they are the foundations or anchorings of Western rationality (of what I have called "phallogocentrism" [as the complicity of Western metaphysics with a notion of male firstness]). Such recognition should not make of either the truth value or femininity an object of knowledge (at stake are the norms

of knowledge and knowledge as a norm); still less should it make of them a place to inhabit, a home. It should rather permit the invention of another inscription, one very old and very new, a displacement of bodies and places that is quite different.[89]

Yet Derrida's desire for the new choreography of sexual difference also makes him wary of any attempt to introduce a new concept of representation of Woman to replace the ones we have now, because this change would again turn her into an object of knowledge. Woman would again be normalized, her proper place established. Thus, in response to Christie McDonald's question as to whether and how we can change the representation of Woman through "stage two" of deconstruction, in which the dichotomous hierarchy of the masculine and the feminine is reversed, Derrida responds:

> No, I do not believe that we have one [a new concept of Woman], if indeed it is possible to *have* such a thing or if such a thing could exist or show promise of existing. Personally, I am not sure that I feel the lack of it. Before having one that is new, are we certain of having had an old one? It is the word "concept" or "conception" that I would in turn question in its relationship to any essence which is rigorously or properly identifiable.[90]

Derrida, in other words, does not want feminism to be another excuse for passing out "sexual identity cards."[91] There is no ultimate feminine concept of Woman that can be identified once and for all. But this suspicion also prevents Derrida from proclaiming the Truth of Woman as absence or more specifically as the absence of Truth. This is Lacan's "concept." Derrida is instead celebrating the potential in the feminine to refuse castration, and by so doing to allow actual woman to dance differently:

> "Woman"—her name made epoch—no more believes in castration's exact opposite, anti-castration, than she does in castration itself. . . . Unable to seduce or to give vent to desire without it, "woman" is in need of castration's effect. But evidently she does not believe in it. She who, unbelieving, still plays with castration, she is "woman."[92]

The misinterpretation of Derrida that insists that he, in spite of himself, evokes Woman as the absence signified by the lack of the phallus, stems from the failure to note the full implications of Derrida's reversal of the Lacanian relationship of Truth and fiction as it relates to Woman.

Again, this does not mean the relationship of Truth and fiction is simply reversed, because it is precisely Lacan's point, in one sense, that Woman is a fiction. Derrida is not saying that there is nothing to be said about Woman written within this system of gender representation. Although he is clearly more interested in what women write for themselves. He is simply exposing that the claim that there "is" a truth of Woman that establishes her lack as fact of sexual difference itself takes place in the textuality of the referent woman. Derrida exposes the metaphorical transference that hides itself in the *literal* assumption that "there is" inescapable castration.

Stated within the technical language of Lacan's own analysis, the Real itself as the operational force of impossibility cannot be completely severed from the linguistic code of the unconscious.[93] A linguistic code cannot be frozen because of the slippage of meaning inherent in the metaphoricity of language. Lacan, in other words, belies the force of his own insight into the linguistic formation of the unconscious. There "is no pure beyond to the Symbolic," but there is also not a complete cut from either the imaginary, and the idealized woman, or the Real, because they only "are" in language.[94] The three realms Lacan differentiates are intermingled and thus the Law of the Father is marked and contaminated by what it needs to shut out to achieve the imaginary self-presence of phallic authority. To quote Derrida:

> That does not mean (to say) that there is no castration, but that this *there is* does not take place. There is that one cannot cut through to a decision between the two contrary and recognized functions of the fetish, any more than between the thing itself and its supplement. Any more than between the sexes.[95]

The erection of the Ça, Lacan's own term for the erection of sexual difference in the unconscious, is just that—an erection, fated to fall: The Law of the Father "is" only against what it represses, the idealized symbolic relationship of the infant to the mother. But this moment of repression marks the Law of the Father itself—indeed, makes it what *it is*—as authoritative because it is *phallic,* therefore *not* feminine. Lacan's assertion of the self-presence of the Father is exposed as a mechanism of denial to protect against the "return" of the feminine. The fantasy of self-presence of the male authority figure who pronounces what the Law "is" is exposed as precisely that, fantasy. The Law rests on the repressed underside of the feminine which, even when held down, continues to disrupt the purported unity of the Law. The feminine "operator" can intensify the effect of her disruption. Derrida's *Spurs* is a hymn to her power of disruption, which belies Lacan's attempt to pin down her Truth.

> The question of the woman suspends the decidable opposition of true and non-true and inaugurates the epochal regime of quotation marks which is to be enforced for every concept belonging to the system of philosophical decidability. . . . Truth in the guise of production, the unveiling/dissimulation of the present product, is dismantled. The veil no more raised than it is lowered. Its suspension is delimited—the epoch. To de-limit, to undo, to come undone, when it is a matter of the veil, is that not once again tantamount to unveiling? even to the destruction of a fetish? This question, *inasmuch as it is a question*, remains—interminably.[96]

Derrida's allegorical reading of the feminine is itself utopian in that it refuses the so-called realism of castration. In *Spurs,* Woman is the very figure of the constitutive power of the not yet, the beyond to Lacan's Symbolic. The play of difference does exactly the opposite of what it is thought to do; it does not make utopian thinking impossible, it makes it absolutely necessary, because the meaning of Woman, and of sexual difference, is displaced into the future. Lacan's pretense that we know Her truth and establish Her as a fact is revealed as an expression of the desire to know her so he can capture her. This desire is not the truth of reality, but rather the pretense he must play out to assuage his longings. What Derrida writes of the male generally can be read as a description of this Lacanian phenomenon:

> (Perhaps at this point one ought to interrogate and "unboss"—the metaphorical full-blown sail of truth's declamation of the castration and phallocentrism, for example, in Lacan's discourse).[97]

Moreover, Lacan's delusion is to see himself as the master of Woman. Woman continually plays with her truth, taking up through performance the position he has supposedly reduced her to. But, in Derrida, Woman engages with this performance, knowing that she is "playing":

> She takes aim and amuses herself (*en joue*) with it as she would with a new concept or structure of belief, but even as she plays she is gleefully anticipating her laughter, her mockery of man. With a knowledge that would out-measure the most self-respecting dog-

matic or credulous philosopher, woman knows that castration *does not take place*.[98]

Derrida realizes that stabilized gender representations exist and are enforced in social conventions so as to become "true." Indeed, without such stabilized representations it would not be possible to give a critical account of the treatment of the feminine and of women within law. The point is that the "truth" of feminine "reality," once we understand its inevitable metaphorical dimension, does not and cannot lie in properties of the object Woman. This "truth" rests in the systems of representation that have become so stabilized that they appear unshakable. Once we do away with the notion of a female nature that can be known, we can see that it would be a mistake to conclude that all interpretations of the feminine are equal, so that competing interpretations of the feminine can be judged for their adequacy to the object Woman. Instead, the criteria for judgment must be ethical and political. We can operate through the language of the feminine—by using the feminine affirmatively—to displace the stereotypes associated with gender difference.

Derrida's engagement with the language traditionally associated with the feminine body, then, is not a coincidence. Derrida, knowing that what he does is not the same as when a woman does it, positions himself through the feminine. But his style of writing in a chorus of "polysexual" voices also expresses his desire for the disruption of the prescriptive order of gender identity associated with the reification of literal gender identifications. For Derrida, an "answer" to the question of who we are sexually, if indeed it should even be risked, cannot even be approached if the standpoint of either male or female is reified so that the author speaks and writes from a unified position:

> At the approach of this shadowy area, it has always seemed to me that the voice itself had to be divided in order to say that which is given to thought or speech. No monological discourse—and by that I mean here mono-sexual discourse—can dominate with a single voice, a single tone, the space of this half-light, even if the "proffered discourse" is then signed by a sexually marked patronymic. Thus, to limit myself to one account, and not to propose an example, I have felt the necessity for a chorus, for a choreographic text with polysexual signatures.[99]

This attempt to achieve a "choreographic text with polysexual signatures" should obviously not be confused with an attempt to reinstate a sexually neutral position from which to write. Derrida consistently argues that such a position within our system of gender identity is impossible, which is why the choreographic text still involves designatable masculine and feminine voices at the same time that it tries to blur the traits and lines of thought traditionally associated with the gender opposition. Thus, even though Derrida deliberately resexualizes the supposedly neutral language of philosophy, and does so by using words which carry associations with the feminine body, hymen and invagination, for example, he also hesitates before the danger that such a use of language, while recognizing the repressed feminine, nevertheless reinforces rigid gender identity. Derrida recognizes that one can never know for sure whether any attempt to shift the boundaries of meaning and representation through a reinvention of language is complicit with or breaks with existing ideology. The use of words associated with the feminine body could only too easily reinstate phallocentric discourse by perpetuating myths of what that body is from the masculine viewpoint. Derrida believes he has chosen his words carefully to disrupt traditional associations that would seem to be determinate of the feminine. The introduction of such language carries a performative aspect that can never be totally assessed, but which unmasks the pretense of neutrality and at the same time questions the current line of cleavage between the sexes that would rigidly designate, this is masculine, this is feminine. The hymen "is" between male and female, but as what gives way "in love." To quote Derrida:

> One could say quite accurately that the hymen *does not exist*. Anything constituting the value of existence is foreign to the "hymen." And if there were hymen—I am not saying if the hymen existed—property value would be no more appropriate to it for reasons that I have stressed in the texts to which you refer. How can one then attribute the *existence* of the hymen *properly* to woman? Not that it is any more the distinguishing feature of man or, for that matter, of the human creature. I would say the same for the term "invagination" which has, moreover, always been reinscribed in a chiasmus, one doubly folded, redoubled and inversed, etc.[100]

The link between the Other, Woman, as the more (*mehr/mère*) of a given state of affairs is the threshold. We are constantly invited to cross through the essentialist conceptions of sexual difference, which in turn creates the opening for new interpretations. This link, evoked as the hymen, is both the invitation to cross over and yet also a barrier to full accessibility. The hymen, however, if inseparable from the feminine cannot just be reduced to a property of the female body.

Derrida also understands the ethical risks inherent in the gender-neutral position. Traditionally, ethics has been conceived as involving a universal position attainable for all subjects and thus independent of their sexual markings. Ethics then, involves the ability, at least for the purposes of morality, to speak of humanity in general and in a language that reflects that generality:

> [T]he possibility of ethics could be saved, if one takes ethics to mean that relationship to the other which accounts for no other determination or sexual characteristic in particular. What kind of an ethics would there be if belonging to one sex or another became its law or privilege? What if the universality or moral laws were modelled on or limited according to the sexes? What if their universality were not unconditional, without sexual condition in particular?[101]

If we do not accept the possibility of achieving a neutral position, then by definition morality itself will be sexually marked. More important, if we understand the sexual opposition not only as a dichotomy but as a hierarchy in which the feminine is pushed under, morality will be marked by the privileging of the masculine. This hierarchy establishes us as the counterpart of the masculine which is what Luce Irigaray has called the "old dream of symmetry." As Derrida explains,

> One could, I think, demonstrate this: when sexual difference is determined by *opposition* in the dialectical sense (according to the Hegelian movement of speculative dialectics which remains so powerful even beyond Hegel's text), one appears to set off "the war between the sexes"; but one precipitates the end with victory going to the masculine sex. The determination of sexual difference in opposition is destined, designed, in truth, for truth; it is so in order to erase sexual difference. The dialectical opposition neutralizes or supersedes . . . the difference. However, according to surreptitious operation that must be flushed out, one insures phallocentric mastery under the cover of neutralization every time. These are well known paradoxes.[102]

The only way out of this paradox is to work within the hierarchy to reverse the order of repression. This is why Derrida positions himself through the feminine, understood as a position, not a description of actual women. Because rebellion against metaphysical oppositions cannot simply take the form of denial that they exist in already-established "neutral" discourse, there must be a "phase" of overturning. This phase is necessary for the intervention into the hierarchical structure of opposition. It is not a phase that one simply surpasses, because the oppositions continually reassert themselves. The phase is structural, not temporal. We never just get "over it." We can not settle down once and for all. In this sense, deconstruction is interminable and there cannot be a clear line between "phase one" and "phase two." As Derrida explains,

> I am not sure that "phase two" marks a split with "phase one," a split whose form would be cut along an indivisible line. The relationship between these two phases doubtless has another structure. I spoke of two distinct phases for the sake of clarity, but the relationship of one phase to another is marked less by conceptual determination (that is, where a new concept follows an archaic one) than by a transformation or general deformation of logic.[103]

Deconstruction seeks to disrupt the deformation of the logic of sexual difference as opposition and the repression of the feminine upon which it rests. Therefore, in spite of his recognition that the phase of overturning is necessary, Derrida does not seek a new concept or representation of Woman. Even the metaphors that give body to the feminine, including, as we have seen, those of the feminine body, are suspect in that they seem to assert what Woman is.

The Critique of Catharine MacKinnon: Feminism Always Modified

The system of gender representation is not a prison from which we cannot escape. It is there, as Joyce reminds us, as the world of "fici-fact."[104] Catharine MacKinnon presents a powerful account of the oppression experienced by women in a system of gender repression in which the masculine is everywhere privileged. The feminine is ignored when we are passive and obliterated when we resist.[105] MacKinnon's theoretical mistake is her failure to recognize the status of our current system of gender identity as "fici-fact." MacKinnon characterizes any attempt to affirm the feminine as a misguided effort to find consolation within the gender roles that shackle us. Her view is, as we will see, in tension with her own understanding of the social and genderized construction of truth. MacKinnon's point is that we are in chains; there is absolutely nothing to celebrate in that condition. We must, as a result, confront our own distortion by the male power that denies us the lives available to men. MacKinnon does not want us to *pretend* that things are different now so that the world seems more bearable. She wants to destroy the pretense of femininity as a justification for any further complicity inn our oppression. Therefore, we must, in an unmodified way, condemn our situation as it is now. To quote MacKinnon:

> Feminists say women are not individuals. To retort that we "are" will not make it so; it will obscure the need to *make change so that it can be so*. To retort to the feminist charge that women "are" not equal, "Oh, you think women aren't equal to men" is to act as though *saying* we "are" will make it so. What it will do instead, what it has done and is doing, is legitimize the vision that we already "are" equal. That *this* life as we live it now is equality for us. It acts as if the purpose of speech is to say what we want reality to be like, as if it already is that way, as if that will help more reality to that place. *This may work in fiction, but it won't work in theory.*[106]

The central purpose of this essay is to show that the reality of Woman cannot be separated from the *fictions* in life and in theory. When we write of Woman, we are indicating the "not yet." Feminist theory, in other words, cannot be separately maintained from fiction. Feminist theory, insofar as it involves an appeal to Woman, demands poetic evocation. I agree with MacKinnon that we should not justify our current system of gender representation. We must condemn our oppression. Moreover, there is no doubt that MacKinnon's vivid narrations of women's position in patriarchy have made a significant contribution to our ability to see the world as genderized on all levels. The *power* of MacKinnon's writing lies in the different way of seeing that she gives us. I do not, in any way, want to deny or to mitigate the full extent of women's suffering under patriarchy. Our suffering has either gone unnoticed or been rendered acceptable as the inevitable result of femininity for too long, far too long. But MacKinnon's theoretical mistake carries its own dangers, not the least of which—and in spite of her intent—is the privileging of the masculine position.

MacKinnon's central error is that she reduces feminine reality by *identifying* the feminine *totally* with the real world as it is seen and constructed through the male gaze. On one level, MacKinnon does explicitly reject the idea of an objective reality beyond social construction. For MacKinnon, the objective standpoint is the male point of view in disguise:

> The *kind* of analysis that such a feminism is, and, specifically, the standard by which it is accepted as valid, is largely a matter of the criteria one adopts for adequacy in a theory. If feminism is a critique of the objective standpoint as male, then we also disavow standard scientific norms as the adequacy criteria for our theory, because the objective standpoint we criticize is the posture of science. In other words, our critique of the objective standpoint as male is a critique of science as a specifically male approach to knowledge. With it, we reject male criteria for verification. We're not seeking truth in its female counterpart either, since that, too, is constructed by male power. We do not vaunt the subjective. We begin by seeking the truth of and in that which has constructed all this—that is, in gender.[107]

My disagreement with MacKinnon is that feminism dislocates the very reality of the gender hierarchy upon which "truth" is built. There is no "truth" to Woman. Feminism is *always* modified differently as different groups of women insist on their reality. Being cannot be separated from seeing, but it cannot be reduced to it either. Indeed, it is precisely because of the impossibility of this separation that what "is" cannot be reduced to the way one particular group sees reality. Other visions are always possible. There is always the possibility of slippage between what is seen and what "is," even if we can only understand the significance of the slippage from another point of view.

MacKinnon, on the other hand, gives us an unshakable, objective, unmodifiable reality, constructed by the male gaze. I am suggesting that that reality is not as unshakable as it might look, for that reality cannot be separated from its metaphors. Through metaphor we can modify the world because the world as it "is" appears in the language in which it is represented. The feminist visionary who sees the world differently and tells us of her world may be ignored, but her vision cannot be taken away from her. The deconstructive allegory of the feminine indicates that Woman is the *seer* precisely to the degree that she skirts castration by the symbolic order. Cassandra saw "the truth" of Troy.[108] In the feminist retelling of the myth, she was not mad, only "true" to her reality.

If it were not possible for feminism to confirm a different view of the world through women's solidarity, feminism would lose its critical edge. There would be no viewpoint other than the one established as the "real" masculine world. If the feminine view is repudiated, the masculine stance is the only one possible. Feminism ironically becomes the call to stand up like a man. I agree with MacKinnon that there cannot be a third neutral position from which one can look down upon gender. But unlike MacKinnon, I recognize the danger of the reassertion of the masculine, which blocks all other visions, and so I insist on the affirmation of the feminine.

I envision not only a world in which the viewpoint of the feminine is valued, I also see a world peopled by individuals, sexed differently, a world beyond castration. Through such visions we can affirm the "should be" of a different way of being human. The goal of ethical feminism, which sees the "should be" inherent in the feminine viewpoint, is not *just* power for women, but is the redefinition of all of our fundamental concepts, including power. Feminine power should not, in other words, be separated from the different, ethical vision of human beings sought after in the feminine. When "Anna Stessa rises" it is not in the form of an erection.[109]

Within the sadomasochistic system of gender representation in which the masculine is on top and the feminine is on the bottom, the only alternative is reversal of *power*. One is either a slave, or a master. The political goal of empowerment can only be obtained by reversing the hierarchy. But the hierarchy is not dismantled, even if women were to take the upper position. Ethical feminism refuses this alternative as itself an expression of phallogocentrism within sexual difference. Without an ethical affirmation of the feminine as the skirting of castration we cannot, I am arguing, move beyond the replication of hierarchy inherent in the master/slave dialectic. As a result, our political struggle for power must be informed by a challenge to phallic logic itself.

A real danger inherent in MacKinnon's brilliant transposition of the Marxist paradigm to gender is that it must reject as distortion any re-figuration of the feminine and, therefore, leave us only with the struggle for power within the pregiven hierarchy. But another more subtle danger is the implicit privileging of masculine values, such as freedom, as more important than love and intimacy, and the masculine concept of the self. Andrea Dworkin tells us that the literary character Emma Bovary *really* wanted *freedom:* "Romance was her suicidal substitute for action; fantasy her suicidal substitute for a real world. And intercourse her suicidal substitute for freedom."[110] Her death was the result of her false consciousness, her supposed impotence. But what kind of freedom does Dworkin interpret her to want? The freedom to be Charles Bovary? The freedom to enter into the realm of the symbolic and by so doing assume her own castration? To dream of herself as the castrator? As bell hooks remarks, the very rhetoric of freedom has all too often reflected the desire to achieve the imagined position of phallic power. Feminism teaches us that this is only an imagined position. No "body" has the phallus. What we have is the fantasy of what having the phallus might mean as that meaning has been established and perpetuated by the patriarchal order. Dworkin's message, symbolized by her interpretation of the fate of Emma Bovary, is that *we*—women—would be better off if we stopped desiring intimacy. But would we, or for that matter, would anyone be better off? Indeed, *can* we even stop our desire in a system of gender representation in which the feminine as the Phallic Mother and the intimacy she figures are cut off by the order of the symbolic? I do not want to emphasize the *can*, but the should. We *should* not want to cut off our desire for intimacy in the name of a fantasy of masculine freedom. I refer to Dworkin's interpretation of Emma Bovary and to bell hooks careful analysis of the phallic logic often struggled with the rhetoric of freedom, to reinforce the inevitable reinstatement of the masculine when the feminine is repudiated, and to question Dworkin's concept of freedom. If the choice is between suicide and the assumption of castration, then the very use of the word choice is *truly* a mockery.

Perhaps my central disagreement with MacKinnon can be stated as follows: MacKinnon writes, "[w]e would settle for equal protection of the laws under which one would be born, live, and die, in a country where protection is not a dirty word and equality is not a special privilege."[111] I agree with MacKinnon that we should fight for equal protection under the law, but I would not *settle* for it. With Derrida, I will continue to dream of a new choreography of sexual difference, in which love and intimacy are other than the lackluster lassitude of tired and cynical collusion in women's oppression.

> [W]hat if we were to reach, what if we were to approach here (for one does not arrive at this as one would at a determined location) the area of relationship to the other where the code of sexual marks would no longer be discriminating? The relationship would not be a-sexual, far from it, but would be sexual otherwise: beyond the binary difference that governs the decorum of all codes, beyond the opposition masculine/feminine, beyond bisexuality as well, beyond homosexuality and heterosexuality which come to the same thing. As I dream of saving the chance that this question offers I would like to believe in the multiplicity of sexually marked voices. I would

like to believe in the masses, this indeterminable number of blended voices, this mobile of non-identified sexual marks whose choreography can carry, divide, multiply the body of each "individual," whether he be classified as "man" or as "woman" according to the criteria of usage.[112]

The Art of Losing

There is a theoretical reason for the affirmation of the dream of a new choreography of sexual difference. The psychoanalytic framework, particularly as it has been developed by Lacan, teaches us that the law and the legal system cannot be separated from the Law of the Father through which gender identity is established. It also follows from MacKinnon's own position that we can only achieve legal equality if we challenge the very basis of sexual difference. This intertwinement of law with the Law explains that we cannot settle for changes in the legal system, because these reforms must themselves involve a challenge to gender identity. Otherwise—and we have certainly lived to testify to this reality—even the most modest legal reforms will be undermined at every stage by the reassertion of the Law.

MacKinnon reminds us that *all* of our concepts are genderized. Under her *own* unmodified feminism, the idea of the self would have to be genderized as well. For MacKinnon, the feminine self is the one "who gets fucked."[113] Femininity is the trap in which we ensnare ourselves in our distorted desire "to be fucked." To quote MacKinnon: "I'm saying femininity as we know it is how we come to want male dominance, which most emphatically is not in our interest."[114] The masculine self is defined as the "one who fucks" and "fucks over" the other. What is the worst imaginable disaster to this masculine self? To be fucked. The *man* is the one who penetrates, not the one who is penetrated. That's what, according to MacKinnon, makes him a man. But we now have to ask why it is the end of the world "to be fucked" if you are a man.

The obvious answer is that this is what happens to women. Whatever happens to women is to be avoided in the name of being men. That is how a man *knows* he is a man and so he does not let *that* happen to him. This may provide a partial explanation of the homophobia directed toward gay men.

But why is it the end of the world "to be fucked"? Why do we think of all forms of oppression in terms of "getting fucked"? Is the problem with "getting fucked," or is it with the system of gender representation that defines the masculine and the corresponding self as the one who does not "get fucked"? MacKinnon, of course, has an answer to these questions: To "be fucked" is to be turned into an object of masculine desire in which the woman, not the man, loses her subjectivity. But, as Bataille continually reminds us, eroticism demands nothing less than risking one's self.[115] In erotic passion, the boundaries of selfhood yield to the touch of the other.[116] Does MacKinnon successfully distinguish the inherent value, ability, and risk to the self involved in eroticism from the specific feminine position of "being fucked"? I think she does not. Indeed, she cannot as long as she recasts the subject as seeking a freedom which is defined through the longing for the imagined phallic power of men. As long as it is accepted that to be masculine, to be a self, is to not "be fucked," then if women are "fucked," we cannot be *individuals*. Therefore, women cannot be individuals until they give up "getting fucked." The only conclusion that can follow from this acceptance of the definition of the self as the one who does not "get fucked" is MacKinnon's slogan "out now."[117]

I completely agree with MacKinnon that in a system of gender representation like our own we do not choose heterosexuality. The reality of the sanctions against those who attempt to define their sexuality differently makes meaningful choice impossible. One *cannot choose* homosexuality then either. The ideology inherent in the words "sexual preference" is exposed as ideology. MacKinnon remarks,

> Those who think that one chooses heterosexuality under conditions that make it compulsory should either explain why it is not compulsory or explain why the word choice can be meaningful here. And I would like you to address a question that I think few here would apply to the workplace, to work, or to workers: whether a good fuck is any compensation for getting fucked.[118]

I take MacKinnon's question with all the seriousness it deserves. Having experienced both, I want to insist that "getting fucked" and working in a factory do not yield the same experience of domination. I differ from MacKinnon insofar as I reject the transposition of the Marxist paradigm *without modification* into the realm of gender identity. Of course, we cannot escape the reality of the economics of sex, and the way exploitation affects the very definition of sex and sexuality. Yet when we go on strike against an employer, we do not risk living mutilation in the same way we do when we cut ourselves off from the affective and, if we interpret ourselves as heterosexual, the erotic relationships we have with men. But I wish to ask an even more fundamental question: Why should we endorse a view of selfhood, defined from the side of the masculine, as the one who does not "get fucked"? If this is what a self consisted of, why would a woman desire to become "it"? (I use the word "it" deliberately.)

In this view of the individual or the subject, the body becomes the barrier in which the self hides and the weapon (read *phallus*) that asserts itself against others. The feminine self, as it is celebrated in myth and allegory, lives the body differently. The body is not an erected barrier, but a position of receptivity. To *be* accessible is to be *open* to the other. To shut oneself off is *loss* of sexual pleasure. If one *views* one's body in this way, then to "be fucked" is not the end of the world. The endless erection of a barrier against "being fucked" is seen for what it "is"—a defense mechanism that creates a fort for the self at the expense of *jouissance*.[119] It is not that a "good fuck" is compensation for "being fucked." It is not even that the economic rhetoric of the rational man is not adequate to *jouissance*. My suggestion is, instead, that it is only if one accepts a masculine view of the self, that "being fucked" *appears* so terrifying.

Elizabeth Bishop, in her poem "One Art," notes, "It's evident the art of losing's not too hard to master / though it may look like (write it!) like disaster."[120] To "be fucked" is to lose the self. But those of us who have mastered the "one art" know that there are more important things to do—like loving—than maintaining the self against all comers.

I agree with MacKinnon that within patriarchy gender is not just a matter of difference but of domination. But MacKinnon draws the wrong conclusions from this insight:

> I am getting hard on this and am about to get harder on it. I do not think that the way women reason morally is morality "in a different voice." I think it is morality in a higher register, in the feminine voice. Women value care because men have valued us according to the care we give them, and we could probably use some. Women think in relational terms because our existence is defined in relation to men.[121]

MacKinnon's rhetoric gives her away. Men may well value "getting hard," because that is the example par excellence of masculine assertion. Why should we seek this impossible form of assertion ourselves?

MacKinnon argues that sex for women does not bring empowerment.[122] If empowerment is defined as self-assertion and if, in turn, self-assertion is identified with "getting hard," then clearly sex for women does not bring empowerment. But again, I want to suggest that "sex" in the best of all possible worlds should *not* bring empowerment. Empowerment is not and should not be the ultimate goal in any relationship. Perhaps, if nothing else, the identification of empowerment as the sole political goal of feminism shows how profoundly we remain under the sway of masculine symbolism.

Furthermore, I disagree with MacKinnon that feminine desire can be completely identified with masculine constructs. Desire is enforced by the power of negativity; desire does not, by definition, simply confirm what is. To argue that feminine desire loses its *power* of negativity because it is socially constructed from the male point of view implicitly asserts that a social construct can be turned into a fortress sturdy enough to fend off the transformations inherent in the metaphoricity of language in which it is built. Why bolster the fortress by asserting its unshakability? Instead, let us seek the new idiom in which we can speak of feminine desire. I am not advocating that we deny male power. I am only suggesting that we not make the masculine *our* world by insisting that we "are" only what men have made us to be. As Cixous writes, "She is a woman, heaven knows, / What is the difference? It isn't only the sex, / It's the way that love loves, above walls, despite armour, after the end of the world, / But I don't know how to say it."[123] I don't know how to say it either. But if there is a reason to keep writing, it is for the sake of trying to say it. When I engage with MacKinnon I must take on the world of heterosexual male violence that MacKinnon makes us see. Certainly, engagement with other women potentially offers us release from this world. But, then, as Irigaray reminds us,

> [f]or women to undertake tactical strikes, to keep themselves apart from men long enough to learn to defend their desire, especially through speech, to discover the love of other women while sheltered from men's imperious choices that put them in the position of rival commodities, to forge for themselves a social status that compels recognition, to earn their living in order to escape from the condition of prostitute . . . these are certainly indispensable stages in the escape from their proletarization on the exchange market. But if their aim were simply to reverse the order of things, even supposing this to be possible, history would repeat itself in the long run, would revert to sameness; to phallocratism. It would leave room neither for women's sexuality, nor for women's imaginary, nor for women's language to take (their) place.[124]

The very language of MacKinnon's either/or, "getting fucked" or casting "them" out, envisions feminine desire within the constraints of heterosexuality. If we are to open the space for feminine desire, we need to affirm our desire as *difference,* and it is precisely the affirmation of the feminine sexual difference that MacKinnon disallows. Once "they" are out, MacKinnon offers us no other world in which we could speak from feminine desire. The vision of the body as a wall against, rather than as a connection to, creates a stark phallic image. Irigaray, on the other hand, has envisioned a different, feminine view of the body—and the body of Irigaray should itself be understood as metaphor and not as the *basis* for female reality—as she imagines two women making love:

> No surface holds. No figure, line, or point remains. No ground subsists. But no abyss, either. Depth, for us, is not a chasm. Without a solid crust, there is no precipice. Our depth is the thickness of our body, our all touching itself. Where top and bottom, inside and outside, in front and behind, above and below are not separated, remote, out of touch. Our all intermingled. Without breaks or gaps.[125]

Again, to quote Irigaray:

> How an I speak to you? You remain in flux, never congealing or solidifying. What will make that current flow into words? It is multiple, devoid of causes, meanings, simple qualities. Yet it cannot be decomposed. These movements cannot be described as the passage from a beginning to an end. These rivers flow into no single, definitive sea. These streams are without fixed banks, this body without fixed boundaries. This unceasing mobility. This life—which will perhaps be called our restlessness, whims, pretenses, or lies. All this remains very strange to anyone claiming to stand on solid ground.[126]

To think beyond the phallic imagery of sexuality we have to transform from within the cultural symbols of desire. We have to dare to be out of step, to dance differently. MacKinnon tells us that we must give up collaboration.[127] A crucial aspect of this collaboration is the attempt to succeed within their system, to seek to become like them.

> I'm evoking for women a role that we have yet to make, in the name of a voice that, unsilenced, might say something that has never been

heard. I will hazard a little bit about its content. In the legal world of win and lose, where success is measured by other people's failures, in this world of kicking or getting kicked, I want to say there is another way. Women who refuse to forget the way women everywhere are treated every day, who refuse to forget that *that* is the meaning of being a woman, no matter how secure we may feel in having temporarily escaped it, women as women will find *that way*.[128]

First, I am advocating that mastering the art of losing is necessary if we are to find "that way." I am also arguing that there is an underpinning to collaboration that MacKinnon herself does not notice. Collaboration can be interpreted to result from the *desire* to assume the imagined phallic position which is necessarily denied to women as a group. Appropriation of the phallus becomes the goal. The Woman collaborator fantasizes that she has achieved the power of the so-called masculine position. But this is a fantasy, allowed to her precisely because of her usefulness as a collaborator.[129] Feminism, in other words, must seek a different economy of desire if feminism is not ultimately to be reinscribed into the phallic logic of patriarchy.

To give one's self up is to relinquish the phallic notion of the self as *selbststaendig*, as the subject who stands up against the other and strives desperately to be on top. This alternative has also been beautifully evoked by Joyce: "Sea, Sea! Here, weir, reach, island, bridge, Where you meet I."[130] Returning to the beginning of the essay, if we do not bring the "feminine" reality from the "rere" to the front we will be imprisoned in the genderized reality that MacKinnon so eloquently describes, in which everywhere we look we find the male.[131] But the project of bringing the "feminine" from the "rere" to the "fore" is dangerous. Throughout this essay I have warned against the reinstatement of naturalist theories of Woman. Yet, even in my debate with MacKinnon, I have relied on myth to defend the deconstructive, ethical allegory of the feminine. As Barthes rightfully describes myth, "We reach here the very principle of myth: it transforms history into nature."[132]

Have I not, by defending the allegory of feminine sexual difference through myth, fallen into a naturalist theory, if even in the form of a myth of Woman? I am aware of the danger. But, I am also indicating—indicating, rather than asserting, because, after what I have just written, I cannot assert—that the best weapon against myth is to signify it in turn, and to produce an artificial myth: and this reconstituted myth will in fact be mythology.[133] I am suggesting that even an allegory of woman that protects the beyond as beyond can only express itself through an interchange with a mythology of the feminine. I am also suggesting that this coexistence is acceptable if we are to give "body" to the figure Woman. We must give Woman "body" if we are to affirm feminine sexual difference as giving us a new economy of desire, beyond phallic logic. The danger, as Kristeva reveals, is of turning Woman into a religion.[134] But, if Bataille is right, and I endorse his interpretation, religion itself is an expression of the desire for intimacy that we associate with the fantasy figure Woman.[135] Religion and Woman may well go hand in hand if both are understood to represent the desire for intimacy. The danger of turning Woman into religion is precisely the danger of feminism unmodified. The only solution to this danger is to understand myth as artificial mythology so that the structure of second nature reinstated by myth will appear as our mythology. Nothing more, nothing less. There can always be other mythologies.

The Significance of Myth and the Feminine as an Imaginative Universal

The role of myth in feminist theory is essential to the reclaiming and retelling of "her story" because of our inability to escape our genderized context. The word *myth* emphasizes the hold that representations of the feminine have over both individuals and cultures. They are remarkably unchanging. Hans Blumenburg has defined myth as follows:

> Myths are stories that are distinguished by a high degree of constancy in their narrative core and by an equally pronounced capacity for marginal variation. These two characteristics make myths transmissible by tradition: their constancy produces the attraction of recognizing them in artistic or ritual representation as well [as in recital], and their variability produces the attraction of trying out new and personal means of presenting them. It is the relationship of "theme and variations," whose attractiveness for both composers and listeners is familiar from music. So myths are not like "holy texts," which cannot be altered by one iota.[136]

Myth is one important way in which the feminine achieves what Blumenburg calls significance. Significance is myth's capacity to provide symbols, images, and metaphors which give us an inspirational and shared environment. Myth's constancy allows us to recognize ourselves in the great mythic figures of the feminine and to engage with them as touchstones for a feminine identity. Cixous, for example, has powerfully evoked mythical figures to give significance to the deliverance of the feminine writer, seeking to find her way beyond a system of gender representation she finds crippling.[137] The appeal to the mythic heightens the intensity of our own struggles to survive within patriarchal society. Our engagement with mythical feminine figures heightens the shared sense that our struggle really matters.

This memory is recollective imagination. We re-collect the mythic figures of the past, but as we do so we reimagine them. It is the potential variability of myth that allows us to work within myth to reimagine our world and, by so doing, to begin to dream of a new one. In myth we find Woman with a capital letter. We construct her to indicate the impossibility in the Lacanian Real. But in their very excess, the figures of the feminine in myths betray their imitation of the masculine fantasies they supposedly express. These myths, as Lacan indicates, may be rooted in masculine fantasy, but they cannot, as he would suggest, be reduced to it.[138] The "reality" presented in myth cannot be separated from the general metaphoric capacity of language. This is why we can work within myth to create an artificial mythology. As a result, even in myth, "reality" is always shifting as its metaphors yield a different and novel interpretation of the myth's meaning.

The feminist reconstruction of myth, which we find in novels such as Christa Wolf's *Cassandra* and in Carol Gilligan's discussions on love,[139] involves recovering the feminine as an imaginative universal which will feed the power of the feminine imagination. This use of the feminine as imaginative universal does not, and should not, pretend to simply tell the truth of Woman as she was, or is. Indeed, it does the opposite. It insists that the truth of Woman is always an impossibility. This is why our mythology is self-consciousness and artificial mythology: Woman is continuously re-created as she is re-written. Better to love like Dido, than to found the Roman empire. Similarly, we have no doubt after reading Wolf's *Cassandra* that Achilles had his priorities all wrong and that we should have listened to Cassandra because she saw the connection between destruction and masculine subjectivity.[140] In this sense, the reconstruction of myth can bring into the light and out of the shadows, the differend. Moreover, the reconstruction of myth also involves making explicit the utopian aspiration which the reinterpretation expresses. As Wolf explains, "The Troy I have in mind is not a description of bygone days but a model for a kind of utopia."[141] That utopian Troy is Cassandra's Troy, not that of Achilles! When we speak of Cassandra, of her experience, of her Troy, we do not return to essentialism. We redeem the feminine from the shadows in which it has been obscured. We bring the feminine from the "rere" to the "fore."

We can now see how Catharine MacKinnon has obscured the real power of the celebration of the utopian potential of the feminine. In her discourse with Carol Gilligan, MacKinnon challenged her opponent for affirming the conditions of women's oppression.[142] In her empirical work Gilligan had argued that women speak about ethical questions in a different voice from that of the young men in her study.[143] Women, as she put it, enacted an "ethic of care," rather than a morality of rights.[144] MacKinnon did not challenge Gilligan's empirical findings of whether this "ethic of care" was actually correlated with women. As we have seen, she argued instead that to the degree that women demonstrated these characteristics, it was because they had been subordinated.[145] As a result, these characteristics should be rejected as suspect. MacKinnon recognized that we might accept these values on an independent basis (though, under her own analysis, what would such a basis be?), but not because they were feminine.[146] As we have seen, for MacKinnon, what is feminine is only there as the male point of view. She argues that, as women, we only accept these values because men tell us this is what they want us to do. In a free world women might still accept these values, but it would only be in such a world that the choice would be meaningful.

I want to return to MacKinnon's disparagement of the feminine, which can itself be a reflection of the acceptance of feminine castration as the inevitable price we pay for entering the realm of the symbolic so as to play ball with the men. In her discourse with MacKinnon, Gilligan claims not only that men and women love and care about people differently, but also that women's difference should be valued if not as a better, then at least as an equal mode of intersubjectivity. Within the perspective I have offered here, it is not important whether women have actually achieved a different way of loving that is superior and, therefore, to be valued. Gilligan's narrations may be a part of our artificial mythology. As we tell the *story*, however, we are beginning to create the *reality* in which the very economy of desire perpetuated by phallogocentrism is undermined. What matters is that the recasting of the feminine as an imaginative universal gives body to the "doubly-prized world" which makes this one appear hopeless and gives us the hope and the dream that we may one day be beyond it. If there is a last word in feminism, it is not the testimonial to an unmodified reality. Feminism, instead, calls us to the dream of a utopia of sensuous ease, in which the *reality* of the castrated subject appears as a nightmare from which we are trying to awaken. Feminism allows us to "see" the doubly prized world which might be ours. The world recast in Wolf's *Cassandra* is truly doubly-prized, not only as a disruptive power of difference, but also as the opening of the space of the feminine so "herstory" can be told, in all its suffering and pain and in all its glory.

5

Sexual Difference, the Feminine, and Equivalency

Introduction

Catharine MacKinnon's *Toward a Feminist Theory of the State*[1] is a provocative challenge to conceptions of liberal jurisprudence and to the traditional Marxist critique of liberalism. Both stand accused of erasing the centrality of gender, sex, and sexuality in the development of a modern legal system. This erasure, MacKinnon believes, can only perpetuate injustice to women through the pretense that equality has already been achieved—as in the case of her version of liberalism—or reduce it to a category of class domination which makes gender a secondary form of subordination—as in the case of her interpretation of Marxism. Despite my criticism of MacKinnon, she clearly deserves tribute for relentlessly insisting that any theory of equality for women will fall short of its own aspirations if it neglects the question of how sexuality, and more specifically femininity, is constructed through a gender hierarchy in which women are subordinated and subjected. I share her insistence that we must conceptualize a theory of equality that truly envisions the end of the domination of women by confronting the relationship between sex and sexuality as these have been constituted by the gender identity imposed upon women by patriarchy. We cannot, in other words, sanitize gender by removing it from the way in which "sex" is lived. MacKinnon's contribution has not been mere criticism of existing theories that refuse to examine the connection between sexuality and gender, she has also been a proponent of specific doctrinal changes. Her efforts were key in achieving recognition of sexual harassment as a matter of sex discrimination and gender inequality.[2] This is only one of many areas in which her understanding of the constitutive role of sexuality in the creation and perpetuation of male dominance has led to advocacy for legal and doctrinal reform.

My critique of MacKinnon, however, is that ultimately she cannot fully develop her program, which attempts to justify state intervention in current social arrangements of gender hierarchy and sexual identity. She cannot develop her own feminist theory of the state with any success because she is unable to affirm feminine sexual difference as other than victimization.[3] Of course, we need a program that legally delegitimates gender hierarchy and exposes the seriousness of sexual abuse. But we also need a more expansive, positive program, for the reduction of feminine sexual difference to victimization cannot, ultimately, sustain a feminist theory of the state. I propose a program which recognizes and incorporates equivalent rights.[4] Such a program would be irreducible to an intermediary set of privileges such as affirmative action—as important as these steps may be[5]—and would go beyond addressing inequality in the name of making it possible for women to be more like men.

I do not deny the horror and *the reality* of the story MacKinnon tells us about the extent to which sexual abuse perpetrated against women is treated as the way of the world,[6] but I must argue against reducing Woman to the figure of victim, and of feminine sexual desire to its "place" in the gender hierarchy. The result of this reduction is not only that MacKinnon cannot develop adequate programs of reform, but also that she cannot account for the very feminist point of view that she argues must be incorporated if we are to struggle for a state in which equality between "the sexes" would be more than mere pretense for the perpetuation of masculine privilege and female subordination.

Equivalent rights, although meant to challenge gender hierarchy, do not do so by erasing sexual difference or the specificity of feminine desire. Further, equivalent rights should not be understood only as a means to end sexual difference. Instead, a program of equivalent rights seeks to value the specificity of feminine[7] sexual difference, beyond the current stereotypes of femininity imposed by the gender hierarchy. MacKinnon cannot take us beyond a "negative" program without an affirmation of the feminine within sexual difference which is irreducible to the current patriarchal trappings of her own understanding of femininity.

My fundamental disagreement with MacKinnon is that she reads women's sexuality as constituted *only* by and for men and, therefore, as contrary to women's freedom from the chains of an imposed femininity which constitutes "our" sex, and can only justify women's domination.[8] Even if I agree with her that rape, battery, sexual abuse, and pornography must be seen not only as questions of criminal law, but also as barriers to the equality of women when the law has the ideological capacity to reinforce the devaluation of the feminine "sex," I disagree with MacKinnon's structural analysis of feminine sexual difference and of feminine sexuality. More important, she fails to take into account how feminine sexuality and desire are constructed not only by gender, but also by race. In our racist society, sexual domination is always already colored.

As I have already indicated, it is not simply that MacKinnon's analysis cannot sustain a positive program for state intervention in gender arrangements. MacKinnon's own stance toward the feminine reflects the devaluation of feminine within sexual difference which in turn prevents the feminine from being affirmed legally through a program of equivalent rights.[9] This devaluation is structural, and is, perhaps, the very hallmark of the logic of phallogocentrism. As a result, the phallic logic, *if not the experience of it,* cuts across race and class lines. My criticism of the division MacKinnon creates between freedom and sexuality is that this division rejects a conception of the self as a being of the flesh. For such a sexual being, sexual expression cannot be separated from freedom. Women have been forced to deny their own sexuality for too long. We have been silenced from articulating our own desires by enforced patriarchal assumptions about what a "normal" woman should want. It has been difficult for us even to know our desires given the internalization of patriarchal taboos. Women have had to pay an extremely high price for refusing to be "normal" women whose sexuality neatly matches the so-called standard of normal heterosexual femininity. The silence imposed upon us is so profound that we frequently do not know of what we wish to speak. For women, then, freedom cannot be separated from the struggle against the devalorization of the feminine and the erasure of the specificity of feminine sexual desire.

As a result, consciousness raising, which is crucial to fostering the dream of women's freedom, must involve more than the exposure of the "truth" of our victimization. It demands the refiguration of the feminine within sexual difference as sexual difference has been constituted "to be" within patriarchy. The feminine within sexual difference is what must be symbolized in and through the social practice of feminism, as well as through the demand for a program of equivalent rights. The feminine, in other words, has yet "to be" in law, other than as a stereotypic conception of femininity. MacKinnon is right about that, but it is precisely the stereotypes of femininity that must be challenged through a positive program that values the feminine within sexual difference.

I use the expression "the feminine within sexual difference" deliberately, because I believe the feminine should not be identified as a property or characteristic of women. Indeed, a crucial aspect of gender hierarchy is that it enforces rigid gender identity, so that the feminine, as it is imagined, is necessarily repressed by men who seek to live up to the fantasy ideal of a "pure" masculinity. The consolidation of rigid gender identity and imposed heterosexuality is itself a prison from which feminism must seek to free us. To realize the dream of women's freedom, we must think through the conditions of women's equality of well-being and capability, in light of the recognition and value of the feminine within sexual difference.

Simply put, women's sexuality cannot be reduced to women's "sex," as our "sex" has been defined, once we understand both the limit to institutionalized meaning, and the endless possibility of remetaphorization and of metonymic displacement.[10]

MacKinnon's understanding of feminine sexuality accepts what Luce Irigaray has called "the old dream of symmetry."[11] For Irigaray "the old dream of symmetry" exposes the fantasy that our sexuality is symmetrical to that of men. In other words, what men fantasize women want is what we actually do want. But women's sexuality is irreducible to the fantasy that we are only what MacKinnon calls "fuckees." MacKinnon's reduction of feminine sexuality to being a "fuckee" endorses "the old dream of symmetry" as "truth," thereby promoting the prohibition against the exploration of women's sexuality and "sex" as we live it, and not as men fantasize about it.

Men may imagine that what they think women want, what they want women to desire because of their own fears and fantasies about the "feminine sex," *is* what women desire. However, feminine writing on feminine sexuality has recognized "the old dream of symmetry" is just that: a fantasy and, more specifically, a masculine fantasy. I want to emphasize the political and personal significance that challenging MacKinnon's view of feminine sexuality has for women. The possibility of celebrating women's "sex" and sexuality can keep us from the tragic disjuncture between sex, sexuality, and freedom that MacKinnon's analysis leads us to.

But such a recognition of the feminine within sexual difference is also necessary if we are to meet the aspiration to legitimate and recognize the feminist point of view in law, in the name of equality, and not by appeal to special privilege. MacKinnon's own analysis cannot meet her own aspiration if it denies the equivalent value of the masculine and feminine, particularly as the masculine is privileged within the current gender hierarchy. Equivalent rights do not repeat the "separate but equal" argument, but challenge the idea that sexual difference can or should be eradicated through the pretense that the human "being" is currently constituted as sex-neutral, or as if man is the human. I rely on Amartya Sen's view of equality to justify my understanding of equivalence as equality of capability and well-being.[12] As Sen reminds us, "Capability reflects a person's freedom to choose between different ways of living."[13] Sen's view of equality is valuable to feminists precisely because it allows for a "positive" program to guarantee women's equality of well-being and capability. Capability of well-being demands the affirmation of "sex" and sexuality, and, in the case of women more specifically, of living without shame of our "sex."

Mackinnon's Analysis of the Social Construction of Women's Sexuality

MacKinnon's analysis of the social construction of femininity is an expression of male dominance and, more specifically, of male sexual desire. To quote MacKinnon: "Male dominance is sexual. Meaning: men in particular, if not men alone, sexualize hierarchy; gender is one. As much a sexual theory of gender as a gendered theory of sex, this is the theory of sexuality that has grown out of consciousness raising."[14] Thus, for MacKinnon, inequality *is* sexual, and sexuality and the engagement in "sex" perpetuates that inequality. An analysis of inequality that does not frame inequality as a sexual dynamic in which male domination reduces women to their sex will ultimately "limit feminism to correcting sex bias by acting in theory as if male power did not exist in fact."[15] It will "limit feminist theory to the way sexism limits women's lives: to a response to terms men set."[16] As a result, MacKinnon argues,

> A distinctively feminist theory conceptualizes social reality, including sexual reality, on its own terms. The question is, what are they? If women have been substantially deprived not only of their own experience but of terms of their own in which to view it, then a feminist theory of sexuality which seeks to understand women's situation in order to change it must first identify and criticize the construct "sexuality" as a construct that has circumscribed and defined experience as well as theory. This requires capturing it in the world, in its situated social meanings, as it is being constructed in life on a daily basis.[17]

The study of the construct of sexuality is, for MacKinnon, the examination of how women come to have a "sex." To put it simply, women are defined as women because "we get fucked."

> First sexual intercourse is a commonly definitive experience of gender definition. For many women, it is a rape. It may occur in the family, instigated by a father or older brother who decided to "make a lady out of my sister." Women's sex/gender initiation may be abrupt and anomic: "When she was 15 she had an affair with a painter. He fucked her and she became a woman." Simone de Beauvoir implied a similar point when she said: "It is at her first abortion that a woman begins to 'know.' " What women learn in order to "have sex," in order to "become women"—women as gender—comes through the experience of, and is a condition for, "having sex"—women as sexual object for man, the use of women's sexuality by men. Indeed, to the extent sexuality is social, women's sexuality is its use, just as femaleness is its alterity.[18]

Femininity is the "sex" imposed on us by a world of male power in which men seek the fulfillment of their desire through us. Female gender identity is this imposed sexuality, reinforced in all gendered social arrangements and through the state, which reflects male sexual desire and legitimates sexual dominance as the rule of law. The challenge, then, to femininity as imposed sexuality, as the subjection of our "selves" to our "sex," *is* feminism, and ultimately this forms the basis of the feminist theory of the state.

> In feminist terms, the fact that male power has power means that the interests of male sexuality construct what sexuality as such means, including the standard way it is allowed and recognized to be felt and expressed and experienced, in a way that determines women's biographies, including sexual ones. Existing theories, until they grasp this, will not only misattribute what they call female sexuality to women as such, as if it were not imposed on women daily; they will also participate in enforcing hegemony of the social construct "desire," hence its product, "sexuality," hence its construct "woman," on the world.
>
> The gender issue, in this analysis, becomes the issue of what is taken to be "sexuality"; what sex means and what is meant by sex, when, how, with whom, and with what consequences to whom.[19]

"Sex" difference is the consequence of this imposed sexuality. To celebrate women's difference is a form of "false consciousness," because women's so-called difference is only women's status as "fuck-ees," and the affirmation of difference is only an excuse for reducing women to those who "get fucked" in whichever way men want. This reduction of women to "fuckees" is what MacKinnon means when she argues that our social reality is fundamentally pornographic.

We can now begin to understand why, according to MacKinnon, pornography is absolutely central to the way in which the state enforces the male viewpoint, and particularly the male vision of women as sexual objects. Representing men as forcing themselves down women's throats is not just a male masturbatory fantasy, but is the truth of women's reality. *Deep Throat*, in other words, depicts what we are forced to become under our current system of gender domination. This is why MacKinnon can say in all seriousness that we are all Linda Lovelace,[20] with oral sex being the essence of women's subordination.

Yet this reality of subordination is not only ignored by the state, it is protected as a matter of right—the right of free speech under the First Amendment.[21] Pornography, for MacKinnon, is not a matter of speech at all, but a matter of the systematic silencing of women. The image of men being shoved down women's throats is the very symbol of silencing us and of what is used to do so.

> Thus the question Freud never asked is the question that defines sexuality in a feminist perspective: what do men want? Pornography provides an answer. Pornography permits men to have whatever they want sexually. It is their "truth about sex." It connects the centrality of visual objectification to both male sexual arousal and male models of knowledge and verification, objectivity with objectification. It shows how men see the world, how in seeing it they access and possess it, and how this is an act of dominance over it. It shows what men want and gives it to them. From the testimony of the pornography, what men want is: women bound, women battered, women tortured, women humiliated, women degraded and defiled, women killed. Or, to be fair to the soft core, women sexually accessible, have-able, there for them, wanting to be taken and used, with perhaps just a little light bondage. Each violation of women— rape, battery, prostitution, child sexual abuse, sexual harassment— is made sexuality, made sexy, fun, and liberating of women's true nature in the pornography.[22]

That pornography is seen as the "right to speak" is another sign of the way in which the state and the law simply reflect the male point of view and the right of men to subordinate women to their sexual desires. As MacKinnon explains,

> The state is male in the feminist sense: the law sees and treats women the way men see and treat women. The liberal state coercively and authoritatively constitutes the social order in the interest of men as a gender—through its legitimating norms, forms, relation to society, and substantive policies. The state's formal norms recapitulate the male point of view on the level of design.[23]

The feminist point of view, on the other hand, is impossible, because, according to MacKinnon, the male "point of view" enforces itself as true and as the totality of a pornographic social reality. As MacKinnon tells us,

> Feminism criticizes this male totality without an account of women's capacity to do so or to imagine or realize a more whole truth. Feminism affirms women's point of view, in large part, by revealing, criticizing, and explaining its impossibility. This is not a dialectical paradox. It is a methodological expression of women's situation, in which the struggle for consciousness is a struggle for world: for a sexuality, a history, a culture, a community, a form of power, an experience of the sacred.[24]

For MacKinnon, the impossibility of a woman's point of view is constantly reinforced by the state, which reflects the male point of view as the rule of law, and which erases what it has done in the name of neutrality. The rule of law is then transformed into ideology, further enforcing the male viewpoint, not only as perspective, but as the definitive interpretation of the Constitution.

MacKinnon's Marxism Summarized

MacKinnon uniquely transposes the Marxist critique of liberalism into her analysis of imposed sexuality as the basis of female gender identity.[25] For MacKinnon, our current law is clearly not neutral vis-à-vis the gender divide. Instead, law reinforces the legitimacy of the male viewpoint as the standard upon which the law is based, and which is bolstered by the myth of the legal person. The myth of the legal person erases the continuing reality of the gender hierarchy and the terrible suffering imposed by male domination. The myth itself is a form of domination. The Marxist application here turns on MacKinnon's argument that the liberal state is based on a pretense of gender equality in the name of a legal person, when, in reality, the underlying social stratum of gender inequality remains as the truth of woman's condition. It is precisely in its perpetuation of the myth of equality that the liberal state further silences women who try to challenge it as a reflection of its masculine *constitution*. For this is exactly what our Constitution is for MacKinnon: The protection of the right of men to silence and to subordinate women. The so-called abstract equality of the individual must, therefore, be challenged by feminism. This is one interpretation of a Marxist analysis transposed into the context of gender. As Marx argued that the establishment of legal rights hides the continuing reality of class subordination, so MacKinnon argues that the constitution of "the rights of man" erases the subordination of women as the basis of social life.

> In Anglo-American jurisprudence, morals (value judgments) are deemed separable and separated from politics (power contests), and both from adjudication (interpretation). Neutrality, including judicial decision making that is dispassionate, impersonal, disinterested, and precedential, is considered desirable and descriptive. Courts, forums without predisposition among parties and with no interest of their own, reflect society back to itself resolved. Government of laws, not of men, limits partiality with written constraints and tempers force with reasonable rule-following.[26]

As a result, MacKinnon identifies the so-called neutrality of the liberal state not only as a *prop* to the male point of view, but as its fundamental expression. Thus, she can argue that

> [t]he state is male jurisprudentially, meaning that it adopts the standpoint of male power on the relation between law and society. This stance is especially vivid in constitutional adjudication, thought legitimate to the degree it is neutral on the policy content of legislation. The foundation for its neutrality is the pervasive assumption that conditions that pertain among men on the basis of gender apply to women as well—that is, the assumption that sex inequality does not really exist in society. The Constitution—the constituting document of this state society—with its interpretations assumes that society, absent government intervention, is free and equal; that its laws, in general, reflect that; and that government need and should right only what government has previously wronged. This posture

is structural to a constitution of abstinence: for example, "Congress shall make no law abridging the freedom of . . . speech." Those who have freedoms like equality, liberty, privacy, and speech socially keep them legally, free of governmental intrusion. No one who does not already have them socially is granted them legally.[27]

Before turning to my own story of the constitution of feminine "sex," sexuality, and gender difference, which I will use to counter MacKinnon, I want to demonstrate some of the contradictions within her analysis.

The Contradictions Inherent in MacKinnon's Devaluation of the Feminine

My first and most important criticism of MacKinnon is that she is mistaken when she says that it does not matter whether and how the feminine "sex" is affirmed or disparaged. As she puts it,

> Difference is the velvet glove on the iron fist of domination. The problem then is not that differences are not valued; the problem is that they are defined by power. This is as true when difference is affirmed as when it is denied, when its substance is applauded or disparaged, when women are punished or protected in its name.[28]

In MacKinnon's own terms, this difference matters precisely in relation to what it might mean to incorporate the feminist point of view into the state—MacKinnon's stated program.

> Law that does not dominate life is as difficult to envision as a society in which men do not dominate women, and for the same reasons. To the extent feminist law embodies women's point of view, it will be said that its law is not neutral. But existing law is not neutral. It will be said that it undermines the legitimacy of the legal system. But the legitimacy of existing law is based on force at women's expense. Women have never consented to its rule—suggesting that the system's legitimacy needs repair that women are in a position to provide.[29]

How can one incorporate the feminist point of view into the state if sexual difference is not recognized? More specifically, in MacKinnon's own terms, how could women provide the needed repair? If women as a gender are defined as victims, as "fuckees," as voiceless, and if, as MacKinnon argues, the feminist "point of view" is an impossibility within our system of male dominance, then it would be impossible to provide the condition for repair. Thus, women, defined as we are by MacKinnon, cannot possibly play the role she allots us.

The second contradiction in MacKinnon's analysis is that she advocates a positive program of state intervention into gender arrangements, and yet her own political slogan, "Out now!" is, and *must remain*, negative. Positive rights for women should not just involve the end of sexual abuse, or even restrictions on pornography, as crucial as these are to any program of legal reform. Such rights would also involve, for example, a full program of maternity rights, which would value, and not force women to pay for, their reproductive capacity. MacKinnon has successfully advocated a city ordinance which makes the propagation of pornography actionable as a matter of sex inequality. In *Virginia v. American Bookseller Association, Inc.,*[30] the harm to women was recognized by the Court, yet pornography was protected as speech. As she has argued, the "law of the First Amendment secures freedom of speech only from governmental deprivation."[31] For MacKinnon, the limit on governmental intervention not only applies to the First Amendment, but also to the concept of law. As a result, we have what MacKinnon calls a "negative" state, which ironically guarantees the positive "freedom" of men precisely by limiting state intervention. MacKinnon argues that "the offspring of proper passivity is substanceless. Law produces its progeny immaculately, without messy political intercourse."[32]

I agree that the harm to women caused by pornography should be legally recognized, even if I do not accept MacKinnon's own legal solution. But without the affirmation of feminine sexual difference, we cannot develop a concept of "positive" freedom for women, which MacKinnon herself recognizes is needed to rectify the inequality of women. As she herself has said, the negative state has sweeping implications: "For women this has meant that civil society, the domain in which women are distinctively subordinated and deprived of power has been placed beyond reach of legal guarantees."[33] But if we are to truly intervene in civil society to restructure the gender hierarchy, we must insist that the specificity of the feminine within sexual difference be valued legally. MacKinnon's analysis, in other words, can criticize the negative state, but she cannot successfully justify the move beyond it given her own repudiation of the feminine within sexual difference. I agree with her, however, that the negative state is clearly not enough to end the inequality of women.

We need a full program of rights that will provide women with the conditions for equality of well-being and capability. I advocate Sen's theory of equality for two reasons. First, the emphasis on well-being allows us to take sexuality and its expression into consideration when thinking about equality for women. Second, such a view of equality allows for "positive" legal intervention on the part of the state to guarantee "well-being." In other words, this view of equality allows us to move beyond the negative state that MacKinnon describes as inadequate, in order to provide equality for women. Equality of well-being and capability also prevents the recognition of sexual difference from degenerating into the justification of special privilege for women. Equivalent rights are a part of equality defined as the recognition of equivalence between "sexed" beings. They should not be seen as special privileges. This vision of equality has the substance that allows for positive intervention and does more than just perpetuate stereotypes. The rhetoric that fits equivalent rights into a view of equality is important, because in the end, the rhetoric provides us with philosophical justification for the conditions of women's equal well-being and with a cultural framework in which recognition of feminine sexual difference need not be reduced to an appeal for "special" treatment.

To summarize, MacKinnon's refusal to affirm the feminine within sexual difference means that her negative political program cannot be turned into "positive," affirmative legal reform. Her analogy to the Nicaraguan struggle,[35] does not provide a blueprint for a legal program for women. The Nicaraguans were fighting for socialism and for national independence. They were not fighting to keep the United States out, but to realize a dream of a different social order. The slogan "Out now!" was addressed to a nation that was struggling against that dream and against that fight. If our dream is to recognize women as full, individuated human beings, then the negative program MacKinnon offers is not and cannot be enough.

The Critique of MacKinnon's Conception of Liberalism—The Example of Pornography

MacKinnon's analysis of liberalism is limited to a conception of neutrality that even many liberal thinkers reject. Thinkers as diverse as Bruce Ackerman, C. Edwin Baker, Ronald Dworkin, Sylvia Law, Thomas Nagel, John Rawls, Steven Shiffrin, and Wendy Williams,[35] all of whom would continue to designate themselves as liberals, have long since abandoned the traditional concept of neutrality defined by

Robert Bork and Herbert Wechsler.[36] I do agree, however, that none of these scholars have adequately addressed the significance of the gender hierarchy as it continues to limit our thinking on equality. This is important, because even within their own terms of analysis, it would be possible to reach very different conclusions on, for example, the question of pornography. In order to see the harm to women as relevant to a theory of equality, we do not even need an account of the relationship of inequality, the gender hierarchy, and the feminine "sex." Rae Langton, for example, has argued that Ronald Dworkin's own principles, as he has developed them most recently in *Law's Empire*, could be used to justify at least some limited time and place restrictions on pornography.[37] Ronald Dworkin has himself defended limited time and place restrictions on pornography.[38] However, Thomas Nagel's understanding of an "offense," and his argument for reasonableness within the context of a much more traditional legal argument about "free" speech, may give us the most powerful liberal defense for time and place restrictions on pornography, even though Nagel himself does not give the feminist position the attention it deserves.

I'd like to explore the relationship between Nagel's concept of offense and the wrong to women in pornography more fully. My argument using Nagel's categories is as follows: Pornography is a harm to women because it is inescapable and public. Do I have the choice to avoid pornography? Not if I choose to go out of my apartment in New York City. I cannot escape images which devalorize my "sex," which appear everywhere, including the supermarket where I shop, the public transportation I ride, and wherever I might choose to buy my Coca-Cola. These images continuously assault my own self-conception. They portray my "sex" as shameful, as something to be despised. They challenge my self-respect as a woman. Nagel himself distinguishes between two kinds of offense. The first is the kind of offense I have just described. But I insist that I am not only offended, I am violated by pornographic depictions from which I cannot escape. When I am forced to see my "sex" ripped apart, I have already been violated in my very sense of myself as a person whose inviolability must be respected. Pornography is unavoidable; it is only too literally "in my face," and is therefore, my business. The second kind of offense involves behavior that I do not have to confront. An example that Nagel uses is the "offense" of just having to live in a society with homosexuals. For Nagel we can demand legal protection from the first kind of offense but not the second. Indeed, the further problem with the very idea of offense is that it appeals to a constructed interiority that is vague at best. My argument, which transcends Nagel while if using his analytical distinction, is that pornography should be considered not only an offense in the first sense, but also a violation which warrants legal restriction. I am violated in the specific sense that I am forced to confront the reality—yes, symbolically presented—that my "sex" has been denied its inviolability. Inviolability, as Nagel himself recognizes, is the very basis of a legal order in which an individual claims the right to remain alive. The body is, in this very basic sense, a legal construct from the outset. We are beings who can be assaulted or killed. All of the myths of the social contract start with the basic agreement that we join together for protection from murder. What I am forced to see in pornography is myself as a being whose "sex" is portrayed not only as violable, but "there" for violation.

The violation, then, is first in that I am forced to see what I do not want to look at, and second in the content of what I am forced to see. The symbolism of the woman in "bits and pieces" whose body is not only not inviolable, but is instead there to be violated, *attacks me right then and there when I am forced to see it*. It assaults my projected image of myself as an individual worthy of inviolability. To forcibly strip someone of their self-image, particularly when that projected image is as basic as that of bodily integrity, is a violation, not just an offense. The distinction I would offer between erotica and pornography begins with the separation of depictions that do involve explicit violence to women, the body in "bits and pieces," from those that do not. All "sexist" representations that offend women's projected self-images are not equal, because they are not so fundamentally violative of our claim, in this most basic sense, to equal protection. I am offended, for example, by the annual *Sports Illustrated* swimsuit issue. Indeed, I participated in a demonstration that protested against this obvious perpetuation of the worst kind of female bodily stereotypes. But I am sickened and threatened by images of myself in "bits and pieces." Such images do not just suggest a threat, they actually threaten my claim to inviolability.

Although we need a much stronger condemnation of the wrong in pornography than the one offered by Nagel, his theoretical framework and his concept of reasonableness is helpful in examining the legitimacy of time and place restrictions on pornography, once we understand pornography as violation. His theory is important because we need a concept of legal legitimacy. Without such a concept, we are left with random balancing devoid of standards. It is essential to explain why and how we recognize not only the way pornography violates women, but also why that violation can justify time and place restrictions on pornography. This "weighing" process demands a guiding principle by which to proceed in the social field of profound erasure to which MacKinnon points us. Nagel's reasonableness gives us such direction; he gives us standards by which judges can assess "competing" harms and viewpoints under which harm is defined.

Under Nagel's theory, we weigh the extent of the *wrong* and the degree of the *suffering* of competing parties having opposing moral positions. For example, who is wronged more profoundly and suffers more intensely—the homosexual who is repressed or the puritan who believes that homosexuality is an evil that contaminates the puritan's social reality, his children's well-being, etc?[39] This conception of reasonableness allows the law and the state to make the difficult decisions between competing moral and ethical positions when there is no moral consensus, and there is a "war" between different moral visions and different perspectives on life in which these visions are embedded. I am arguing here that the feminist position, particularly on the issue of pornography, clearly deserves the hearing that Nagel himself has not given it.[40] It is interesting to note that Nagel does not show the same compassion for the feminist argument against pornography that he does for the homosexual's argument for freedom of sexual expression. I would argue that the reason for this "blindness" is Nagel's inability to see the harm to women, precisely because he does not integrate a psychoanalytic theory of the construction of feminine sexual difference into his analysis of pornography.

By pornography, adopting Cass Sunstein's definition,[41] I mean the explicit connection of sex with violence that in no way denies that pornography is sexual and not just violence. Why am I adopting Cass Sunstein's definition? As I have already suggested, we need to distinguish between erotica and pornography. Sunstein's definition allows us to make this distinction. We must think about the definition we adopt within the context of current politics. The National Endowment for the Arts' campaign to repress certain forms of erotic expression is only too well known. Ironically, this censorship has been directed against feminist artistic attempts to expose and then to critique the reduction of women to sexual objects of masculine desire. I adopt Sunstein's definition because it allows us to distinguish between erotica and pornography, and because it protects feminist artists who may choose to depict women's sexual objectification in such a graphic way as to fall victim to censorship themselves. But even if one adopts Sunstein's definition, his own argument for time and place restrictions on pornography lacks a crucial philosophical dimension.

Sunstein's argument is strengthened in defense of the possible legitimation of time and place restrictions if he works within Nagel's concept of reasonableness. Indeed, the weakness of Sunstein's argument is that he does not have a concept of legal legitimacy. Nagel's reasonableness can provide him with such a concept. Sunstein argues that the periphery of pornography within the traditional context of First Amendment arguments, combined with evidence that pornography promotes violence in men, might lead us to accept legal restrictions, notwithstanding the concern with censorship and the constraints such restrictions must place on men in their access to pornography. Sunstein explains that

> there is a quite straightforward argument for regulating at least some pornographic materials. The first point is that much pornographic material lies far from the center of the first amendment concern. If the first amendment is, broadly speaking, a safeguard against governmental suppression of points of view with respect to public affairs, at least some forms of pornography are far from the core of constitutional concern. Under current doctrine, and under any sensible system of free expression, speech that lies at the periphery of constitutional concern may be regulated on the basis of a lesser showing of government interest than speech that lies at the core.
>
> To say this is hardly to say that the definition of the core and the periphery will be simple. Under nearly any standard, however, at least some pornographic materials will be easily classified as belonging in the periphery.[42]

If under traditional doctrinal analysis pornography is at the periphery of free speech, and there is evidence that it perpetuates the *legitimation* of violence against women, and, in my sense, is itself a violation, while the "suffering" to the pornography reader is limited, particularly if access is restricted and not banned, then "reasonableness" demands time and place restrictions even before we have an adequate account of the relationship between gender hierarchy and the devalorization of the feminine "sex." This account, however, is ultimately necessary if we are to understand fully the seriousness of the wrong to women of pornography.

The Critique of MacKinnon's Incorporation of Marxism in the Context of Gender

I have criticized MacKinnon for her identification of liberalism with principles of neutrality, and for her failure to recognize arguments consistent with the liberal concern for individuality for some of the legal reforms she seeks to make. In this difficult period, we need to choose our allies carefully. But there is, perhaps, a more important critique to be made of her own transposition of Marxism into the context of gender. I agree with MacKinnon that the Marxist tradition has tended to reduce gender and sex to a secondary question. And I agree with her, as so many others have, that this reduction is a disservice to women.[43] Yet I still believe MacKinnon's own use of Marxism may be criticized on three separate grounds.

The first is related to the "pragmatic"[44] and "postmodern"[45] critique of attempts to develop empiricist, positivist, or materialist accounts of women's situations that can claim to be scientific, if by scientific we mean "free" of the mediation of narration.[46] MacKinnon does not recognize the status of her own analysis as a story, but rather as a materialist conceptualization of gender inequality. Such accounts are never simply descriptions, but are always narrations, and part of a discourse that gives meaning to reality. Reality is presented in a discursive field. I want to emphasize the phrase "in which reality is presented." To address the question of how reality is presented in no way denies that it is *there*. It is a serious misreading of the "postmodern" position to argue that it denies reality, let alone that it disavows the materiality of violence to women. As a woman who lived through an attempted rape, I cannot forget the materiality of that violence. Laclau and Mouffe have succinctly captured the meaning of the proposition that reality is presented to us in a discursive field:

> The fact that every object is constituted as an object of discourse has nothing to do with whether there is a world external to thought, or with the realism/idealism opposition. An earthquake or the falling of a brick is an event that certainly exists in the sense that it occurs here and now independently of my will. But whether their specificity as objects is constructed in terms of "natural phenomena" or expressions of "the wrath of God" depends upon the structuring of a discursive field. What is denied is not that such objects exist externally to thought, but the rather different assertion that they could constitute themselves as objects outside any discursive condition of emergence.[47]

In law, competing narratives and discourses can never be free of an evaluation of that reality, which is what gives the story its normative meaning, and, in the case of law, its legal meaning. A classic example is "date rape." In order to define a certain kind of sexual abuse to women as date rape, we must rely on a seeming oxymoron: putting the idea of a date—with its implied concept of consent—together with rape. The behavior may have always been "there," but it took a different story, with a different evaluation of those acts—such as locking a woman into a dorm room until she agreed to have sex—to define this behavior as rape.

To say that the philosophical status of MacKinnon's account is a narration in no way takes away from its "truth," if by truth one means an illumination of an existing "reality" that previously was invisible, because it had not been told or evaluated in a way that made that particular behavior "appear" as a legal wrong or harm to women.[48] MacKinnon's story helps us to see that what was once thought of as normal was and remains the systematic sexual abuse of women. I agree with that part of the story which emphasizes the "normalcy" of sexual violence to women as a physical reality. The story tells us why it is abuse, and not just "boys being boys."[49] As one of the many reflected in the unfortunate statistic that at least one-half of all women will undergo a sexual assault,[50] I cannot deny this story myself. I know only too well the "truth" of MacKinnon's chapter on rape in which she discusses the long-term trauma that such attacks leave in their wake. But her story is limited precisely because she figures women only as victims, and feminine sexual difference as *only* the velvet glove on the iron fist of domination."[51] I do not see myself as my attacker saw me. And I must defend the "reality" of my way of seeing my "sex" as other to masculine fantasy.

The figure of Woman as victim is an important one, but it is not the *only* figure of feminine sexual difference. MacKinnon tells us a profound story, but it is only partially true. This is the second criticism of MacKinnon's Marxist transposition which can only understand women's "material" oppression through the reduction of feminine sexual difference to Woman as the "fuckee."

For MacKinnon, having a "sex," particularly a female identity, cannot be separated from "having sex," and "having sex" cannot be separated from domination and sadomasochism. If we have "sex" with men we allow ourselves to be objectified. The rejection of this reality, the struggle against it, must include the end to "heterosexual sex," at least in the sense that having sex is identified with intercourse. There can be no two ways about it:

> Feminism has a theory of power: sexuality is gendered as gender is sexualized. Male and female are created through the erotization of dominance and submission. The man/woman difference and the dominance/submission dynamic define each other. This is the social meaning of sex and the distinctly feminist account of gender inequality. Sexual objectification, the central process within this dynamic, is at once epistemological and political.[52]

If "heterosexual" women continue to get "fucked," they are collaborators in their own oppression and not just its victims. I put "heterosexual" in quotation marks because if we challenge the gender hierarchy with its rigid structures of identity, there can be no pure "heterosexual sex," only different combinations of the masculine and the feminine in "sex" and within each "sex." The disavowal of homosexuality is what makes the clear division between homosexuality and heterosexuality possible.

The third criticism, which is primarily political, is that despite the limits of Marxism as a "science," its emphasis on class, race, and national difference remains extremely important to a feminism that is *always modified* through its respect for difference, and which continually allows new narrations of feminine sexual difference and how it is lived, experienced, and represented. As Audre Lorde has succinctly argued,

> By and large within the women's movement today, white women focus upon their oppression as women and ignore differences of race, sexual preference, class, and age. There is a pretense to homogeneity of experience covered by the word *sisterhood* that does not in fact exist.[53]

In other words, feminine sexual difference, if it is not to fall into the erasure of race and class difference, must always be modified. Indeed, put even more strongly, the openness to modification through, or modification by, the "other woman," is what provides the very basis of feminism as an aspiration to an ethical relationship to the Other, irreducible to a set of established rules or any currently accepted political slogan.

Indeed, Mackinnon overlooks the way in which gender and race interact in the construction of sexuality, as well as in the very description of oppression. As bell hooks explains,

Race and sex have always been overlapping discourses in the United States. The discourse began in slavery. The talk then was not about black men wanting to be free so that they could have access to the bodies of white women—that would come later. Then, black women's bodies were the discursive terrain, the playing field where racism and sexuality converged. Rape as both right and rite of the white male dominating group was a cultural norm. Rape was also an apt metaphor for European imperialist colonization of Africa and North America.[54]

An analysis of rape, then, demands an understanding of how sexual violence is crucial to imperialist domination and to racist justifications. "Blackness" and "whiteness" are part of the very construction of desire. The structure of desire in turn feeds the fantasies which justify racism and privilege some of us as "white." The very figure of the "white" woman and who she becomes in fantasy has to be analyzed. We cannot even begin to understand gender unless we understand how gender is "colored" and how "color" is in turn engendered, in the psychosexual dynamics of desire. As hooks argues, if we are to adequately understand racism we must also understand its sexualization in and through a phallic logic which reinforces race as much as it does gender. hooks has analyzed the way in which black liberation has been identified with sexual, masculine domination precisely because of phallogocentrism.

Oppressed black men and women have rarely challenged the use of gendered metaphors to describe the impact of racist domination and/or black liberation struggle. The discourse of black resistance has almost always equated freedom with manhood and the economic and material domination of black men with castration, emasculation. Accepting these sexual metaphors forged a bond between oppressed black men and their white male oppressors. They shared the patriarchal belief that revolutionary struggle was really about the erect phallus, the ability of men to establish political dominance that could correspond to the sexual dominance.[55]

At first glance, hooks's analysis of how the very struggle against racism is itself sexualized would seem to reinforce MacKinnon's projection of the male sadist as the figure of masculinity. But for hooks, masculine domination as established by phallogocentrism does not diminish or erase the difference between "black" and "white" men, it demands that we think *dynamically* about how desire is constructed through race as much as it is through gender.

The Affirmation of Feminine Sexual Difference

Overcoming the Repudiation of the Feminine

I can summarize my disagreement with MacKinnon as follows: For MacKinnon, feminism must involve the repudiation of the feminine; for me, feminism *demands* the affirmation of the feminine within sexual difference, and the challenge to women's shame of their "sex" which flows inevitably from the repudiation of the feminine. Without this challenge, we are left with the politics of revenge and lives of desolation, which make a mockery of the very concept of freedom. But to understand how we can make this challenge without simply replicating the pattern of gender hierarchy, we must first give a different account of why a gender hierarchy cannot completely capture feminine sexual difference.

MacKinnon's own analysis of femininity does not turn on a naturalist account of anatomy as destiny or on appeal to natural libidinal drives as the basis of male desire and domination. She moves within accepted "postmodern" insight by recognizing that femininity as imposed sexuality is a social construction. But, social construction or not, the constitution of the world through the male gaze as reinforced by male power totalizes itself as our social reality. Thus, if MacKinnon clearly rejects naturalism, she nevertheless remains a specific kind of essentialist. Under this patriarchal social reality, women's imposed "sex" is women's "essence," her only "being."

The Lesson of Deconstruction

I have argued at length elsewhere that MacKinnon fails to understand the critical lesson of deconstruction.[56] The lesson is that no reality can perfectly totalize itself, because reality, including the reality of male domination, is constituted in and through language in which institutionalized meaning can never be fully protected from slippage and reinterpretation.[57] MacKinnon believes that a feminist theory of sexuality must be studied in its experienced empirical existence, not just in the texts of history (as Foucault does), in the social psyche (as Lacan does), or in language (as Derrida does). Sexual meaning is not made only, or even primarily, by words and in texts. It is made in social relations of power in the world, through which process gender is also produced.[58]

Jacques Derrida does not argue that sexual meaning is made in and through words and texts in the limited way MacKinnon defines them. Derrida shows us that social reality (including the very definition of power) and "empirical" experience cannot be separated from the meanings they are given, while simultaneously exposing the inevitability of the limit on those meanings that have dominated our social life. The relevance of the limit[59] to institutionalized meaning in this context is that it allows for the affirmation of feminine sexual difference as other than its stabilized definitions within gender hierarchy. This, in turn, is precisely what allows us to develop a feminist celebration of women's "sex," rather than its repudiation, as well as a feminist "perspective" which, even under MacKinnon's own program, must be the very basis of a feminist theory of the state.

More specifically, I have argued that "seeing" and "being" can never be separated.[60] This argument would, at first glance, seem to bolster MacKinnon's argument: As we are seen, so we are. But, as Paul Ricoeur has convincingly argued, we do not "see" reality directly. Instead, we "see" through language and, more specifically, through the metaphors in which "being" is given to us.[61] "Being" for Ricoeur is itself a metaphor. This means that the "being" of femininity can never just be described as "there."

The Significance of the Rule of Metaphor

As a result, the rule of metaphor has specific implications within the context of feminism.[62] I have argued that "feminine being" cannot be separated from the metaphors in and through which it is figured. Metaphor as transference and analogy always implies both the like and the not like. The definition of the feminine, including MacKinnon's definition, *is* only as metaphor. Metaphor, in turn, allows both for expansion of meaning and for reinterpretation. The characterization cannot be cemented in stone precisely because it is designated as metaphor. Therefore, the realization of "feminine being" as metaphor is what allows us to reinterpret, and, more important, to affirm, the feminine as other, and *irreducibly other,* to any of the definitions imposed by patriarchy. Thus we can challenge MacKinnon's position on feminine sexuality.

For MacKinnon, as we have "seen," a feminist perspective is impossible as anything other than the recognition of the totalization of the masculine viewpoint. Therefore, the most we can do is simply to reverse the meaning of the totality, rather than challenge it in the name of the feminine imaginary which seeks a new symbolization of the meaning of sexual difference. The problem with this solution, as Luce Irigaray has explained, is that the possibility of feminine desire—and let me use the beautiful French word *jouissance*[63]—that is irreducible to being fucked by men and liking it, is foreclosed by MacKinnon's analysis.

Sexuality Rethought

I will return to lesbianism and love between women as an alternative shortly. For now I am operating within MacKinnon's own heterosexual framework, because, given MacKinnon's analysis, that is the framework that defines social reality. I want to emphasize that, given MacKinnon's repudiation of the feminine, there can only be the inescapable totality of male violence, the world of the "fuckees" and the "fuckors."[64] "True love" between women is always blocked by the totality of an imposed pornographic heterosexual reality. As a result, the utopian vision of lesbianism developed by innumerable writers such as Cixous, Irigaray, and Wittig, is foreclosed.[65] We are left instead with a disjuncture between sex and freedom. To quote MacKinnon:

> So long as sexual inequality remains unequal and sexual, attempts to value sexuality as women's, possessive as if women possess it, will remain part of limiting women to it, to what women are now defined as being. Outside of truly rare and contrapuntal glimpses (which most people think they live almost their entire sex life within), to seek an equal sexuality without political transformation is to seek equality under conditions of inequality. Rejecting this, and rejecting the glorification of settling for the best that inequality has to offer or has stimulated the resourceful to invent, are what Ti-Grace Atkinson meant to reject when she said: "I do not know any feminist worthy of the name who, if forced to choose between freedom and sex, would choose sex. She'd choose freedom every time."[66]

Maybe. But what is the content of this freedom? More specifically, what kind of conception of the person would we need to think that the disjuncture between "sex" and freedom could lead to freedom? One central theme of feminist philosophy has been to challenge conceptions of freedom that pit freedom against the reality that we are beings of the flesh, and necessarily sexual. The argument, simply put, has been that we cannot rise above our empirical selves of the flesh in order to be *free*. Such a conception has been critiqued as repression, not freedom, and has been connected to the devaluation of women—just as women have come, in Western philosophy, to be associated with the flesh.[67] If this is women's "choice"—and choice would hardly seem to be the right word since, in MacKinnon's analysis, it is forced upon women—it would seem rather to be a "choice" between desolation[68] or sacrifice and "sex," not between "freedom" and "sex." The celebration of the feminine "sex" and women's sexuality, on the other hand, suggests that our sexuality is not represented by any of the current male fantasies of woman and sex within patriarchy. By "having sex," then, I do not mean "getting fucked" in MacKinnon's sense. Such a reduction obviously envisions an act perpetrated by men upon women: the man fucks, the woman "gets fucked"—with all the negative connotations "getting fucked" takes on within our culture of so-called heterosexuality; so-called because the feminine as Other is denied its otherness under the rigid identity dictates of the gender hierarchy. Instead, by "sex" I mean the physical intimacy necessary for creatures of the flesh. Sex is the caressing, the kissing,[69] the embracing that can bring comfort and connection to two mortal, sexual creatures clinging to one another against the darkness and finding in one another a moment of protection and safety. Irigaray beautifully imagines two women making love as an alternative to MacKinnon's vision of "getting fucked." As Irigaray writes,

> No surface holds. No figure, line, or point remains. No ground subsists. But no abyss, either. Depth, for us, is not a chasm. Without a solid crust, there is no precipice. Our depth is the thickness of our body, our all touching itself. Where top and bottom, inside and outside, in front and behind, above and below are not separated, remote, out of touch. Our all intermingled. Without breaks or gaps.[70]

I am not arguing that lesbianism can simply take us away from male domination. Even so, as Wittig has brilliantly argued, lesbianism *can* provide us with a politically significant vision of a different engagement with a woman's own body and with a lover in which a woman's "sex" is not repudiated.[71] Indeed, for Wittig, the lesbian is not a woman, precisely because a woman traditionally defined cannot be separated from her role within heterosexuality. Simply put, the lesbian need not engage with her "sex" from within the psychosexual dynamic MacKinnon describes to live her life or explore her love. Ironically, given MacKinnon's move to totalize her own description of heterosexuality, she excludes Wittig's promise of lesbianism as a different practice of sexuality, other than by comparison to the sadomasochism which MacKinnon defines as heterosexuality.

Nor am I arguing that the practice of heterosexuality is reducible to MacKinnon's and Dworkin's view of "sex" as "intercourse" or of "intercourse" as "getting fucked."[72] Here again, we are returned to the possibilities of reinterpretation, even if we simultaneously recognize the institutionalization of certain sexual practices, particularly within heterosexuality, as "normal," when they may have nothing at all to do with women's desire. But I insist on the need to affirm the feminine within sexual difference and feminine sexuality, because it is necessary to challenge the conception of a free person as one who has been cut off from her own sexuality. Such an affirmation allows us to avoid the tragedy into which MacKinnon's analysis inevitably leads us.

But does this mean that she is not right to remind us at every step that, under gender hierarchy, to use Lacan's famous phrase, "fucking . . . [is] not working"?[73] The answer is no. I, too, want to emphasize the suffering women must endure and, more specifically, expose the relationship in our society between sexual shame and women's lives. However, the story I relate is a narration very different from MacKinnon's.

I turn now to Lacan because his story lies at the base of how gender hierarchy (and with it sexual desire) is constructed, and goes beyond MacKinnon's limited vision of gender hierarchy as only a matter of social psychology.[74]

The Lacanian Account of Sexual Shame in Women

According to Lacan, the genesis of linguistic consciousness occurs when the infant recognizes itself as having an identity separate from the mother, because the mother is Other to herself or himself. The primordial moment of separation is experienced by the infant as both loss of unity and the gaining of an identity. The pain of this loss results in a primary repression that simultaneously buries the relationship to the mother in the unconscious and catapults the infant into the Symbolic realm to fulfill its desire for the Other. Once projected into language, this primary identification with the mother is experienced only through the disruptive force of the unconscious. The unrepresented desire for the Phallic Mother is only remembered in the fantasy projection that compensates for Her absence. So far on this account it would seem that both sexes suffer a primordial separation from the mother and would be marked by this separation in the same way.

Although Lacanians maintain the difference between the penis and the phallus (the phallus represents the lack that triggers desire in both sexes), it remains the case in Lacan's analysis that because the penis can visibly represent the lack, the penis can appear to stand in for the would-be neutral phallus. This establishes the basis of the illusion that having the penis is having the phallus, with all its attendant symbolic power. In this culture of gender hierarchy, the male child "sees" his mother's lack, which gains significance as her castration. Sexual difference and gender identity are based on the cultural significance attributed to this experience of "sighting." The penis is identified with potency, able to satisfy the mother's desire. Woman, on the other hand, is identified as the castrated Other. If the penis, at least on the level of fantasy, is identified with the phallus, then Woman, who lacks the penis, is also seen as lacking the affirmative qualities associated with the phallus. Her "sex" is seen as both fearful and shameful.

Lacan's speculative insight has been reinforced by such empirical research as the work of Eleanor Galenson.[75] Galenson's nurseries provided the arena for observing the actual behavior of little girls. Her studies argue that sexual shame in girls is associated with the recognition of themselves as the castrated Other. Lacan helps us to understand why this recognition is not the result of biology but of a symbolic order in which the feminine is devalued. Galenson's work draws the connection between this early experience of sexual shame as inherent in feminine identity and some of the symptoms and behavioral patterns in mature women, including depression, profound feelings of inadequacy, feeling like a "fake," or fear of being "found out" despite a record of accomplishment. The fear that one will be discovered reflects the shame of and devaluation of the feminine "sex."[76] One of the most significant expressions of sexual shame is the denial of the value of feminine sexual difference which is irreducible to the current cultural trappings of femininity.

It also is important to note that Lacan understands male superiority as a "sham," meaning that it is not mandated by a person's "sex" but instead rests on the fantasy identification that having the penis is having the phallus. This illusion also means that the symbolic "Daddy" can always take the phallus away and, with the phallus, the affirmative qualities associated with potency. This fear is the basis of the designation of the male as the "wimp," beautifully allegorized in Samuel Beckett's *Happy Days*. The man crawls around on all fours unable to face the woman:

> *Winnie:* "What is a hog exactly? What exactly is a hog, Willie, do you know, I can't remember. What *is* a hog, Willie, please!"
>
> *Willie:* "Castrated male swine. Reared for slaughter."[77]

The analysis of the fear of the "wimp" in no way takes away from the cruelty and the violence of the "male swine." But it does explain this violence and cruelty as rooted in fear and not in power, especially if one defines the empowerment of personality as innovative capability rather than beating up the other.[78] It would be accurate in this analysis to say that pornography is what wimps need, not what men want. Thus, I disagree with MacKinnon when she argues that "[p]ornography permits men to have whatever they want sexually. It is their 'truth about sex.' "[79] Nonetheless, for me, as I have already argued, pornography is clearly a violation.

Sexual Shame and the Violation of Pornography

How can we more profoundly understand pornography as a violation of women under the story of gender hierarchy I have just developed? Pornography reinforces the very sexual shame that, as Galenson and others have shown, makes it difficult for women truly to find equality of capability and well-being. We can only truly understand pornography as a violation within a context that explains gender hierarchy as the basis of sexual shame. Pornography, in this most basic sense, symbolizes the devalorization and fear of women's "sex." Pornography prevents women from feeling like equal members of the community because it reflects our "sex" in a way that no woman can affirm. To live in a community where pornography is everywhere graphically impinges on women's space, in which we could invent our fantasies, redraw, and refigure our "sex." I have already defined the enforced viewing of pornography which is inseparable from the reality that it's everywhere as a violation. The first major gain from restriction is that women will no longer have to undergo this forced viewing. We can be freed from this one violation. But there is also an extremely important symbolic gain. The view of the feminine "sex" portrayed in pornography cannot as easily proclaim itself as an obvious "truth," reinforced by its very pervasiveness. When it is *restricted,* the restriction makes a normative evaluation of what is portrayed in pornography, the violation against women is recognized as they are protected from it. Thus, the harm to women is understood to far outweigh the claim of the man who desires that pornography be available to him free of any restrictions, particularly once we understand the idea that pornography is not only a violation to women, but also an insult to men.

Pornography insults men in that it depicts them as having to violate women in order to imagine having sex with them. It gives us a vision and reinforces a view of the man as the "wimp," afraid of women and, therefore, needing to have them in chains, which is hardly a flattering picture. I distinguish insult from offense and violation because I do not want to pretend that its insult to men imposes the same kind of suffering as its violation of women, but it must be noted. Finally, it is important to recognize that the fear of the "wimp"—the fear of losing the supposed all-powerful phallus—is so overwhelming because in the context of gender hierarchy, the worst thing that can happen to a person is to become a "girl," or rather a "cunt."

The identification of Woman as the castrated Other explains the fear in the "wimp" as well as the devalorization of Woman. The assumption of masculine gender identity thus depends upon the devalorization of Woman, which, in turn, explains the repudiation of the feminine as the basis for patriarchal culture. The result for women is that we are left in a state of *délaissement,* which means that the little girl cannot positively understand her relationship to her mother, and, therefore, to her own "sex." Thus, Lacan's account of gender differentiation into two "sexes" explains why the gender divide becomes a hierarchy in which the feminine is repudiated and despised, by women as well as men. Lacan leaves us with a world of "wimps" (men) and ghosts (women) unable to meet, speak, touch, ally. Beckett's depiction of the male crawling on all fours and the woman slowly sinking into the "same old shit" in *Happy Days* allegorizes the Lacanian understanding of the reality of gender hierarchy. "Fucking," for both Lacan and MacKinnon, cannot be separated from the subjection of women. But, if Lacan recognizes the subjection of women, he also believes that the problem is insoluble.

Ironically, MacKinnon also expresses the insolubility of the problem of women in her own writing. Her politics of revenge only reinforces the very structure of domination with its divide between the castrators and the castrated. Her desire cannot be expressed, it can only be negated. It is the inevitability of negation within this brand of feminism that has led some Lacanians to insist that feminism only expresses the lesson that there cannot be an affirmative evaluation of feminine sexual difference and of feminine sexual desire. Irigaray reminds us over and over again of the cost of denying the specificity of our desire. To respond to both Lacan and MacKinnon, I return to Derrida's intervention into Lacan, because he shows why the affirmation of feminine sexual difference cannot be foreclosed by the institutionalized meanings of patriarchy.

Derrida's Intervention into Lacanian Theory

Derrida teaches us that Lacan's own understanding of gender identity, constituted in and through the linguistic structures of the Symbolic realm—the conventional meanings given to gender in patriarchy— can be turned against Lacan's own political conclusions. Derrida's intervention shows us that the phallus only takes up its privileged position through a reading that is dependent on a chain of signifiers inseparable from the meaning of patriarchy, which bolsters the illusion that by itself the phallus generates and engenders the continuity of life through patriarchical lineage. What is read can always be reread. Derrida shows that the very slippage of meaning inherent in language breaks up the coherence of the gender hierarchy and allows for resignifying the phallus. Deconstruction, on the reading I have just offered, challenges the inevitability of the reestablishment of the patriarchal order which would reduce the feminine "sex" to the castrated other. In French feminist writing and in my own recent work, another step has been taken beyond deconstruction, to advocate the need not only to open the space for the reevaluation of the feminine within sexual difference, but also to write its celebration through refiguration and remetaphorization of feminine figures.[80]

Equivalent Rights: A New Context for Sex, Sexuality, and Gender Identity

Challenging the "Sameness" Ideology

I believe my own program of equivalent rights can develop a different theory of equality and overcome the deficiency in MacKinnon's analysis. We need a theory of equality which does not end by reinforcing the privileging of the masculine as the norm. MacKinnon has correctly and profoundly challenged the "sameness" ideology that informs so much of the law of sex discrimination.[81] She explains that if we can show that women are like men, then we can show that we have been discriminated against if and when we are in fact like them, but are treated differently. As women we must continually analogize our experience to men's if we want it to be legally recognized as unequal treatment. For MacKinnon, "sameness" and "likeness" analysis is itself a reflection of discrimination because it demands that women meet the male norm without questioning why the masculine was identified as the norm in the first place. My argument insists further that unless we recognize the value of the feminine within sexual difference we cannot adequately challenge the acceptance of the male as the human, and, therefore, we cannot ultimately challenge gender hierarchy. In other words, we need the affirmation of feminine sexual difference if we are to challenge the likeness analysis without reducing our insistence on women's rights to an appeal for special privilege.

A program of equivalent rights is the legal expression of the affirmation and valuation of sexual difference. "Equivalence" means of equal value, but not of equal value *because of likeness*. Equivalence does not demand that the basis of equality be likeness to men. Such a view would once again deny that we are, sexuate beings. Hopefully, this will continue to change as we challenge the reality of rigid gender identity. The human species is of two genres, not one species without differentiation. Equivalent rights can then be distinguished from the dominant analysis of sex discrimination that has been reflected in recent federal-court and United States Supreme Court opinions. Moreover, equivalent rights recognize the irreducibility of sexual difference to some universal conception of the asexual person. As Luce Irigaray has explained,

> I know that some men imagine that the great day of the good-for-everyone universal has dawned. But what universal? What new imperialism is hiding behind this? And who pays the price for it? There is no universal valid for all women and all men outside the natural economy. Any other universal is a partial construct and, therefore, authoritarian and unjust. The first universal to be established would be that of a legislation valid for both sexes as a basic element in human culture. That does not mean forced sexual choices. But we are living beings, which means sexuate beings, and our identity cannot be constructed without a vertical and horizontal horizon that respects difference.[82]

The "legislation valid for both sexes" as a basic element in human culture" to which Irigaray refers must include equivalent rights as rights, and not as privileges needed to correct the imposed inequality of women. Equivalent rights are not merely a means to help women become more like men in order to promote one species undivided by sexual difference. Equivalent rights do not have as their sole or even main goal the allowance of entry into a male world from which we have previously been shut out. Rather, they are designed to enable women to value the choices we make about our lives and work without shame of our "sex," even if such choices do not fit into the preestablished social world. Such rights, then, demand the restructuring of, not just accommodation to, the current world of work. MacKinnon has criticized the patriarchal culture which imposes "forced sexual choices." Yet she fails to see that one of these forced sexual choices is the very repudiation of the feminine within sexual difference.

I want to avow what has been disavowed, affirm what has been repudiated, *as one moment* in the political struggle of feminism. This affirmation is explicitly ethical in that it deliberately challenges the gender hierarchy in which the feminine within sexual difference is refused, or, perhaps more precisely, is identified as refuse. But the affirmation necessarily operates within a performative contradiction precisely because the feminine within sexual difference is what is not "there," except as the projected Other to man, as the abject, as the refuse. It is a mistake to identify my version of ethical feminism with any appeal to the myths of a primary femininity.[83] Ethical feminism operates within the paradox of the aporia that I have just indicated inheres in the affirmation of what has been "erased" through the projected fantasies of Woman perpetuated, and indeed, demanded, by the gender hierarchy. Ethical feminism denies the "truth" of the gender hierarchy by affirming the feminine within sexual difference as other to its current identifications. The emphasis *must* be on the other to what has become identified as the femininue within gender hierarchy. The remetaphorization of the feminine within sexual difference does not try to capture the truth of femininity. We are not to accommodate to what we have been forced "to be" under the gender hierarchy. The opposite is the case. The process of refiguration, remetaphorization, and metonymic displacement denies that there is such a "truth" as a primary femininity, as the process itself slides away from and shifts the boundaries of our current identities imposed by our engendered "reality." I can only suggest here how the program of equivalent rights, once it is put into the context of this understanding of sex, sexuality, and gender identity, can help further the analysis of specific issues of doctrinal concern.

Pornography and the Equivalent Protection of Inviolability

I have argued through my reading of Lacan and the reinforcement of his theory in the empirical research of Eleanor Galenson that the repudiation of the feminine, and, more specifically, the reinforcement of sexual shame, harms women in a very specific sense, and that this harm is reinforced by pornography. Moreover, pornography is not the projection of all-powerful men but, as Laccan would tell us, of the "wimps" who are afraid of women. Ultimately, pornography amounts only to a compensatory fantasy to make up for fear of women, the "dark continent."[84] I will not deny that fear often leads to cruelty. We see this in the horrifying reality of race relations as well as in gender hierarchy. But, when MacKinnon speaks of the all-powerful man—and of pornography as his vision and his desire—she accepts the psychical fantasy of macho compensation as truth. Who but a "wimp" would fantasize about sex with a woman in chains, tied, bound, and gagged, so he would, in the most profound sense, not have to face her, let alone hear her?

My argument has been that the recognition of the equivalent protection of women's inviolability demands some time and place restrictions on pornography. To summarize: Restrictions on pornography are necessary for the guarantee of women's equality of well-being and capability, given the way in which pornography reinforces sexual shame and denies us equivalent protection of inviolability.

Equivalent Rights and Abortion

The right of abortion is a classic example of equivalent rights for women and should be included in what Irigaray has called "the right to 'motherhood' " (as should rights such as maternity leave and prenatal care). Without such a right, women cannot aspire to achieve the most basic sense of well-being, because we are denied the power to enjoy pregnancy and motherhood without sacrificing other aspects of our lives. Men clearly do not need the right of abortion. But that does not mean that women should not have such a right guaranteed if we are to have equality of capability and well-being. To understand why the

right of abortion is crucial as an equivalent right, we must understand
ourselves as sexual beings whose freedom can never be separated from
an affirmative relationship to our "flesh." Such an affirmative relationship is impossible without a right of bodily integrity. I should add
here that bodily integrity in any complete sense, is, of course, always
imaginary. But as Lacan has reminded us, this imaginary projection of
bodily integrity is crucial, indeed, the very basis of individuation. As a
result, an assault against this projected image of bodily integrity is an
assault on the very process of individuation which provides us with a
sense of self. Justice Blackmun in his dissent in *Webster v. Reproductive
Health Services*[85] voiced his fear of the loss of freedom to women if we
were to lose this right of abortion, which I would include under the
right to bodily integrity.[86] I want to stress here the suffering which will
be imposed on women as creatures of the flesh if we lose that right and
yet find ourselves in circumstances in which we are unable to raise and
mother a baby, and, therefore, must impose upon ourselves a self-
inflicted abortion. The abortion movement of the early 1970s docu-
mented how many women were forced to rely on this as an option
when abortion was illegal. In her horrifying novel—horrifying because
it depicts so brilliantly the toll of the sexual shame on women—
Torborg Nedreaas describes the physical anguish of a self-inflicted
abortion:

> Then I set to. Drops of sweat ran down the bridge of my nose, and
> I noticed that I was sitting there with my tongue hanging out of my
> mouth. Because something burst. I could hear it inside my head from
> the soft crunch of tissues that burst. The pain ran along my spine
> and radiated across my loins and stomach. I screamed. I thought I
> screamed, but there wasn't a sound. More, more, push more, find
> another place. It had to be wrong. And I held the very tip of the
> weapon between my thumb and forefinger to find the opening to my
> uterus once more. It was difficult but I thought I'd succeeded. The
> steel needle slid a little heavily against something. It went far up.
> Then a piercing lightning of pain through my stomach, back and
> brain told me it had hit something. More, more, don't give up.
> Tissues burst. The sweat blinded my eyes. I heard a long rattling
> groan come out of me while my hand let the weapon do its work
> with deranged courage.[87]

Whether self-inflicted or not, the pain is not just physical, and yet
there is very little discussion in psychoanalytic literature of the psychic
cost that is often paid in the decision to have an abortion. This erasure

is obviously not surprising, and it makes it more difficult for women to come to terms with abortion. The burial of how individualized the experience of abortion actually is, is due to the prevasiveness of the stereotypes and their imposition upon women who do not bring their pregnancies to term. But in one of the few psychoanalytic papers to address the issue, Graciela Abelin-Sas[88] argues from her clinical experience as an analyst that the stereotypic reasons assumed by analysts to explain the decision to have an abortion—denial of the maternal function, a troubled relationship with the patient's own mother—are completely inadequate, and the pain, in turn, is rendered inexpressible in a culture which implicitly or explicitly condemns abortion. From her own work with her patients, Abelin-Sas argues convincingly that the woman's ability to articulate the actual experience of her abortion is crucial for her psychic well-being. There is obviously no more powerful condemnation of abortion than that of making it illegal. The devastating effect of such a legal regression on women's ability to articulate their experience and integrate it into their psychic lives is probably incalculable. In such a case, the interpretation of their decision to have an abortion can only too easily be reduced to silence before their imposed sexual shame. It's not at all surprising, given the sexual shame associated with abortion, that one of the first early actions to make abortion a legal right was for women to publicly admit to their abortions.[89]

Feminine flesh is not the same as masculine flesh. It is important to note here that I am using flesh as a metaphor, not as a literal description of the body. But still there is an inescapable, if ultimately inexpressable to full definition, psychicality to human "being." Flesh is the metaphor of psychicality that can never be fully articulated. There is no body that is just there, particularly when we are writing of the significance given to sexual difference. The law is one area in which the contest over how sexual difference is to be symbolized takes place. The law is one powerful reading of the body that marks and defines it. The right to bodily integrity as this is, in turn, related to psychic well-being and individuation, is a right necessary for both "sexes" under the vision of equality of capability and well-being. The right to bodily integrity does not mean the same rights, but rather the guarantee of its equivalent scope for both "sexes." The right of abortion is most definitely necessary to guarantee bodily integrity for women. Rights should not be based on what men, as currently defined, need for their well-being as sexual beings of the flesh, as if there were only one genre of the human species.

Conclusion

If MacKinnon ultimately repudiates the feminine within sexual difference, she perpetuates rather than challenges the gender hierarchy which lies at the base of women's inequality. If the feminist point of view is to be incorporated into the state, we must have an account of its possibility. I have argued that such an account is possible once we correctly understand the role of deconstruction and, beyond this, the place of remetaphorization and refiguration of the feminine in reinventing, and thus affirming, sexual difference. This affirmation allows us to identify the wrongs to women within a context of sexual shame imposed upon women by gender hierarchy. It also allows us to challenge the idea that the human species is of only one genre and therefore that the "rights of man" give us a full conception of rights. To argue for equivalence is not to advocate special privilege, once we value the feminine within sexual difference as necessary for women's equality of capability and well-being, and recognize sexuality itself as necessary for a creature of the flesh to enjoy a full life.

6

Sex-Discrimination Law and Equivalent Rights

In this chapter I will suggest that we should understand the wrong in sex discrimination as the imposed law of gender identity on lived possibilities, whether those oppressed are women who seek to be truck drivers or prison guards, or homosexual men who are denied the right to be fathers or to have access to desperately needed medical treatment such as AZT. Under current sex-discrimination law, as conventionally interpreted,[1] the wrong of discrimination is the imposition of a universal on an individual who does not match that universal. I will argue against this interpretation as underinclusive of what should be considered sex discrimination. Secondly, I will advocate a program of equivalent rights that allows us to respect diversity and different lifestyles and, by so doing, challenge the reigning doctrine of discrimination in the Supreme Court.

Under that doctrine, the wrong of sex discrimination is not the imposition of stereotypes per se, but the imposition of stereotypes when they are not "true"—that is, when the stereotypes are not an adequate description of the actual life of the person. So, for example, if a job requires that the employee lift two hundred pounds, and a woman can lift two hundred pounds, she should be able to take on the job even if women generally could not meet the job requirements. Difference, in the sense of being unable to meet the norm, must be shown, not just assumed on the basis of generalizations about gender. Equality, in this definition of discrimination, turns on the demonstration that a woman is *like* her male counterparts. Discrimination, so defined, is based on an inherently comparative evaluation between the genders.

Under this conception of discrimination, heterosexual white men can sue because of the imposition of an inaccurate stereotype by which they are judged exclusively on the basis of their gender. Thus, heterosexual white men have been granted jurisdiction under Title VII of the

147

Civil Rights Act of 1964.[2] The irony is that gay men have been denied jurisdiction under the statute because their complaints have been found to involve discrimination on the basis of what is called sexual preference. Thus, their complaints as gay men have not been understood as sex discrimination for Title VII purposes. This supposedly follows from the comparative analysis that focuses on the relationship between the genders rather than within the genderized group. Under this reasoning, the differentiation would be between two groups of men, heterosexual and homosexual, and not between men and women. But, of course, to point to the established definition of discrimination only pushes the problem one step further back. We still need to question a conception of the relationship among sex, sexuality, and gender that denies a gay man the right to seek redress under Title VII. We also have to question why, when women are "truly" different, they cannot claim that they have been discriminated against or treated unequally. This issue is not merely a question of why women should have to meet an already-established male norm which, of course, assumes that in a patriarchal society what appear as neutral standards will often implicitly assume the male as the norm. The question is how difference will be taken into account when that difference is an "accurate" stereotype.[3] This problem has been central to feminist debates as to how the issue of maternity, including maternity leave, prenatal care, and abortion, should be legally addressed.

First however, let us take the problem of whether or not the gay man's denial of jurisdiction under the statute can be justified because the discrimination of which they complain is supposedly not based on sex. As we have seen, the argument is that the complaint is not based on "sex" or gender, but on a division within the group of men themselves due to sexual preference. But there is also the implied assumption that heterosexuality is "normal." This assumption is necessary to justify the appeal to the reality that homosexuality has been historically and legally condemned. Some judges at least have relied upon an appeal to the past history in which heterosexuality has been established as normal as the basis for their justification for the state's right to make homosexuality a crime.

The best example of the logic of this particular circle is in Justice White's majority opinion in *Bowers v. Hardwick*.[4] There, White concludes that the "privacy right" established in the line of cases from *Griswold*[5] through *Roe*[6] and *Carey*[7] did not cover homosexual activity.[8] He also argued that there was nothing in the Constitution or the Bill of Rights, in spite of the interpretation of precedent, that guaranteed any fundamental right to homosexual activity. As a result, Justice White rejects the Eleventh Circuit's holding that the Georgia statute violated the respondent's fundamental rights "because his homosexual right is a private and intimate association that is beyond the reach of state regulation by reason of the Ninth Amendment and the Due Process Clause of the Fourteenth Amendment."[9] Clearly suspicious of the basis of the privacy right itself, White further concludes:

> Accepting the decisions in these cases and the above description of them, we think it evident that none of the rights announced in those cases bears any resemblance to the claimed constitutional right of homosexuals to engage in acts of sodomy that is asserted in this case. No connection between family, marriage, or procreation on the one hand and homosexual activity on the other has been demonstrated, either by the Court of Appeals or by respondent.[10]

Of course, if one is a homosexual, the right to engage in homosexual activity has everything to do with "family, marriage, and procreation," even if the standard rights of heterosexual engagement have been denied to gay and lesbian couples, and even if gay and lesbian couples seek other forms of intimate association. Can Justice White's blindness to this obvious reality be separated from his own acceptance of an implied heterosexuality as the "natural" and, therefore, right way to live? Here we see the impact of implicit conceptions of human nature and, more specifically, sexual identity, on a concrete decision. Without such an implicit appeal, Justice White can only rely on the "fact" that most states—and this remains true today—impose sanctions on homosexual activity. In itself, this reasoning represents the mistake of deriving an "ought" from an "is."

But Justice White returns us to the state statutes and to the explicit appeal to what is natural and, therefore, "right" in terms of sexual identity. Homosexual activity is outlawed by the state statutes because it is "unnatural," "abnormal," or "perverted." Without this distinction, the opinion rests on a tautology. We can see more clearly the validity of Justice Blackmun's conclusion in his dissent. For Blackmun, the right involved in *Bowers* is the right of consenting adults to be left alone in their intimate associations.[11] For Blackmun, this right could not legitimately be withheld without some justification, other than that it had always been so.[12] If, however, we go one step further and say that there is no identity based in our "sex" that makes homosexuality "unnatural," then there can be no such justification for "outlawing" such engagement. I will discuss why a psychoanalytic perspective and, more specifically, the analysis of sexuality, sex, and gender in the works of Jacques Lacan and Jacques Derrida can help us dismantle the legitimation of heterosexuality as natural.

But before doing so, I want to explore the second problem in discrimination law: the difficulty of finding discrimination under Title VII when women seem to be actually different and, thus, accurately stereotyped. What this means concretely under our current law is that if a stereotype can be shown to be true—"true" here understood as an accurate description of reality (i.e., women cannot meet the long hours required by law firms when they have children and therefore fall short of the requirements for partnership—then there is no legal discrimination. How are we to solve these problems?

To do so, I want to suggest that we need a new analysis of the relationship among gender, sex, and sexuality. As I have already hinted, such an analysis is already available to us in Jacques Derrida's specific deconstructive intervention into the theoretical work of Jacques Lacan. Both Lacan and Derrida deconstruct the identification of gender, sex, and sexuality, but they arrive at very different political conclusions. The deconstruction of rigid gender identities can give us a new approach to the two problems I have just described, as well as help us reconceptualize the wrong of "sex" discrimination. Of course, to suggest the relevance of deconstruction to an analysis of "sex" discrimination is also to indicate the necessity of psychoanalytic theory in political thought more generally, and to a feminist politics more specifically. But let me turn now to what this deconstruction entails within the context of psychoanalytic theory. To begin, we have to look more specifically at Derrida's intervention into the theory of Jacques Lacan.[13] In Lacan, sexual difference and gender identity are based on the cultural significance attributed to the experience of the "sighting" of the fact that the mother does not have the penis. Having the penis is identified with being potent, able to satisfy the mother's desire, which is why Lacan associates the "reality" of having the penis with the fantasy that having the penis is having the phallus.

If the penis, at least on the level of fantasy, is identified with the phallus, then Woman, who lacks the penis, is also seen as lacking the affirmative qualities associated with the phallus. The result for women is that we are left in a state of *délaissement,* which technically means that given the definition of Woman as the castrated Other, the little girl cannot positively represent her relationship to the mother and, thus, to her own "sex." In this way, Lacan's account of gender differentiation into "two" sexes explains why the gender divide becomes a hierarchy in which the feminine is repudiated.

But for my purposes here, it is important to note three aspects of Lacan's own analysis of the division of human beings into two "sexes." The first is that Lacan's recognition of the constitutive force of language denies any attempt to root sex, sexuality, and gender identity in a pregiven nature or set of libidinal drives. Thus, there is no biologically based gender identity and, corrrespondingly, no normal, mature sexuality that can be understood as the culmination of the proper development of the libidinal drives. In this sense, Lacanianism undermines the *traditional* Freudian conception of sexual perversion, which turns on an account of the "normal" maturation of sexuality into heterosexuality. Secondly, Lacan understands male superiority as a "sham," meaning that it is not mandated by nature, but instead rests on the fantasy identification that having the penis is having the phallus. Lacan undermines the claim that patriarchy is in any way mandated by the nature of biological sex. Third, because Lacan recognizes the role of fantasy in the assumption of gender identity, he also understands that there can be no perfect identification of oneself with one's gender. The very idea of gender is itself always shifting, because there can never be any end to the divergent interpretations of the meaning of gender in an "accurate" description of sex or sexuality. In spite of his recognition that gender as a culture structure determines sex and sexuality, and not the other way around, Lacan's analysis emphasizes the way the law of this division is self-replicating. Thus, even if Lacan understands the situation of women within patriarchal culture and society as an unnecessary subjugation—if by unnecessary we mean not by nature—he still sees change in the gender structure as well nigh impossible.

Derrida's intervention into Lacanianism is against the conclusion that the problem of Woman is "insoluble" because her definition as lack is continually reinforced given the meaning of sexual difference in our current structures of gender identity. Even if Lacan recognizes the fantasy dimension of sexual difference, he emphasizes the power of gender structures to give significance to the reality that women do not have a penis. Derrida, on the other hand, emphasizes the political and ethical significance of the way in which lived sexuality never perfectly matches the imposition of gender identity. He does so first by showing us how Lacan fails to take note of the implications of his own insight into the constitutive force of language. Second, he gives us another interpretation of Lacan's infamous statement "Woman does not exist," which, within Lacan's own framework, means that the libidinal relationship to the Phallic Mother cannot be represented precisely because it has been repressed into the unconscious.

Derrida reinterprets Lacan's insight into what is perceived as the inability to separate the truth of Woman from the fictions in which she is represented and in and through which she portrays herself. Lacan teaches us that any concept of sexuality cannot be separated from what shifts in language, what he calls *significance*.[14] For Lacan, there is no outside referent in which the process of interpretation of sexuality comes to an end, such as nature or biology, or even conventional gender structures. As a result, we can never discover the "true," authentic ground of female identity to counter the masculine erasure of the feminine.[15] For Derrida, Lacan's insight into the linguistic code of the unconscious undermines his own pessimistic political conclusions. As Derrida shows us again and again, this linguistic code cannot be frozen because of the slippage of meaning inherent in the metaphoric aspect of language. Deconstruction also demonstrates that within the Lacanian understanding of the linguistic structure of gender identity, Woman cannot just be reduced to lack because the metaphors through which she is represented produce an always-shifting reality. Against Lacan, Derrida shows us that what shifts in language, including the definition of gender identity and the designation of the feminine as the lack of the phallus, cannot definitively be stabilized.

Derrida also shows us that the phallus takes on the significance it does for the child only as the metaphor for what the mother desires. Because the erection of the phallus as the "transcendental signified" is based on a reading or an interpretation, the significance of the phallus can be reinterpreted. Thus, the significance of the discovery of anatomical sexual difference can also be reinterpreted (if the phallus is not read through the fantasy projection of what it means to have a penis). As a result, the divide into two genders may also yield to other interpretations.

For Derrida, heterosexuality and homosexuality are only given the meaning they are within this current structure, which divides the human race sexually into two. The possibility of reinterpretation of the meaning of the feminine, as well as of the significance of the gender divide itself, is what keeps open the space for Derrida's new choreography of sexual difference. Thus, the emphasis on the performative power of language, in and through which gender identity is constituted, allows for the transformation of current structures of gender identity.

It is a mistake, then, to think that Derrida reduces Woman to the definition of lack or fundamental nonidentity.[16] Rather, he argues that "sex" and "gender" are not identical. In the space of that separation we can open up further transformative possibilities. Moreover, the recognition of the constitutive, performative power of language means that Woman cannot be imprisoned in the current definitions of herself as lack, because such an analysis of Woman turns on the assumption that the phallus will necessarily be erected as the "transcendental signifier." The reading of Derrida that insists that he advocates Woman's nonidentity conflates his position with Lacan's and fails to appreciate the full political and ethical significance of Derrida's "dream of a new choreography of sexual difference."

We can now return to why both Lacan and Derrida's intervention into the Lacanian analysis of the gender divide can help us rethink the wrong in discrimination and, more specifically, help us solve the two problems in discrimination law I indicated earlier.

First, the psychoanalytic perspective I have developed here can help us think differently about "sex" discrimination against gay men. As we have seen, Lacan's own denial that there is a pregiven sexual nature which determines gender rejects the validity of the concept of perversion or even the concept of a normal, mature social identity. Therefore, the division between normal and abnormal "sexual identity"—as long as that identity is based on consent between adults—is a cultural construction, not a natural necessity. Therefore, the appeal to what is natural cannot be the justification for the state's right to outlaw homosexuality.

Now I want to introduce the first sense of equivalent rights. First, homosexuals should be given the *equivalent right* to be left alone in their intimate associations, whether or not they choose to mimic the life patterns of traditional heterosexuals. This recognition of the equivalent rights of homosexuals is, to my mind, the best interpretation of Blackmun's dissent in *Bowers*. I advocate *equivalent* rather than *equal* rights to recognize the difference of homosexuality, which should not have to match itself to heterosexual arrangements in order to justify itself.

In terms of the question of jurisdiction under Title VII, if gay men do not fit into the traditionally defined properties of the masculine— and they are discriminated against for not doing so—they are discriminated against because of their supposedly "aberrant" sexuality and for not living up to their "sex." Thus, this condemnation should be understood as sex discrimination. Derrida shows us in his intervention into Lacanianism not only that such a rigid designation of a human being is ontologically arbitrary, but that it also curtails the possibilities of a sexuality lived differently. As such, it is normatively suspect for limiting possibilities when a limit is not only unjustifiable by reference to a pregiven nature or gender identity, but also "causes the misery."[17] Against the possibility of a "new choreography of sexual difference" that can never be foreclosed, we can then redefine the wrong in discrimination. The wrong in discrimination is the imposition of rigid gender identities on sexual beings who can never be adequately captured by any definition. Under this definition, gay men suffer "sex" discrimination precisely because the reality of their "sex" and sexuality is denied in the name of a gender identity that is imposed upon them.

I have already discussed how the standard definitions of discrimination define the illegal harm as the imposition of a "false" stereotype. But if we accept that the wrong in discrimination is the imposition of gender identity when it cannot be adequate to enjoyed sexuality or lived individuality, we can begin to rethink whether or not discrimination should be limited to the imposition of a false stereotype. The imposition of rigid gender structures may well mean that women have been forced to define their lives within these structures. In other words, women are imprisoned by stereotypes because their options are limited by those stereotypes. Thus, against the backdrop of a new choreography of sexual difference, the very reinforcement of stereotypes can be understood as discrimination. The "purpose" of Title VII can then be understood to disrupt the status quo of gender hierarchy rather than to establish its reinforcement.[18] The very process of stereotyping can be understood itself as a wrong, because it forecloses individual possibilities in the name of "gender" that rests on the implied identification of gender and "sex."

The "mommy track"[19] is wrong because it reinforces the very gender divide in which "mommies" mother. The "mommy track" is one way of allowing women to have limited rights within the job market, given the imposed truth of the stereotypes. But, of course, women are still expected to make sacrifices in their lives because they mother. As a result such "rights" are not "equivalent." If "mothering" is valued social activity, then there should be no sacrifice of either status or pay and, of course, in the name of collapsing the gender divide and imposed stereotypes, we should encourage men to take up this activity.

Even if we can interpret Title VII to challenge gender stereotypes, we still have to face those circumstances in which the difference between men and women, masculine and feminine, cannot be reduced to imposed convention, even the imposed convention that women are primary caretakers of children. The obvious examples are, of course, those that seem inevitably to characterize sexual difference as anatomical difference, not just role difference. As of now, women and men must still have a different relationship to reproduction because it is women who physically bear children. How can we take this actual difference into account? We are returned to the way in which gender hierarchy leaves women in a state of *délaissement,* in which feminine difference is ignored, repudiated, or stereotypically limited. The only way in which feminine difference can gain legal status under the current standards is, ironically, to obliterate itself or to define itself in already-accepted conventions like the "mommy track." We continually have to analogize our experience to men's if we want it recognized. If we can show that a pregnancy is like a hernia, we can legitimately claim that we are discriminated against as women when our insurance program covers hernias and not pregnancies. The political struggle against *délaissement* involves the recognition of feminine difference in those circumstances when we are different, as in our relationship to pregnancy, while simultaneously not reinforcing the stereotypes through which patriarchy has attempted to make sense of that difference and has limited our power because of it. If, however, we challenge the devalorization of childbearing as itself a sign of *délaissement,* then we can insist that the recognition of feminine difference should not be interpreted to devalue us as different from them. Here we are returned to the second category of equivalent rights, now understood to cover those aspects of life and lived sexuality which allow women to live full lives. These rights are equivalent because they allow difference to be recognized without women having to show that they are like men for legal purposes or having to make sacrifices because of the specificity of our "sex," which makes us "unlike" men. If there is a vision of equality that justifies equivalent rights, it is equality of welfare.[20] We need a vision of equality if we are to protect equivalent rights from degenerating into a new defense of separate but equal. The best vision of equality by which to justify equivalent rights is Amartya Sen's equality of welfare and capability. Sen defines equality of welfare and capability as follows: "Capability reflects a person's freedom to choose between different ways of living."[21] Such a view of equality is important for two reasons: First, it allows for the respect and recognition of diversity and different lifestyles. Second, it allows for affirmative measures on the part of the state to restructure current work arrangements to guarantee equality of welfare and capability. For our purposes here, we need only a very thin theory of the good to fill in what constitutes well-being. It must only include the need to have the value of one's sex and sexuality recognized as of equivalent worth to the lifestyle of white heterosexual men.

7

Gender Hierarchy, Equality, and the Possibility of Democracy

My argument will have three steps. First, I will argue that Hannah Arendt's understanding of the *polis* perpetuates the gender hierarchy so as to make her own ideal of politics impossible and gives us a conception of politics inseparable from the subordination of women. Second, I will show how psychoanalysis in general and the theory of Jacques Lacan in particular are crucial in explaining the reproduction of the gender hierarchy so that we can understand that the dilemma inherent in Arendt's understanding of politics is not a coincidence nor superficial to her central argument. Third, I will suggest that Jacques Derrida's deconstructive intervention into Lacan not only opens a space for a redefinition of gender, but does so in such a way as to provide a concept of participatory democracy and of civic friendship uncontaminated by the erasure of women.

I begin with a summation of Arendt's conception of law and politics. Here is her description of the view of law accepted by the Greeks:

> To them, the laws, like the wall around the city, were not results of action but products of making. Before men began to act, a definite space had to be secured and a structure built where all subsequent actions could take place, the space being the public realm of the *polis* and its structure the law; legislator and architect belonged in the same category. But these tangible entities themselves were not the content of politics (not Athens, but Athenians, were the *polis*), and they did not command the same loyalty we know from the Roman type of patriotism.[1]

In terms of Arendt's own earlier distinction between action and making, legislation and law making were defined as *poeisis*, not *praxis*. Legislation and law making were, in this sense, pre-political determinations, even if they were understood as the background conditions of politics. The laws, in other words, provide the foundation of the *polis,* but they are not part of the *polis,* the place of political engagement itself. Law, in this sense, was subordinate to politics. It was only in the *polis* that "men" overcame the realm of necessity to achieve the realm of freedom in which they realize themselves as citizens and not just as social "animals" forced to toil in order to survive.

> In other words, men's life together in the form of the *polis* seemed to assure that the most futile of human activities, action and speech, and the least tangible and most ephemeral of man-made "products," the deeds and stories which are their outcome, would become imperishable. The organization of the *polis,* physically secured by the wall around the city and physiognomically guaranteed by its laws—lest the succeeding generations change its identity beyond recognition— is a kind of organized remembrance.[2]

This remembrance, however, does not depend on the actual, physical space of the *polis* as, for example, the city of Athens. What is recollected is the political life of the citizens meeting together to continually reaffirm their own capacity for self-rule. The *polis* is not just a state- or city-oriented concept, but a political one as well. Thus, as Arendt reminds us,

> The *polis,* properly speaking, is not the city-state in its physical location; it is the organization of the people as it arises out of acting and speaking together, and its true space lies between people living together for this purpose, no matter where they happen to be. "Wherever you go, you will be a *polis*": these famous words became not merely the watchword of Greek colonization, they expressed the conviction that action and speech create a space between the participants which can find its proper location almost any time and anywhere.[3]

The *polis,* in other words, is the public sphere in which human beings act as citizens. Where such interaction is taking place, the *polis is.*

If, as understood by Arendt, the *polis* is a form of human interaction based on speech and action and not just on the locale of the state, let alone of the official government, then there could be many spaces within civil society in which "political," not just social, action could take place. Arendt's ideal of politics, if it is not to be legitimately attacked for a pre-modern bias, demands that we rethink the very idea of where we might find and/or create "public space" for true engagement among peers. Although a modern/postmodern reinterpretation of her work compels us to rethink what a truly democratic public space would be, and the conditions necessary to guarantee it, Arendt herself, because of her sharp divide between the political and the social, cannot help us in understanding how civil society could be turned into a sphere of political action.

As a result, it has been difficult for Arendt's own conception of politics to survive the challenge that it is incompatible per se with a complex, socially differentiated modern society. The result is that her theorizing has been condemned as nostalgic for a world long since lost. Andrew Arato and Jean Cohen, however, have developed a powerful response to this criticism.[4] I refer to Arato and Cohen's work to answer this preliminary objection before turning to my own feminist critique, because, like Arendt, I believe that there is continuing value in the civic-republican understanding of democracy.

Arato and Cohen have argued that the new social movements battle for the creation of a "public space" within the sphere of civil society so as to allow meaningful political arrangement irreducible to strategic empowerment. Under this advocation of the need to create many "public spaces," the National Labor Relations Act (NLRA), which protects the right to organize unions, can be understood as an example of the way law can serve as the foundation for a public space in which peers can interact and engage in self-rule. If Arendt's *polis* is a form of human interaction based on speech and action and not just the locale of the state, the union hall can become a *polis* so long as discussion does not degenerate into addressing solely questions of economic gain.

Such economic questions would, in Arendt's terms, be social not political. But for writers such as Arato and Cohen, who believe that the new social movements play a crucial role in opening up "public space," the union hall is only one example among many of the spaces that can be turned into places of political action. The key idea is that there could be many spaces within civil society in which "political," not just social, action could take place. Aristotle expressed it best in *Politics:* "the *polis* is a community of equals for the sake of a life which is potentially the best."[5] Arato and Cohen reject the conclusion that engagement in a civil society need degenerate into economic jostling. Politics need not be reduced to the kind of social engineering we associate with the welfare state. The revival of the ideal of politics as understood by Arendt and others demands that we rethink the very idea of *where* we might find and/or create "public space" for true engagement among peers.

Even if the state and the government cannot be conceived of as the *polis,* but rather as the complex institutions we associate with the modern, democratic, Western states, there can still be places of "public space" where engagement between citizens remains possible. Very simply put, the civic-republican vision may be one-sided, but it contains an important truth. Democracy without some institutionalization of the guarantees of political self-government hardly lives up to its promise, the promise Aristotle so eloquently described. Arato and Cohen's work shows us how to reconcile the reality of the complexity of a modern society with respect for such traditional American constitutional ideals as the independent judiciary. There need not be the acceptance that modernity simply belies the possibility of participatory democracy, rendering it a nostalgic dream of those who cannot face reality.

In the recent civic-republican literature, the conception of the engagement between equal citizens has been referred to as civic friendship. Jacques Derrida has also presented a vision of democracy as civic friendship.[6] What is emphasized in the idea of civic friendship is the engagement between equals, the positive participatory aspects of democracy, and not just the negative ones, the protections against encroachment on the conditions of equality for all citizens, and the degeneration of a vision of civic friendship into a conservative elitism.

Derrida is unique, and certainly differs from Arendt in that he explicitly worries about whether this conception of democracy as civic friendship might involve a masculine bias.[7] His concern is that the very idea of friendship, particularly civic friendship, was modeled on relations between men. Derrida explicitly critiques the acceptance of the division between the political realms of women and men which informs the traditional Aristotelian conception of the very possibility of the *polis,* defined as the self-rule of equal citizens.

But to fully understand the significance of the concept of civic friendship and particularly how it differs from Arendt's, we need to return to how Arendt addresses this division as inherent in the Aristotelian ideal of politics:

> Unlike human behavior—which the Greeks, like all civilized people, judged according to "moral standards," taking into account motives and intentions on the one hand and aims and consequences on the other—action can be judged only by the criterion of greatness because it is in its nature to break through the commonly accepted and reach into the extraordinary, where whatever is true in common

and everyday life no longer applies because everything that exists is unique and *sui generis*. Thucydides, or Pericles, knew full well that he had broken with the normal standards for everyday behavior when he found the glory of Athens in having left behind "everywhere everlasting remembrance [mnēmeia aidia] of their good and their evil deeds." That art of politics teaches men how to bring forth what is great and radiant—*ta megala kai lampra,* in the words of Democritus; as long as the *polis* is there to inspire men to dare the extraordinary, all things are safe; if it perishes, everything is lost. Motives and aims, no matter how pure or how grandiose, are never unique; like psychological qualities, they are typical, characteristic of different types of persons. Greatness, therefore, or the specific meaning of each deed, can lie only in the performance itself and neither in its motivation nor its achievement.[8]

For Arendt, the conditions for equality between white male citizens were based on the separation of the realm of necessity and the realm of freedom. As she points out, Aristotle clearly recognized that even white men were not just citizens; they belonged to two orders of social reality. To quote Aristotle: "[E]very citizen belongs to two orders of existence. . . . [T]he *polis* gives each individual . . . besides his private life a sort of second life, his *bios politikos.*"[9] The household community was what kept day-to-day life together. The household was the realm of necessity. But it was only on the basis of control of necessity that men were allowed to achieve the freedom to be citizens. As Arendt explains,

> The mastery of necessity then has as its goal the controlling of the necessities of life, which coerce men and hold them in their power. But such domination can be accomplished only by controlling and doing violence to others, who as slaves relieve free men from themselves being coerced by necessity. The free man, the citizen of a *polis,* is neither coerced by the physical necessities of life nor subject to the man-made domination of others. He not only must not be a slave, he must own and rule over slaves. The freedom of the political realm begins after all elementary necessities of sheer living have been mastered by rule, so that domination and subjection, command and obedience, ruling and being ruled, are preconditions for establishing the political realm precisely because they are not its content.[10]

As it was necessary to have slaves, it was also necessary, in a very profound sense, that women be enslaved, at least in the sense of being imprisoned in the realm of necessity. The idea of the *polis,* as Arendt recognizes, was based on patriarchy. The household was a monarchy, as we are told in the *Economics*.[11] The "many rulers" of the *polis* were men freed from necessity by the wives and the slaves they ruled at home. Democracy stopped at the doorway of the household.

> The "many rulers" in this context are the household heads, who have established themselves as "monarchs" at home before they join to constitute the public-political realm of the city. Ruling itself and the distinction between rulers and ruled belong to a sphere which precedes the political realm, and what distinguishes it from the "economic" sphere of the household is that the *polis* is based upon the principle of equality and knows no differentiation between rulers and ruled.[12]

While clearly recognizing the patriarchal basis of the one-man rule in the household as necessary to the creation of the *polis* as the sphere of freedom, Arendt herself felt it was crucial to separate the realm of necessity and the realm of political freedom. Her critique of Marxism, simply put, is that Marx reduced the political to the realm of the social. He no longer has the dignity of the political citizen.

> In the modern world, the social and the political realms are much less distinct. That politics is nothing but a function of society, that action, speech, and thought are primarily superstructures upon so-cial interests, is not a discovery of Karl Marx but on the contrary is among the axiomatic assumptions Marx accepted uncritically from the political economists of the modern age. This functionalization makes it impossible to perceive any serious gulf between the two realms; and this is not a matter of a theory or an ideology, since with the rise of society, that is, the rise of the "household" (*oikia*) or of economic activities to the public realm, housekeeping and all matters pertaining formerly to the private sphere of the family have become a "collective" concern. In the modern world, the two realms indeed constantly flow into each other like waves in the never-resting stream of the life process itself.[13]

To summarize, Arendt's criticism of Marxism is that Marx reduced "Man" to *homo faber*. Politics, as a result, lost all its grandeur. The focus instead was on work and on how to change the social conditions. Her criticism of Marx can certainly be interpreted as one-sided. But for my own purposes here, Arendt's insistence on the separation of the realm of necessity and the realm of freedom is crucial to a concept of politics irreducible to wrangling over social conditions. For Arendt, it is what she calls *viva activia* that allows "men" to become truly human.

Arendt's focus on the revival of politics, of the *viva activia,* of speech and action in the public realm as what truly make the "man," can be subjected to a number of feminist critiques. First, one has to note that the line between the social and the political can itself be interpreted as a political question. The line between the social and the political is a question, in other words, to be decided in the course of the debate between citizens. Therefore, the line Arendt draws between the social and the political is too rigid. She writes as if it were a line that was just "there." Surely that line has shifted in recent years, precisely because of political struggle.

Arendt's assumption that politics demands equality between partici-pants cannot be separated from her own insistence on separating the realms of freedom and necessity. Arendt insists that for the realm of freedom to exist, the realm of necessity must be *conquered.* But she also assumes that conquering *must* take place in the private realm, in the household, if it is not to contaminate the realm of freedom. That assumption about how the realm of necessity is to be conquered is the object of one feminist critique of Arendt.

This critique begins with the principle that any meaningful concep-tion of equality must provide all women with political, social, and economic rights. Certainly many of the feminist battles in the late 1970s were directed at socializing certain aspects of life that had previously been relegated to the privacy of the household. Battles were waged over maternity leave, child care, and decent collective care for the aging. These battles were not just about social empowerment in the realm of necessity, they were political battles waged to secure the conditions necessary to ensure women's citizenship. Yes, these political battles were about shifting the line between the political and the social, and they emphasized that without the shift in that line, women could not be full citizens. *Viva activia* was denied to women because of their relegation to the realm of necessity; this relegation, in turn, denied women the freedom to be political actresses. Unfortunately, the victo-ries were meager, even when won, and in the last ten years we have even seen many of these meager victories erased. The result is the notorious "double burden" on women who enter the work force, let alone the political arena.

A second feminist critique is grounded in the question of why it is only in the *viva activia* that we truly become human. We need to ask not only why women are assigned the "dirty work," but also why the endless battles for equality fought by women for generations, if not for centuries, to socialize that work and to have it valued, seem to have brought so little progress in their wake. To address this question, I will focus on the contribution of psychoanalysis in general, and the theories of Jacques Lacan in particular, to the problem of the apparent inevitability of the continuous reconstitution of masculine privilege and the concordant devalorization of women's work.

Psychoanalytic theory emphasizes the foundational role of inevitable infantile narcissistic wounds. These wounds are structured by the infant's encounter with "mommy" as other, as in possession of an identity of her own, as wanting something which is "not me," but rather wanting "daddy." Lacan locates the advent of an originary narcissistic wound with the emergence of the Oedipus complex and thus he puts the Oedipus complex back at the center of how gender differentiation takes on its meaning. What Lacan helps us to understand is why, once this story becomes a cultural "truth," it becomes so unshakable.

The original narcissistic wound is the basis of all subsequent desire, wanting, whose linguistic form Lacan so notoriously exposes. That linguistic form partakes of a pre-existing symbolic register. The child's desire to speak necessarily includes a desire to summon "mommy," to bring her back. One speaks so as to present oneself as the one she might want. This presentation necessarily includes an impulse toward an identification with "daddy," structurally constituted as what "mommy" does want when she does not want "me."

It might seem that both sexes suffer a similarly primordial separation from the mother and would thus be marked by this separation in the same way. For both sexes, the unattainable mother is the Phallic Mother, omnipotent and phallic because she wants and needs only herself. She thus carries both sexes within, wanting, lacking neither. She needs no one else. Thus, She is a being not marked by desire.

The narcissistically wounded child identifies with the Imaginary Father because the Imaginary Father is what "mommy," now constituted as "incomplete" and also identified-with, desires. What does "daddy" have that "mommy" desires, that symbolizes what mommy wants? Simply put, it is the penis, but Lacanians do not put it quite so simply. Rather, they maintain the difference between the penis and the phallus. The phallus signifies that which initiates desire in both sexes. Identification with the Imaginary "daddy" and with his imaginary phallus, the biological penis which is only a signifier for whatever is finally wanted by "mommy," offers compensation for narcissistically experienced loss of empowerment.

This identification bodes well for the little boy, who can readily fantasize that it is he who now might have the penis that could bring "mommy" back. But the identification strategy is bad news for the little girl. She does not have it, and is thus driven to what Lacan describes as a more radical masquerade of "being" it.

The ground for sexual difference is based on the significance attributed both to the experience of sighting the penis and to the site of its absence. Having the penis is identified with being able to satisfy mommy's desire and bring her back. Its lack is identified as castration, a secondary disempowerment which leans on the primary narcissistic one. Woman cannot identify with her sex in any affirmative manner because her sex is what has devalorized her. Thus, her relationship to the mother easily degenerates into resentment.

Men achieve a masculine identity in this sequence by identifying with the Imaginary Father. Everything that is feminine is repudiated and turned into "otherness." In fantasy, the condition of phallic deprivation gives rise to the necessity for phallic restoration. Thus, in the erotic realm, deprivation, what Freud calls "bitter experience," is yoked to necessity. This equation of deprivation and necessity appears operational in social life as well, where activity in the realm of necessity is devalorized as though it signifies castration. It is devalorized not because *homo faber* is necessarily inferior to the man of political action, but because this is the work of women.

The traditional psychoanalytic claim is clear. Women *cannot* be recognized as equal to men. Lacan's basic point is that Woman exists under the gender hierarchy only as man's other. She has no identity that can be recognized as such by the Symbolic register. She appears under the sign of an absence. One sad result of this, of course, is the epidemic proportions of depression in women.

Lacan's turn away from the biologistic penis and toward the signified phallus provides an important corrective to any essentializing reading of Freud's account of gender differentiation through the castration complex. The penis has no "natural" significance; it becomes identified as the phallus. For Lacan, this identification is like all identification, grounded in fantasy. Therefore masculine privilege is a masquerade, a sham, and in no sense grounded on any natural fact. There is nothing in the penis to envy. What is envied is the easy identification it provides with an Imaginary Father.

Returning for a moment to Arendt's framework, and a discussion of her politics, we can see that her rigid divide between the realm of necessity and the realm of freedom is homologous with an equally rigid divide of male and female, itself constructed in response to an originary narcissistic wound. To the extent that gender identity is grounded in an opposition of narcissistic sufficiency and deficiency, each formed against the other, the derivative realms of freedom and necessity will also be valorized according to narcissistic determinants. Just as masculinity needs to be covertly propped up by the presence of a deprived feminine figure, so the realm of freedom needs to propped up by a devalorized realm of necessity.

Now the question becomes, What are the conditions in which women could be equals in political participation? For orientation, I turn again to Derrida.

Derrida's intervention into Lacan's work is important for two reasons. First, he turns Lacan's understanding of the signifier against Lacan's own pessimistic political conclusions. Derrida argues that the performative aspect of language which defines gender roles cannot be thought of other than through the performance of these roles. As such, the signifier has no essential determining power, and with language, we can play at what we become and not simply submit to determinations whose origins would reside outside that language.

For instance, the uncastratability of Woman is one of the themes Derrida continually plays with throughout *Spurs*[14] and *Glas*.[15] He refuses the "realism" of castration. For him, the feminine is not the symbol of castration, but of the undeniability of the "uncastratable." Woman plays with her truth, taking up the position in which she has been placed. But in Derrida's staging of her performance, she knows that she is playing:

> "Woman"—her name made epoch—no more believes in castration's exact opposite, anti-castration, than she does in castration itself. . . . Unable to seduce or to give vent to desire without it, "woman" is in need of castration's effect. But evidently she does not believe in it. She who, unbelieving, still plays with castration, she is "woman." She takes aim and amuses herself (*en joue*) with it as she would with a new concept or structure of belief, but even as she plays she is gleefully anticipating her laughter, her mockery of man. With a knowledge that would out-measure the most self-respecting dogmatic or credulous philosopher, woman knows that castration does not take place.[16]

Here the primary narcissistic wound need not be compensated for through an identification with the Imaginary Father, nor need the wound be denied. The possibility of reperformance, of actions beyond the fixing determination of the phallic signifier, brings with it the possibility of love that is not just compensation.

Derrida is famous for his innovative writing style, but what is often missed is the way in which his style deliberately pokes fun at macho rhetoric, a rhetoric aimed at calming those who, while indulging in the illusion that to have the penis is to have the phallus, must always fear that "daddy" can always take it away and, thus, reduce them to something like, but less than, a girl.

Derrida's rhetoric undermines the very legitimacy of the macho rhetoric that Arendt herself uses to glorify the realm of freedom. Writing of democracy as friendship, Derrida writes of "feminine" virtues: care, gentleness, an appreciation of heterogeneity.

Arendt, in contrast, uses the rhetoric of macho individualism in describing the *viva activia:*

> No doubt this concept of action is highly individualistic, as we would say today. It stresses the urge toward self-disclosure at the expense of all other factors and therefore remains relatively untouched by the predicament of unpredictability. As such it became the prototype of action for Greek antiquity and influenced in the form of the so-called agonal spirit, the passionate drive to show one's self in measuring up against others that underlies the concept of politics prevalent in the city-states.[17]

Arendt argues that it is through *viva activia* that men become "heroes." They stand out when they stand up. Thus, there is a tension in Arendt between her assertion that any true form of democracy must involve a public space where citizens can actually participate in self-rule and her assertion that what comes out of the engagement is that the individual finds his own chance to become a man. This may well explain why, for Arendt, the virtues that have now become identified as feminine are not suitable to include in the public realm. Her own explanation is that we cannot expect political activity to represent such virtues because it is just too much, for example, to expect citizens to *love* one another. Love is a matter of luck and destiny. Compassion, too, is directed toward individual suffering. Yet it is important to note here that for Arendt, forgiveness does play a role in public life. Indeed, her emphasis on forgiveness may seem surprising. It seems to be introduced out of nowhere and to be inconsistent with her previous descriptions of the *viva activia.* Even so, to quote Arendt:

Without being forgiven, released from the consequences of what we have done, our capacity to act would, as it were, be confined to one single deed from which we could never recover; we would remain the victims of its consequences forever, not unlike the sorcerer's apprentice who lacked the magic formula to break the spell. Without being bound to the fulfillment [sic] of promises, we would never be able to keep our identities; we would be condemned to wander helplessly and without direction in the darkness of each man's lonely heart, caught in its contradictions and equivocalities— a darkness which only the light shed over the public realm through the presence of others, who confirm the identity between the one who promises and the one who fulfills, can dispel. Both faculties, therefore, depend on plurality, on the presence and acting of others, for no one can forgive himself and no one can feel bound by a promise made only to himself; forgiving and promising enacted in solitude or isolation remain without reality and can signify no more than a role played before one's self.[18]

I would suggest that Arendt's emphasis on forgiveness indicates an aspect of the repressed feminine in her own writing in which the vengeance that might seem to follow from her own rhetoric of greatness and men trying to be men is replaced by forgiveness and the importance of the promise. Nevertheless, despite the indication that there is a side of the feminine, particularly in terms of the need for safety, Arendt does not explicitly include what have now become identified as feminine virtues into the concept of public life. Therefore, we need to at least consider that there may be a deeper reason for her rejection of the feminine virtues as part of the public realm. The obvious reason is that Arendt rejects these virtues as part of her own denial of feminism. Why is the feminization of the rhetoric of civic friendship in Derrida's article missed by most readers? Lacan, of course, would answer that this "missing" is symptomatic, grounded in a fantasy that the feminine has its "place," and it is not the place of politics. Such a reading would occur through a lens that essentially denies "castration" and, thus, makes it impossible to see Derrida's introduction of the feminine into the sphere of democracy and politics. For example, even Thomas McCarthy, in his thoughtful discussion of Derrida's work and its political implications, fails to take into account the significance of the feminization of his stylistic innovations.[19] This failure to notice is no coincidence, because it is precisely the feminine that, under our current system of "citing," cannot be "seen."[20] Derrida writes in the style of the dialectic, with a feminine interlocutor who is usually given the last word.[21] For Lacan the dialectic was no longer an acceptable philosophical style:

> For us, whose concern is with present day man, that is, man with a troubled conscience, it is in the ego that we meet . . . inertia: we know it as the resistance to the dialectic process of analysis. The patient is held spellbound by his ego, to the exact degree that it causes his distress, and reveals its nonsensical function. It is this very fact that has led us to evolve a technique which substitutes the strange detours of free association for the sequence of the *Dialogue*.[22]

Written out of *Dialogue,* women cannot write themselves back into it. Derrida undermines Lacan's pessimism by insisting on the availability of the dialectic:

> If I write two texts at once, you will not be able to castrate me. If I delinearize, I erect. But at the same time I divide my act and my desire. I—mark(s) the division, and always escaping you, I simulate unceasingly and take my pleasure nowhere. I castrate myself—I remain(s) myself thus—and I "play at coming" [*je "joue à jouir"*]. Finally almost.[23]

We must return to the question of democracy. We have seen that the leftist challenge to the impossibility of a return to the *polis* has been answered by an emphasis on the democratic possibilities left open in civil society. But what has not been taken up in this analysis is the question of what kind of subject one would have to be to even participate in these experiences. Arendt's pessimism is based on her analysis that the social and the political would become one in a modern society. Lacan's pessimism is that there can be no "real" democracy, if we mean by democracy at least some institutionalization of participatory structures inclusive of women. As long as the gender hierarchy is in place, it will be impossible for women to be recognized as individuals. Derrida's intervention undermines the gender hierarchy that divides us into two "sexes" and casts us on to the stage as automatons, fated to play out our gender roles. Thus, the dream of a new choreography of sexual difference does not just have to do with the possibility of love between human beings—as important as it is to protect that possibility. It also has to do with the possibility of democracy itself, once we include participatory, dialogic structures in democracy. The psychical fantasy of Woman not only prevents love, it also blocks the dialogue we associate with participatory democracy. Indeed, it blocks the recognition of women as citizens. Therefore, it is not enough just to socialize the so-called realm of necessity in order for participatory democracy to exist, although this is clearly an important step in battling against the repudiation of the feminine and the devalorization of feminine virtues. The realm of the political must itself be feminized, but in a more radical way than has often been suggested. It is not just that both the ethic of care and the ethic of right have important roles in political life. It is instead that this division must itself be challenged as we integrate the virtues of the feminine into the very definition of civic friendship. To insist on this kind of integration in no way denies the importance of rights.

To summarize: Psychoanalysis plays a crucial role in helping us understand why women have not been welcomed into the political arena as equal citizens. First, there has been the implicit acceptance that women should do the "dirty work," and this work is, in turn, devalorized because it is associated with women. Secondly, the very rhetoric of the political world reflects the "macho" language that serves as a compensation for masculine anxiety and fear. To change the world in the name of democracy, we need not only to change the rights of man to include the social rights of women, but also to challenge the masculinization of the rhetoric of the ideal of politics itself. Both steps are necessary. Psychoanalysis helps us understand why these steps are so difficult, blocked as they are by the gender hierarchy. And yet, the Derridean deconstruction of the gender hierarchy shows that those of us who continue to dream are not foolishly nostalgic; we are just that: those who continue to dream.

8

What Takes Place in the Dark

Imagining difference (which of course does not mean making
it up, but making it evident) remains a science of which we all
have a need.

—Clifford Geertz[1]

The problems of life are insoluble on the surface and can only
be solved in depth. They are insoluble in surface dimensions.

—Ludwig Wittgenstein[2]

Introduction

The purpose of this essay is to show that psychoanalysis can and
must play a role in Clifford Geertz's "science of imagining differences,"
and more specifically, in imagining the intersection of race and gender
within our own culture.

Geertz shows how the spirit of his own field, anthropology, can
play a crucial role in helping us engage with difference without the
complacent superiority of ethnocentrism. The work of ethnography
demands attention to how the anthropologist understands difference
as irreducible to mere "foreignness" to her own culture and perspective.
This sensitivity to difference, which goes with the job if it is to be done
well, is notably evident in the incorporation of psychoanalysis into
ethnography and into the theory that guides it. Questions of the conditions of universalization, as well as of the usefulness of applying a
method developed in one culture to the study of another, have been in
the forefront of the debate over the use of psychoanalysis in anthropology. These questions are obviously crucial in the effort to think theoretically about how one avoids dressing up ethnocentrism as science and
truth when one adopts a Western methodology to study other cultures.
But my focus will be slightly different. First, I will examine the relation-

ship that psychoanalytically informed anthropology has drawn between ethnocentrism and logocentrism as the specificity of this relationship has been thought through an emphasis on the role of unconscious forces not only in the life of the individual but also in the work of culture. In my discussion of this relationship, I will focus on the work of Gananath Obeyesekere[3] who has explicitly argued for the need for a nonlogocentric approach to the study of the work of culture if we are to advance beyond reductive explanations and avoid the trap of ethnocentrism.

To define logocentrism, I am rephrasing the definition offered by Obeyesekere himself.[4] Logocentrism is characterized by the subscription of all symbolic forms under a *consciously accessible* set of signs within the purportedly synchronic structures of conventional meaning. With Wittgenstein, Obeyesekere always reveals that we cannot understand the problems of life if we insist on studying only their surface expressions. My specific addition to Obeyesekere's use of psychoanalysis in the development of a nonlogocentric approach to the work of culture is to argue that he incorrectly rejects the contribution of Jacques Lacan to that project.[5] As we will see, the addition of the contribution of Jacques Lacan's understanding of the unconscious is not only important for the development of a non-logocentric, antiethnocentric approach to the work of culture, it also has significance for the politics implied by "the science of imagining difference" and specifically for how we conceive of the possibilities of change consistent with the psychoanalytic emphasis on the unconscious.

My concern—a concern I obviously share with Geertz—is how divergent approaches to difference affect our practical politics. As a result, I choose to describe the relevance of the approach to the work of culture I advocate to how gender is "colored" in the psychosexual dynamics of desire. With Geertz, I will argue that our political obligations cannot be separated from our efforts to imagine difference. Thus, I will contrast Geertz's conceptualization of postmodern liberalism to the one advocated by Richard Rorty.[6] Rorty divides the world of "public," political obligation from the purportedly private, fantasy dream world of the individual. This rigid division is explicitly rejected by the psychoanalytic approach to the work of culture I will defend. To show the limits of Rorty's response to Geertz, I will offer my own story—the story of an attempt to build solidarity between "white" and "black" women in an actual union drive. A union drive is clearly a public event, but as we will see, the effort to build the union became inseparable from the need to challenge social fantasies and more particularly, the fantasies which give meaning to the "coloration" of sex, sexuality, and gender. I put "white" and "black" in quotation marks because my argument will be that race is misunderstood as a set of positive characteristics, rather than as a matrix of intertwined signifiers in which the distinction between "white" and "black" womanhood takes on significance. As we will see, we need to put the American feminist debate over the relationship between race and gender into an analysis of the inevitable connection between logocentrism and ethnocentrism.

But let me turn first to the debate between Geertz and Rorty because it sets the stage for feminist discussion of the practical, political significance of a nonlogocentric, antiethnocentric approach to the work of culture.

The Geertz/Rorty Debate

Both Geertz and Rorty consider themselves to be postmodern liberals, yet they profoundly disagree on the obligation of such liberals to imagine difference. Rorty embraces what he calls *anti-anti-ethnocentrism*. Rorty's anti-anti-ethnocentrism has two prongs. First, Rorty explicitly argues that we are members of the culture and language game into which we are born and which defines who we are. We Western liberals are just that, Western liberals. This is the boat into which we have been thrown. But there is an important value in being in this boat and not another. The vehicle provided by the language game of Western liberalism turns out to be the best boat for getting around—and, I might add here, over—in an obviously complex world of cultural difference and diversity. For Rorty, bourgeois liberalism is defined by its very battle against at least one particular kind of vicious ethnocentrism that attempts to justify one cultural vision of the good as having the last word. Liberalism, in other words, by definition, allows for cultural contention. In response to the concern that Western liberalism shuts out divergent viewpoints and by so doing turns itself into a windowless monad, Rorty argues:

> Some human communities are such monads, some not. Our bourgeois liberal culture is not. On the contrary, it is a culture which prides itself on constantly adding more windows, constantly enlarging its sympathies. It is a form of life which is constantly extending pseudopods and adapting itself to what it encounters. Its sense of

its own moral worth is founded on its tolerance of diversity. The heroes it apotheosizes include those who have enlarged its capacity for sympathy and tolerance. Among the enemies it diabolizes are the people who attempt to diminish this capacity, the vicious ethnocentrists. Anti-anti-ethnocentrism is not an attempt to change the habits of our culture to block the windows up again.[7]

But if anti-anti-ethnocentrism is not about changing the habits of our culture what is it an attempt to do? Or more precisely what is it an attempt to defend us against? Rorty gives us his answer; the danger is what he defines as "wet" liberalism.[8]

This bemusement makes us susceptible to the suggestion that the culture of Western liberal democracy is somehow on a par with that of the Vandals and the Ik. So we begin to wonder whether our attempts to get other parts of the world to adopt our culture are different in kind from the efforts of fundamentalist missionaries. If we continue this line of thought too long we become what are sometimes called, wet liberals. We begin to lose any capacity for moral indignation, any capacity to feel contempt. Our sense of selfhood dissolves. We can no longer feel pride in being bourgeois liberals, in being part of a great tradition, a citizen of no mean culture. We become so open-minded that our brains have fallen out.[9]

I prefer to replace Rorty's phrase, wet liberals, with my own expression to designate those whose brains have fallen out. I call such individuals "stiff" liberals, because of the barriers their stiffness erects against the thinking process itself. Geertz agrees with Rorty that we are inevitably a part of some form of life. But he disagrees with what that proposition means when it comes to an assessment of the value of ethnocentrism. As Geertz explains,

The trouble with ethnocentrism is not that it commits us to our commitments. We are, by definition, so committed as we are to having our own headaches. The trouble with ethnocentrism is that it impedes us from discovering at what sort of angle, like Forster's Cavafy, we stand to the world; what sort of bat we really are.[10]

For Geertz the discovery of what kind of bat we really are demands that we recognize "the foreignness" within ourselves. The *unheimlich* is not simply "out there." The very definition of who the "we" is carries within an evaluation of what part of ourselves we are identifying with and what part we are excluding as other. For Geertz the we/they split is a way of avoiding a much-needed confrontation with ourselves, with who we are. It cuts us off from a kind of "self-knowledge," not just from the "outside" world of other cultures.

> "Foreignness" does not start at the water's edge but at the skin's. The sort of idea that both anthropologists since Malinowski and philosophers since Wittgenstein are likely to entertain that, say, Shi' being other, present a problem, but say soccer fans, being part of us do not, or at least not the same sort, is merely wrong. The social world does not divide at its joint into perspicuous we-s with whom we empathize, however much we differ from them, and enigmatical they-s, with whom we cannot, however much we defend to the death their right to differ from us. The wogs begin long before Calais.[11]

My stiff liberal is precisely the one who erects these barriers between the we-s and the they-s in order to achieve the illusion of an identity freed from difference. It leads to a kind of blindness. The stiff liberal invests in the illusion of his own self-identity and the self-identity of the "we" of which he considers himself to be a part. He can not see beyond himself. But this very illusion that I am what I am, we are who we are, and you are, by definition, Other, the dark continent out there, also carries within it an assumption of superiority to which Geertz always returns us. This is why I deliberately used the word "over" earlier. We define others by our standards and assume that others are only there in relationship to us. This relationship is fundamentally hierarchical. In Geertz's words, it reduces difference to mere unlikeness. But I also use the word "over" to indicate the process of repression that pushes parts of ourselves under, to the realm of what, by definition, cannot be known. As we will see, the psychoanalytic perspective takes us one step beyond Geertz. Foreignness does not even start at the skin's edge, it goes far deeper than that. We are called by psychoanalysis to examine our "internal" otherness and to correspondingly analyze the projected apparition of the Other that lies at the heart of the so-called proper, solid I or we. For Geertz, the so-called solid "we" to which Rorty so self-confidently appeals, has become more and more illusionary because of the diversity within each culture or form of life:

> More concretely, moral issues stemming from cultural diversity (which are, of course, far from being all the moral issues there are) that used to arise, when they arose at all, mainly between societies— the customs contrary to reason and morals sort of thing on which

imperialism fed—now increasingly arise within them. Social and cultural boundaries coincide less and less closely—there are Japanese in Brazil, Turks on the Main, and West Indian meets East in the streets of Birmingham—a shuffling process which has, of course, been going on for some time (Belgium, Canada, Lebanon, South Africa—and the Caesars' Rome was not all that homogenous), but which is by now, approaching extreme and near universal proportions. The day when the American city was the main model of cultural fragmentation and ethnic tumbling is quite gone; the Paris of *nos ancêtres les gaulois* is getting to be about as polygot, and as polychrome, as Manhattan, and may yet have an Asian mayor (or so anyway, many of *les gaulois* fear) before New York has a Hispanic one.[12]

To demonstrate his point that the science of imagining differences involves the exploration of who "we" is, Geertz uses the example of the alcoholic Native American and the kidney machine. To make a long story short—and I shorten the story only because I intend to tell another one which emphasizes the intertwinement of race and gender in an economy of desire—the Native American alcoholic was put on the kidney machine because he gained access to it through a lottery that seemed to be the only fair and acceptable way to handle the problem of a shortage of resources. The Native American refused to stop drinking. The doctors became more and more distressed that he refused to play by their rules, but given the fact that he was on the machine because of the lottery, there was nothing they could do about it. The Native American eventually died, unrepentant for his behavior.

For Rorty, this story is an example, par excellence, of the success of Western procedural justice. The doctors were upset but they couldn't do anything about it because they had to play by the rules to which they were committed. So the Native American stayed on the machine. What more could Geertz possibly want? The answer for Geertz is understanding, the understanding he believes is necessary—and I believe he is right—for respect, not just for enforced tolerance. As he argues,

> What tends to take place in the dark—the only things of which "a certain deafness to the appeal of other values" or "comparison with worse communities" conception of human dignity would seem to allow—is either the application of force to secure conformity to the values of those who possess the force; a vacuous tolerance that, engaging nothing, changes nothing; or as here where the force is

unavailable and the tolerance unnecessary, a dribbling out to an ambiguous end.[13]

For Geertz the value of understanding is that it replaces "the dribbling out to an ambiguous end" with the openness to change demanded by an encounter with a different form of life. In this case the openness to the story of how one man dealt with his life as a Native American within a dominant white culture. For Geertz, the story should have been about the doctors' confrontation with their own ethnocentrism. Instead these stiff liberals shut themselves off to the Other and enmeshed themselves in their own self-righteous distress that "some Indian drunk" was using the machine. For Geertz, in other words, the analysis of the situation cannot be separated from the result. The relevant political question is not just whether or not "the drunken Indian" should have been left on the machine, but what kind of world was disclosed by the treatment allotted to him by doctors incapable of understanding his decision to keep drinking. World disclosure becomes a part of politics itself once we understand that the political result cannot be separated from the analysis that precedes it and justifies it. As we see the world differently, so it "is" differently. For Geertz, the way the world is disclosed to us can have a practical effect in that it can change the way we relate to others. Indeed, this openness to difference and thus to the different possibilities inherent in a multicultural society is what separates Geertz's own postmodern liberalism from the stiff liberal's self-enclosure, which, by definition, denies the possibility for change at the moment that it resists an encounter with the Other that is not already prejudged.

Geertz stresses the role of the imagination in the continual move into the future that openness to difference requires of us.

> It is in this, strengthening the power of our imaginations to grasp what is in front of us, that the uses of diversity, and of the study of diversity, lie. . . . If we wish to be able capaciously to judge, as of course we must, we need to make ourselves able capaciously to see. And for that, what we have already seen—the insides of our railway compartments; the shining historical examples of our nations, our churches and our movements—is, as engrossing as the one may be and as dazzling as the other, simply not enough.[14]

The payoff of Geertz's science of imagining difference cannot be calculated in advance because such a science turns us toward the future. We cannot, in other words, know in advance what the ultimate meaning of our attempts to encounter difference will be, precisely because such attempts break the hold of common sense over our imaginations. The doctors could not make sense of the alcoholic Native American's behavior because it did not meet *their* standards of sense. Geertz's point is that if we are to engage with difference other than through the establishment of a contrast effect in which we—surprise, surprise— always end up on top, we have to be able to reimagine the sensible given to us by our own standards of making sense. Hence, as I have suggested, Geertz draws the connection between Rorty's post-Wittgensteinian brand of philosophy and ethnocentrism. Rorty's bazaar with lots of private clubs ultimately protects the "we" from having to face the difference within. The Other is kept over there in her own club. The erected boundaries that allow the club to be "our" club inevitably keep the Other out. In spite of Rorty's better impulses, this is a defense of exclusion. Liberalism becomes the right to club formation, a right supposedly given to everyone. But as our own history of private clubs makes only too evident, this right has not worked equally well for everyone. Could a woman with the experience of being escorted into the "ladies" dining room to avoid disrupting the male bonding going on in "their" dining room not but be suspicious of this definition of liberalism? The challenge to Rorty is that he ultimately skims along the surface of other forms of life in order to feel safe in his own boat. For Geertz, the encounter with "the drunken Indian" demands that the doctors do more than skim along the surface, demands that they at least make the effort to confront what is going on in the dark of their own souls. Moreover, such an effort yields to the pull of psychoanalysis to disclose the difference within that belies the claim that logocentrism gives all the light we need to see what is real and valuable because it makes sense to us.

The Psychoanalytic Challenge to Logocentrism

The insistence that there is only the conscious world, even if we understand this world as only disclosed to us by our form of life or language game, continues to brand a certain kind of post-Wittgensteinian philosophy as logocentric. Yet psychoanalysis has certainly played a role in debunking the neat separation of conscious from the unconscious "mind." Wittgenstein himself took part in the deconstruction of the assumption that it was consciousness that made us "men," as if there were some guaranteed procedure by which we could know that consciousness, thereby ensuring that it would not be false. Even so, Wittgenstein explicitly denied that the unconscious could be analogous to a form of life or language game with its own logic or rules of grammar. In other words, the unconscious cannot be analyzed. What we can know is what we understand and by definition, we cannot understand the unconscious. What we can understand is what is given to us in a form of life or language game. And that's all there is to it. Obeyesekere has explained that Wittgenstein's own professed position had implications for the way in which he viewed "foreign" cultures. The strength of Wittgenstein's approach, at least for those who are just anti-ethnocentrism, is that he refused to judge other cultures as inferior. For example, Wittgenstein blasted someone like Frazer for precisely this kind of ethnocentrism.

> What narrowness of spiritual life we see in Frazer! And as a result: how impossible for him to understand a different way of life from the English one of his time. Frazer cannot imagine a priest who is not basically an English parson of our time with all his stupidity and feebleness.[15]

But his own position elides with positivism because, as Obeyesekere reminds us, for Wittgenstein "[W]hat one can do is describe these forms of life, not 'explain' them."[16] The positivism inheres in the reduction of an engagement with a form of life to a description, as if the form of life were just there. It also fails to take into account what Obeyesekere has called the cultural transference of the one who describes. For Obeyesekere, psychoanalysis not only challenges the very basis of logocentrism on a philosophical plane, it can also be an important and necessary interpretative tool for cultures that have never bought into logocentrism in the first place. In other words, we need psychoanalysis if we are even to approach cultures that do not accept logocentrism and indeed have implicitly or explicitly either denied or overthrown its hold.

Obeyesekere uses his own ethnographic work in Sri Lanka and throughout South Asia to demonstrate the immediate practical significance of psychoanalysis to ethnographic work in cultures that give freer play to unconscious forces within their cultural networks of meaning. This is the first way in which psychoanalysis can play a role in the struggle against ethnocentrism. We cannot even approach certain of the cultures in South Asia without the aid of interpretative tools that take us below the surface of a form of life, if the very form of life in question recognizes the cultural importance of plunging the depths to reach "unconscious thought."[17] Obeyesekere associates the search for truth in anthropology with precisely this effort without fear of reaching the muddy bottom.

For Obeyesekere a nonlogocentric ethnography—this is my expression not his, yet I believe it neatly summarizes his approach to cultural analysis—must be able to grasp the interplay of conscious and unconscious forces as they are played out in symbolic forms. Such a cultural analysis for Obeyesekere is to be modeled on Freud's understanding of the dream work in *The Interpretation of Dreams*,[18] with the caveat that any theory of universal symbolization is to be explicitly rejected. To quote Obeyesekere:

> The dream work constitutes the rules that produce the manifest dream from the dream thoughts (deep motivations); these rules deal with the transformation of complex motives into dream images (or dream symbols if one doesn't confuse 'symbols' with Freud's discussion of representation through symbols). Thus Freud's theory is essentially one of symbol or image formation, albeit confined to the dream as a symbolic set. But dreams are not culture, though they may be the stuff from which some types of cultural forms are psychogenetically derived. Culture is a symbolic order far removed cognitively, ontologically, and ontically from dreams. A psychoanalytic study of cultural forms must move from the dream work to more complex processes that can help us comprehend these more complex forms. One must move from the work of dreams into what, following Freud himself, I call *the work of culture*.[19]

Yet in spite of Obeyesekere's recognition that there are important differences between the work of culture and the dream work, his understanding that there are deep motivations that are continuously translated into the so-called daylight of public life leads him to insist that the principles of symbolic transformation in Freud's work on the interpretation of dreams can and should be used by anthropologists. Otherwise, the best we can do is skim along the surface taking our informants at their word. The question for Obeyesekere is how one reads culture once we accept the most basic insight of psychoanalysis, which is that what appears on the surface may involve cultural defenses, rationalizations, and projective systems that, as such, hide as much as they expose. Following Freud, Obeyesekere argues that the most important principles of symbolic transformation are condensation, displacement, and projection. These principles allow us to read beyond the limits of so-called common sense and the parameters established by conventional meaning so as to trace the associative chains through which what Obeyesekere calls deep motivation is translated into the public realm of culture. According to Obeyesekere, these principles allow us to move beyond the logocentric restrictions imposed by most languages, restrictions such as the law of contradiction, the absence of formal logic in dreams, and the apparent ignorance of negation.

Obeyesekere forcefully argues that the work of culture can only be understood if we move beyond our Western logocentric bias. At the limit of language is the symbol which both represents and is constitutive of experience. Thus, Obeyesekere disagrees with Wittgenstein that the limits of language are the limits of the world. Obeyesekere's own difficulty is that he must develop a prelinguistic *understanding* of symbolic forms if he is to be consistent with his critique of logocentrism at least on his own terms, a conception of an area "below" language which, all the same, is constitutive of experience. Yet if these forms are to be accessible to a "reading" they must somehow or another be susceptible to conditions of representability that can indeed be "read." Obeyesekere recognizes this dilemma in his work and attempts to solve it by returning us to the interpretation of dreams. As Obeyesekere explains,

> The unconscious is never seen; it is inferred from its manifestations. These manifestations are the ideational representatives—dreams, symptoms, fantasies—that are related to the unconscious in *indirect* ways, since direct expression is blocked by threats of censorship (superego) and distortion (*entstellung*). Dreams are the royal road to the unconscious, and they are essentially *images* or "thoughts transformed into images." People in most cultures do not say "I had a dream," but "I saw a dream." These ideational representatives are the elementary forms of the objectifications of the unconscious processes. Their non-lingual nature is due to two important reasons. First, they are pre-linguistic and originate at a time before the child has learnt language. Freud characterized the unconscious as "thinking in pictures." Some people, he said, have the capacity to retain the "visual imagery which is so vivid in the early years" longer than others. Second, as Victor Turner has argued, the images of the unconscious might well be rooted in the primordial structures of the brain.[20]

The second reason given by Obeyesekere is particularly surprising given his insistent rejection of scientistic explanations of deep motivation. He falls back into the very logocentric assumptions he would, correctly to my mind, have us reject when he tries to explain the nonlinguistic "nature" of ideational representatives in dreams and the symbolic forms which stand between *logos* and *bios* in culture. It is the appeal to "nature" which is problematical. Would locating the "images" in the brain really help us in reading them? Ultimately Obeyesekere himself, I believe, would say not. This inconsistency, however, is not serious for Obeyesekere's nonlogocentric approach to the work of culture, once we understand the processes of the unconscious as *analogous* to a language.

To say that the unconscious is *like* a language is not at all to deny that dreams are in images. The emphasis on *analogous* is crucial. As we will see, it is precisely Lacan's contribution to show us that this analogy draws on Freud's own thoughts on how the conditions of representability must be present in dreams if they are to be read.

Lacan's Contribution to Understanding the Unconscious

Following Paul Ricoeur,[21] Obeyesekere rejects the idea that the contents of the unconscious have their own linguistic form, even if not the identical form of conscious language. This is because he ultimately has a logocentric conception of language as a synchronized system of meaning. As a result he misreads Lacan to imply that the processes of the unconscious coincide with Ferdinand de Saussure's *langue*.[22] As we will see shortly, it is precisely Lacan's insight to find in Freud's account of the unconscious the entire structure of language through a unique reinterpretation of the analysis of Ferdinand de Saussure's structural linguistics, which denies the privileging of the synchronic aspect of *langue* over the differential relationality of *parole*. Of course, Obeyesekere is right that Freud understood the content of dreams as ideational representatives, as images. But what he forgets is that Freud also recognized that if we are to "read" such representations we must have some understanding of "the means of representability" which would allow for the expression of chains of association which can be "read," even if only through the thick descriptions provided by the psychic life of the individual and/or the intricate networks of cultural symbolic forms. Thus, Freud compares the dream to a rebus, which is a picture expressing a statement. It is the relationship between the terms, not just the images themselves, that is to be read so as to make the dream a rebus, *analogous* in the form of the expression of a statement.

Lacan takes Freud's comparison of a dream to a rebus one step further. He treats dream elements like words. To quote Lacan:

> Let us say, then, that the dream is like the parlour-game in which one is supposed to get the spectators to guess some well known saying or variant of it solely by dumb-show. . . . [That] the dream run[s] up against a lack of taxematic material for the representation of such logical articulations as causality, contradiction, hypothesis, etc., . . . proves they are a form of writing rather than of mime. The subtle processes that the dream is seen to use to represent these logical articulations, in a much less artificial way than games usually employ, are the object of a special study in Freud in which we see once more confirmed that the dream-work follows the laws of the signifier.[23]

With the phrase "the laws of the signifier," we are returned to Lacan's own interpretation of the structural linguistics of Saussure. It is impossible in the course of this essay to give anything like an adequate summary of Saussure's structural linguistics as appropriated by Lacan.[24] Therefore, I will emphasize only those aspects of Lacan's unique use of structural linguistics that are relevant to resolving the dilemma of Obeyesekere's nonlogocentric ethnography insofar as this approach allows us to deepen our understanding of the political importance of the Rorty/Geertz debate, while keeping in mind the concrete example of race and gender.

Summary of Saussure's Structural Linguistics

Saussere's fundamental insight was that the sign, the simplest unit of semiotics has two components, the signifier, the material aspect— even if it be phonic for Saussure and graphic (the letter) for Lacan— and the signified, the meaningful component. What was new in Saussure was the full recognition of the significance that the sign was not the attachment of the name to a pregiven concept. The sign, in other words, is constitutive of the relation between the signifier and the signified, it does not just represent a pregiven relationship. Neither has a positive identity outside of their relationship. The sign for Saussure is the coupling of difference as the signifier from difference as the signified. The signifier is only what the signified is not and vice versa in this coupling. In like manner, the sign itself signifies, comes to take on meaning and value and, thus, constitutes the significance of our world only in relationship to other signs which it is not. A pen, for example, is not a pencil. A tree is not a shrub, not a flower, not a weed. According to Saussure, it is the mode of difference within a chain of associated terms, for example, leafy green objects growing in a yard, that gives each term its significance. As already suggested, for Saussure the sign is reciprocally defined by its parts. It is his conception of reciprocal determination that allows him in his diagrams to represent each component as reversible.

In Lacan's rejection of the reversibility of the signifier and the signified, we find his first addition to Saussure's conception of the sign. Lacan understands that he materializes Saussure's analysis. For Lacan, the signifier is the letter, not the sound impression, of the word. Lacan defines the letter as follows: "By 'letter' I designate that material support that concrete discourse borrows from language."[25] If the dream elements are to be treated like words, the words themselves are made up of letters. The letter *matters* precisely because it metaphorizes the unconscious which is articulated only as signifiers detached from the signifieds. This detachment is Lacan's linguistic comprehension of the process of repression. Relations between the signifiers, including the one of detachment from the signified which forms the contents of the unconscious, generate the signified for Lacan. Lacan describes the "two orders," that of the signifier and that of the signified, as follows:

> The first network, that of the signifier, is the synchronic structure of the language material in so far as in that structure each element assumes its precise function by being different from the others; . . . The second network, that of the signified, is the diachronic set of the concretely pronounced discourses, which reacts historically on the first, just as the structure of the first governs the pathways of the second. The dominant fact here is the unity of signification, which proves never to be resolved into a pure indication of the real, but always refers back to another signification.[26]

In this specific sense—i.e., that it is the relation between the signifiers that generates the signified and not vice versa—the signifier is privileged over the signified. What this means is that the relationship between signifier and signified is hierarchical, not reciprocal. In psychoanalytic terms the two orders of discourse are always separated by a barrier, a censorship, which can never be traversed once and for all. Lacan thus redraws Saussure's formula of the sign, S/s, to indicate that the signifier is over the signified. Thus, Lacan takes Saussure's insight that language and systems of representation only come to gain significance through the articulation of the differential relation between signs and the elements of signs themselves to its conclusion. For Lacan the privileging of the signifier is the necessary result of the recognition that what is signified is not an ontologically distinct order from the signifiers, and yet even so, its position as under the signifier is what distinguishes the two orders of discourse. The signified, in other words, is just another signifier, but positioned differently underneath. Thus Lacan can argue:

> One can not go further along this line of thought than to demonstrate that no significations can be sustained other than by reference to another signification: in its extreme form this amounts to the proposition that there is no language (*langue*) in existence for which there is any question of its inability to cover the whole field of the signified[.][27]

Meaning is established, pinned down, but, as established in a chain of signifiers, it can always slide, yielding new meanings. The differential relation between the elements of the sign and the signs themselves means that each term needs another term to be understood, and that term needs another, and on and on.

This on and on or horizontal process in which meaning continually glides to create new meaning is what Lacan refers to as metonymy, which is his linguistic interpretation of Freud's principle of symbolic transformation, to which Obeyesekere refers as displacement. Metonymy relies on the endless recreation of the context which results from the juxtaposition to one term with another through contiguity. For Lacan, contiguity is itself a linguistic relation not based on any real relation between objects. Metaphor is also a linguistic relation but, because for Lacan it operates through substitution, metaphor operates vertically and, indeed, frequently operates to erase the term that has been substituted. The term that has been substituted easily falls below the bar of consciousness, thus continually producing the material of the unconscious. This substitution process is identified by Lacan with the principle of condensation. Metaphor, in other words, through the potential erasure implicit in substitution, can make the replaced signifier disappear into the unconscious. The unconscious has no ontological status or real status in Lacan.[28] The unconscious "is" only as the signifiers which have disappeared because the process of condensation has erased the path through which they were pushed under. The sliding process of metonymy is halted when it gets stuck in a congealed sign so that the signifier is not free to generate new meanings. This congealing process is detected in symptoms, or in other unconscious manifestations.

Analysis, on this reading, is the detection of the lost path which the signifier slid down so as to congeal in its detachment from the chain of signifiers that could produce other meanings. It is the relationship between the two functions of metaphor and metonymy, condensation and displacement, that allows for the link between unconscious terms and their preconscious and conscious networks of association so that interpretation is possible. How, then can we interpret deep motivation? How do we have access to what has seemingly been buried and therefore has sunk into the depths? How do manifestations of the unconscious ever become established enough that they can be read? To answer these questions we look *mainly* to the principle of condensation. When the focus is on change we turn primarily to the principle of displacement. Of course, neither principle is truly separable from the other. Their actual operation must be examined in a specific context. This, of course, is a very simple summation of the two key principles of symbolic transformation in the process of analysis itself and in the work of culture. But it emphasizes a process which is by definition endless because linguistic structures both generate the unconscious and allow for its contents to retraverse the pathway of repression. It is precisely this kind of process that Obeyesekere associates with the work of culture.

> In the Sri Lankan case, expression of illness-conflict and the cure both belong to the same order of "representation through images," though the cognitive integration of these images must surely be of a higher order when the oneiric images of the unconscious are transformed, at various levels of symbolic remove, to the status of cultural symbols articulated to a cosmology. Hence, insofar as these culture symbols are removed at various levels from the sources of motivation, one needs the notion of the *work of culture,* over and above the mechanisms of the dream work, to depict the processes of transformation of unconscious motives into cultural symbols that have significance to the individual in respect of both person and culture at the same time. To put it differently, if ideational representatives are the primary objectifications of unconscious processes, we need to describe or identify the mechanisms that are involved in the

more complicated *higher* objectifications entailed in the relationship between unconscious processes and culturally constituted symbolic forms.[29]

What, then, is the significance of Lacan's contribution to Obeyesekere's understanding of the work of culture? The answer is at least twofold. First, Lacan allows us to understand how the unconscious is continually generated as the isolation of usually imagistic signifiers and their corresponding relegation to the position of signified. I use the word "generated" to indicate the process aspect of how the unconscious comes to "be." The unconscious, in other words, *is not,* it is always "coming to be." Repression explains the congealing of the process and allows us to explain why certain signifiers have become so frozen into their status as signifieds that they no longer seem to be governed by principles of metonymy or even of metaphor. They have hardened so as to produce the stiff liberal. This hardened meaning is what gives us the seemingly unshakable structures of culture such as gender differentiation and, I will argue in a moment, "race" and the fantasies and social fantasies expressive of these meanings. These fantasies, as "read" through the process of condensation, allow for an understanding of the work of culture that provides a way to delve below the surface. But secondly, because the analysis of the unconscious through the principles of metonymy and metaphor allows us to trace the repressed trajectory or passageway through which the congelation of meaning took place, it also protects the possibility of change. Without the possibility of change, analysis of an individual patient could not "work" to free the patient from determination by the congealed signifiers expressible only as symptoms. And, in terms of the work of culture, profound social change involving the very restructuring of meanings would also be impossible. Lacan, in other words, gives us a way of thinking about the very principles of condensation and displacement so as to understand both the establishment of meaning and change in the work of culture. Such an understanding of the work of culture, since it does not just skim along the surface, by its very process of analysis does not just leave things as they were. This process of analysis, then, can and should be distinguished from Rorty's brand of post-Wittgensteinian philosophy.

Politics and Divergent Approaches to the Work of Culture

For now, it is important to note that post-Wittgensteinian philosophy does leave things as they are if it refuses to recognize what is other to the consciousness of our surroundings and the rationalizations of culture. Different brands of what has come to be called postmodern philosophy diverge on precisely whether or not the recognition of what is other to consciousness has ethical and political significance. Rorty is implicitly on one side of the divide and Geertz and Obeyesekere on the other, even though Geertz does not explicitly appeal to psychoanalysis at all in his science of imagining difference. This essay's opening quote from Wittgenstein exposes the limits of the kind of skimming along the surface that at other times he indicated was the best we could do because the depths could simply not be plumbed. As I hope to show shortly, the imagining of the future demands that we also reimagine the so-called past, not as an accurate account, but as the fantasy figures that have come to have significance for us in the way they have congealed our definitions of difference. Obeyesekere distinguishes between cultures on the basis of their recognition of the need to take into account the unconscious processes that inform our fantasies. The call in both Geertz and Obeyesekere for such recognition is explicitly ethical. Certainly neither thinker would agree that it is possible to simply banish the unconscious forces that continue to be part of our life. Lacan shows us that language itself generates its own unconscious. Indeed, the effort to thoroughly cleanse unconscious forces in the name of the achievement of a rationalized form of life only pushes them further under, making them less accessible and therefore more forceful, not less so. As Obeyesekere graphically reminds us, everything may smell clean, but that is only because "the shit is flushed into the dark rat-infested sewers that line the belly of the city."[30] To sanitize suffering is not to end it. It is only to refuse it respect.

Race and Gender

There may be no more compelling example of the danger of confusing sanitation with enlightenment than the example of race and gender as these two are played out in the theater of desire. I turn now to my own story which I wish to add to Geertz's example of "the drunken Indian." I tell this story because it does not lend itself to Rorty's easy acceptance of the divide between public justice and private fantasy. I also tell it because it reinforces Geertz's point that we are continuously confronted with difference and diversity within our "own" culture. And last, if certainly not least, I tell it because it helps us to see the relevance of the kind of approach to cultural work advocated by Obeyesekere in the analysis of the intersection of race and gender.

The story is as follows: In 1972–73 I was involved with a union drive in an electronics plant in "Silicon Valley," California. The organizing committee for the United Auto Workers, the union we had chosen to affiliate with, was composed of two hispanics, five African Americans, and four white women, including myself. At the time, we were still in the process of collecting cards and had yet to get the requisite percentage to file for an election. As anyone who has been involved in a union drive will know, this is a very precarious time because the employer has not been officially notified of the presence of the union, and yet the number of workers who know about its presence is constantly expanding. There was an African-American man, whom I will call K, who lived with one of the most active participants in the union drive, a woman I will call P. He had "a thing" for white women and the white women on the committee had been put on notice about K's problem by the sister of the woman he lived with, also an active member of the committee. I will call the sister E. He regularly stood outside the factory when we came out for lunch or to leave the plant after work. The white women involved in the drive systematically ignored his overtures, until a new white worker, C, both joined the organizing committee and took up with K in a rather public way. The report was that they were having sex in his car behind the official company parking lot. The African-American women on the committee asked me to ask C to stop having sex with K. P's deep distress was evident for all to see. The woman carrying on the sexual relationship with K refused to stop, justifying her position with attacks on monogamy as a hopelessly bourgeois institution. I reported back to the other women on the committee. The relationship continued over the next week, unfortunately still taking place mainly in the parking lot. P became increasingly distraught and the organizing committee was thoroughly disrupted by C's behavior. At a crucial point in the drive the needed effort to continue to solicit cards came to a stop. I was again asked to intervene. C again refused to stop the relationship. When I reported back again it was evident that the African-American women thought some kind of further action was necessary. The next evening four African-American women had a physical confrontation with C. I was put in a car during the lunch break and guarded so that I would not try to intervene and therefore end up getting hurt myself. C was delivered back to me and I took her to the emergency room. She was not badly hurt, mainly shaken. The next day she quit. The organizers began the difficult process of trying to rebuild the shattered committee. The African-American women insisted that we could not continue the union drive without an explicit discussion of the dynamics of "whiteness" and "blackness" as they had been played out on this particular field of desire. A series of readings was put together which openly addressed the issues of sexuality, race, and gender as they were themselves part of the brutal history of racial oppression of Afro-Americans within the United States. These meetings were called "purification rites" by those of us who participated. The procedural norms of justice which Rorty celebrates in the case of the "drunken Indian" were not available here. According to Rorty, particularly Freud, but also psychoanalysis generally, is useful in forcing us to face how our private goals are built out of idiosyncratic unconscious obsession and phobias. Psychoanalysis can play no role for Rorty in the public discourse of accommodation to liberal standards of justice. But here the figure of the "white woman-izer" was not seen as idiosyncratic, but part of a social fantasy intricately connected to the oppression of Afro-American women. There could be no neat divide between the public and the private. The public goal of organizing the union was only to be achievable if the psychodynamics of race, sex, and gender were faced as a social fantasy. Like all fantasies, this fantasy has its own logic even if clearly not the logic we associate with *la langue*. In Obeyesekere's terms it is much closer to the logic of dream work, but the consequences of this logic were and are devastating.

Sensitivity to issues of racial and national difference has led many feminists to argue for the "inessential woman."[31] What it means to be a "white" middle-class woman and what it means to be a "black" working-class woman is understood to be so radically different that the very idea of a common experience of womanhood is rejected as part of a racist society that cannot truly confront the other woman. Psychoanalysis, particularly in its current Anglo-American brand of object-relations theory, is indeed forcefully critiqued for its attempt to universalize the experience of white middle-class women as if that experience could tell us something about women per se. For example, Nancy Fraser and Linda Nicholson have effectively critiqued attempts to universalize Nancy Chodorow's sociological account of mothering within North America as a cross-cultural activity that can explain the perpetuation of shared personality characteristics of women. Such characteristics, so the argument goes, can then provide us with a deeper understanding of the gender identity of all women. To quote Fraser and Nicholson:

> Equally troubling are the aporias that this theory generates for political practice. While gender identity gives substance to the idea of sisterhood, it does so at the cost of repressing differences amongst

sisters. Although the theory allows for some differences among women of different classes, races, sexual orientations, it construes these as subsidiary to more basic similarities. But it is precisely as a consequence of the request to understand such differences as second-ary that many women have denied an allegiance to feminism.[32]

I agree with Fraser and Nicholson's critique of this brand of psycho-analysis which is not sensitive to its own ethnocentrism. I would add, however, that this critique should not deny the possibility that gender hierarchy does create some *consequences* which are endured by most, if not all, women. The lesson instead should be that we need to be careful in how we describe gender and then relate gender to these consequences. We need to carefully consider conditions of universalia-bility. But, as I mentioned in the introduction, my focus in this essay is not on this problem, as important as I think it is. I wish to note that for Obeyesekere—and, as I have also argued, implicitly for Geertz—psychoanalysis, as a necessary component of a nonlogocentric under-standing of the work of culture which can take into account the power of unconscious forces as these drive public life, *does not* focus on the attempt to develop universal structures of gender identity. Instead, what is offered is a conception of symbolic transformation that can allow us to understand social fantasies, and the work of culture more generally.

In the case of race and gender more explicitly, this approach to the work of culture, when combined with the Lacanian account of the generation and shifts of the contents of the unconscious, can help us understand race through the dynamics of desire without the attempt to attribute positive, universal characteristics to either race or gender. In the Lacanian understanding of the constitution of identity through difference, what "black" signifies can only be understood through its asymmetrical, differential articulation against whiteness. This is not a definition of blackness as the mirror opposite of whiteness, but as a signifier that only takes on meaning through the principles of condensa-tion and displacement in which what is "black" stands in for a whole series of negative metaphors associated with evil, and displaces very basic fear of otherness into the so-called reality of a color—black. This chain cannot, in turn, be separated from the gendering of sex in which black masculinity is read as the epitome of the symbolization of the bad guy, the black woman devalued (for her supposed accessibility), the white woman projected as the unobtainable other.[33]

In her excellent discussion of the politics of rape and lynching in the

United States, Jacquelyn Dowd Hall has convincingly argued that we cannot understand either of these phenomena as they were constructed in the post-Reconstruction South if we do not grapple with the dynamics of how race and gender are caught in a specific chain of signification. To quote Hall:

> The association between lynching and rape emerges most clearly in the parallel use in racial subordination. As Diane K. Lewis has pointed out, in a patriarchal society, black men, as men, constituted a potential challenge to the established order. Laws were formulated primarily to exclude black men from adult male prerogatives in the public sphere, and lynching meshed with these legal mechanisms of exclusion. Black women represented a more ambiguous threat. They too were denied access to the politico-juridical domain, but since they shared this exclusion with women in general, its maintenance engendered anxiety and required less force. Lynching served primarily to dramatize hierarchies among women. In contrast, the violence directed at black women illustrates the double jeopardy of race and sex. The record of the Freedmen's Bureau, and the oral histories collected by the Federal Writers Project, testify to the sexual atrocities endured by black women as whites sought to reassert their command over their newly freed slaves. Black women were sometimes executed by lunch mobs, but more routinely they served as targets of sex and assault.[34]

This is a classic example of how a crime against women, rape, is played out within the meaning given by race. In the South, the best excuse for a lynching, when an excuse was even rendered, was the supposed rape of an innocent white woman. Hall describes how the Association of Southern Women for the Prevention of Lynching, explicitly recognized the psychosexual dynamics that, in the name of chivalry, oppressed both "black" and "white" women and supposedly justified mob violence of the worst order. Indeed, the differential articulation of "black" and "white" through the structures of desirability and accessibility gave a color to the very basic form of splitting which Lacan has called the physical fantasy of Woman. Under this fantasy woman is signified through the fundamental split of good and bad, in the case of the post-Reconstruction South, "the white," innocent woman with her virtue intact if her sexuality denied, the "black," licentious woman whose purported sexuality made her rape acceptable because she was by definition unrapable. As Hall argues,

In the United States, the fear and fascination of female sexuality was projected onto black women; the passionless lady arose in symbiosis with the primitively sexual slave. House slaves often served as substitute mothers; at a black woman's breast white men experienced absolute dependence on a being who was both a source of wish-fulfilling joy and grief-producing disappointment. In adulthood, such men could find in this black woman a ready object for a mixture of rage and desire that so often underlies male heterosexuality. The black woman, already in chains, was sexually available, unable to make claims for support or concern; by dominating her, men could replay the infant's dream of unlimited access to the mother.[35]

The split is colored and the color differential, in turn, articulates the split. We know what "black" and "white" womanhood means, in part at least, through that fantasy.

In the story I told about the union drive, we see a similar, if not identical, matrix of desire in which what it means to be a woman cannot be separated from how color is itself engendered. It is precisely in the study of how color and "sex" are engendered in a chain of metonymy that we find an approach to the relationship between "black" and "white" women. The figure of the "inessential woman" lets white women off the hook too easily. What we see in the case of both the history of the connection between lynching and rape and the tale of the breakdown of solidarity in the union drive is the differential articulation of "black" and "white." This articulation creates a fundamental asymmetry which would make it a mockery to assume the experience of "black" and "white" women would be the same. But an understanding of this asymmetrical relationship would also deny that color can be reduced to a set of positive characteristics separate from the chain of signifiers in which it is given meaning. In other words there are not just "white" and "black" women who are just there and can be reduced to their "whiteness" and "blackness" as if color could signify separately from the matrix of desire in which it is given meaning. What it means to be "white," in other words, can only be grasped in relationship to the privilege of being "white" within the differential articulation of "white" and "black" womanhood.

Of course we must also grasp the oppressiveness of the so-called meaning given to whiteness which identifies "it" with a fantasized feminine desirability characterized by inaccessibility and so-called virtue. This kind of political challenge was made by the Association of Southern Women for the Prevention of Lynching and by the white women on the organizing committee. But to understand that the differential articulation through which "white" and "black" are given meaning is undesirable for "white" women as well as "black" women, because it is given meaning within the physical fantasy of woman, still does not deny the relative privilege inherent in any relationship of asymmetry. What, then, is shared by "white" and "black" women in these two examples is this differential relation which, precisely because it is asymmetrical, is only held in common through difference. Yet this "in common through difference" is precisely what must be understood through cultural work if there is to be anything like a true solidarity between women. The meaning of "black" and "white" is not engraved in stone even if the meaning of color has become so congealed into the unconscious that change seems well nigh impossible. But change can also not be foreclosed once we understand that the unconscious is always being generated at the same time that its contents are being transformed.

Conclusion

Thus the Lacanian conception of the unconscious, which refuses to ontologize it, has implications for the understanding of the political significance of cultural work. Obeyesekere always reminds us of the trivialization of human suffering that accompanies the confusion of sanitation with enlightenment. We must always remember the dark side that will be with us as long as we are mortal beings.

> What is hidden is dung and death. And like dung and death, pain and human suffering are also confined to a sanitized environment. There are, however, the few who will be attracted to such forms of experience and thought, in spite of the physical and social environment in which they live, because they have searched, as Freud did, the dark recesses of their own lives and from there have had a vision of the dark side of life in general. The moment you label this vision as pessimistic and oppose it to "optimism," you miss the point of it all. Neither Freud nor the Buddha gave way to gloom or nihilism by his recognition that the purpose of all life is death.[36]

Psychoanalysis clearly plays a crucial role in taking us into what takes place in the dark. But in the Lacanian understanding of the unconscious it also allows us to grapple with what gets called dark and, specifically for the purposes of my discussion of race, how dark is itself symbolized through who gets identified as colored "black." In other words, who gets signified as "dark" has itself taken place in the dark. That is at least part of the problem of racism. However, the significance of coloration can shift in political struggle. What has become congealed as the signified can be put into motion again. Part of political struggle is to shift reality through shifting the meaning of our shared symbols. Politics is not just about power but also about the very basis of what can be become "real" and thus accessible to consciousness and change. We delve into the depths not just to understand the dark side but to make fluid the very designations of dark and light. Here we are again returned to the difference between the stiff liberal and the human being who is not afraid of getting a little wet by sinking into what has been pushed under. Of course this process of delving is endless. To emphasize how the Lacanian understanding of the unconscious allows for change in no way denies the reality of dung and death. It does not pit a facile optimism against the pain and suffering of finite creatures whose very efforts to bring everything into the light of reason create new forms of excrement that must again be buried. But it does allow us to remember the ever-shifting nature of our "reality" as it is challenged by those who make us see it differently.

The debate between Geertz and Rorty ultimately turns on how one responds to these challenges. Geertz reminds us that we can not even begin to understand suffering if we don't grasp the limits of our imagination as it has come to be ensnared in the latest conventions. I have suggested that this very effort to free the imagination involves a journey into the depths so that we can see how this process of ensnaring took place. We return to the past through the very process of envisioning "what is" differently. To try to imagine a society without racism demands that we come to terms with the significance "race" has come to be given in our reality. We remember the future as we involve ourselves in this very process of reimaging the past so that the present world seems to give way under our feet in the wake of new meanings we did not dream of before. Psychoanalysis then can play a crucial role in Geertz's "science of imagining difference," a paradoxical phrase which not only captures our responsibility to respect the other, but allows us to understand that our political obligations can not be separated from our dreams and fantasies.

Notes

Introduction

1. See John Rawls, *A Theory of Justice* (Cambridge, Mass.: The Belknap Press of Harvard University Press, 1971).

2. For an excellent review of the "critique" of the subject, see " 'Eating Well,' or the Calculation of the Subject: An Interview with Jacques Derrida," in *Who Comes after the Subject?* ed. Eduardo Cadava, Peter Connor, and Jean-Luc Nancy (New York: Routledge, Chapman and Hall, 1991), pp. 96–118. For divergent positions on the significance of the critique of the subject for a feminist politics, see the essays collected in *Feminists Theorize the Political,* ed. Judith Butler and Joan W. Scott (New York: Routledge, Chapman and Hall, 1992).

3. See Michael J. Sandel, *Liberalism and the Limits of Justice* (Cambridge, Mass.: Harvard University Press, 1982).

4. Stanley Fish, "Anti-Professionalism," *Cardozo Law Review,* vol. 7, no. 3 (1986), pp. 645–77.

5. See chapter 2, "Pragmatism, Recollective Imagination, and Transformative Legal Interpretation."

6. Judith Butler, "The Burning of Gender" (unpublished manuscript on file with author), p. 11.

7. See Richard Rorty, "Feminism and Pragmatism," *Michigan Quarterly Review,* Winter 1991, pp. 231–42.

8. See chapter 4, "The Doubly-Prized World: Myth, Allegory, and the Feminine."

9. See chapter 5, "Sexual Difference, the Feminine, and Equivalency."

10. See chapter 4, "The Doubly-Prized World: Myth, Allegory, and the Feminine.

11. For a thorough explanation of why I renamed deconstruction "the philosophy of the limit," see Drucilla Cornell, *The Philosophy of the Limit* (New York: Routledge, Chapman and Hall, 1992).

12. See chapter 8, "What Takes Place in the Dark."

13. See Jacques Derrida, "Des Tours de Babel," in *Difference in Translation,* ed. and trans. Joseph F. Graham (Ithaca: Cornell University Press, 1985).

14. See chapter 6, "Sex-Discrimination Law and Equivalent Rights."

15. See Amartya Sen, "Inequality Reexamined: Capability and Well-Being," paper

delivered at the Conference on Equality of Life, Helsinki, Finland, July 1988, on file with author, pp. 5–6.

16. See chapter 3, "Disastrologies."

17. See, generally, Jacques Lacan, *Feminine Sexuality: Jacques Lacan and the école freudienne,* ed. Juliet Mitchell and Jacqueline Rose, trans. Jacqueline Rose (New York: W. W. Norton and Company, 1985).

18. See Drucilla Cornell, "The Philosophy of the Limit: Systems Theory and Feminist Legal Reform," in *Deconstruction and the Possibility of Justice,* ed. Drucilla Cornell, Michel Rosenfeld, and David Gray Carlson (New York: Routledge, Chapman and Hall, 1992).

19. See chapter 7, "Gender Hierarchy, Equality, and the Possibility of Democracy."

20. See Jacques Derrida, "The Politics of Friendship," in *Journal of Philosophy,* vol. 80, no. 2 (1988), pp. 632–45.

21. See chapter 8, "What Takes Place in the Dark."

1 "Convention" and Critique

1. These citations come respectively from Ludwig Wittgenstein's *Culture and Value,* ed. G. H. von Wright, trans. Peter Winch (Oxford: Basil Blackwell, 1980), pp. 3e, 77e, and 1e.

2. See Wittgenstein, *Philosophical Investigations,* trans. G. E. M. Anscombe (Oxford: Basil Blackwell, 1968), para. 38, p. 19e. Wittgenstein criticized the philosophy of language that naively identifies words with things as a type of occultism:

> Naming appears as a *queer* connexion of a word with an object.—And you really get such a queer connexion when the philosopher tries to bring out *the* relation between name and thing by staring at an object in front of him and repeating a name or even the word "this" innumerable times. For philosophical problems arise when language *goes on holiday.* And *here* we may indeed fancy naming to be some remarkable act of mind, as it were a baptism of an object. And we can also say the word "this" *to* the object, as it were *address* the object as "this"—a queer use of this word, which doubtless only occurs in doing philosophy.

3. Wittgenstein's antiessentialism is most evident in his discussion of the nature of language. See ibid., para. 65, p. 31e:

> Here we come up against the great question that lies behind all these considerations.—For someone might object against me: "You take the easy way out! You talk about all sorts of language-games, but have nowhere said what the essence of a language-game, and hence of language, is: what is common to all these activities, and what makes them into language or parts of language. So you let yourself off the very part of the investigation that once gave you yourself most headache, the part about the *general form of propositions* and of language."
> And this is true.—Instead of producing something common to all that we

call language, I am saying that these phenomena have no one thing in common which makes us use the same word for all,—but that they are *related* to one another in many different ways. And it is because of this relationship, or these relationships, that we call them all "language."

4. Wittgenstein, *Tractatus Logico-Philosophicus,* trans. D. F. Pears and B. F. McGuinness (New York: Routledge, Chapman and Hall, 1971). The early Wittgenstein attempted to identify general forms of language propositions:

> 3.31 I call any part of a proposition that characterizes its sense an expression (or a symbol).
> (A proposition is itself an expression.)
> Everything essential to their sense that propositions can have in common with one another is an expression.
> An expression is the mark of a form and a content.
>
> 3.311 An expression presupposes the forms of all the propositions in which it can occur. It is the common characteristic mark of a class of propositions.
>
> 3.312 It is therefore presented by means of the general form of the propositions that it characterizes.
> In fact, in this form the expression will be *constant* and everything else *variable.*

Ibid. But the later Wittgenstein explicitly rejected the project of such an undertaking. See Wittgenstein, *Investigations,* para. 97, p. 44e:

> We are under the illusion that what is peculiar, profound, essential in our investigation, resides in its trying to grasp the incomparable essence of language. That is, the order existing between the concepts of proposition, word, proof, truth, experience, and so on. This order is a *super*-order between—so to speak—*super*-concepts. Whereas, of course, if the words "language", "experience", "world", have a use, it must be as humble a one as that of the words "table", "lamp", "door".

5. Stanley Fish, "Anti-Professionalism," *Cardozo Law Review*, vol. 7 (1986), p. 677.

6. Wittgenstein starts his *Investigations* with the observation of the multiplicity of language games or forms of life (para. 7, p. 5e), but then rejects "essentialism"; see note 5 above.

7. For the continuing exchange between Fish and Dworkin, see Ronald Dworkin, "Law as Interpretation," *Texas Law Review,* vol. 60 (1986); Stanley Fish, "Working on the Chain Gang: Interpretation in Law and Literature," *Texas Law Review,* vol. 60 (1982); Ronald Dworkin, "My Reply to Stanley Fish (and Walter Benn Michaels): Please Don't Talk about Objectivity Any More," in *The Politics of Interpretation,* ed. W. J. T. Mitchell (Chicago: University of Chicago Press, 1983).

8. For Owen Fiss's position on interpretation, see Owen Fiss, "Objectivity and Interpretation," *Stanford Law Review,* vol. 34 (1982). For Fish's response, see Stanley Fish, "Fish v. Fiss," *Stanford Law Review,* vol. 36 (1984).

9. See, e.g., Fish, "Fish v. Fiss," p. 1325; Fish, "Working on the Chain Gang," p. 552.

10. Fish, "Working on the Chain Gang," p. 552.

11. Wittgenstein, *Investigations,* para. 23, p. 11e: "Here the term 'language-*game*' is meant to bring into prominence the fact that the *speaking* of language is part of an activity, or of a form of life."

12. Fish, "Anti-Professionalism," p. 651.

13. Wittgenstein, *Culture and Value,* p. 1e.

14. Jacques Derrida, *Dissemination,* trans. Barbara Johnson (Chicago: University of Chicago Press, 1981). Cf. Derrida, *Positions,* trans. Alan Bass (Chicago: University of Chicago Press, 1981).

15. See, generally, Theodor Adorno, *Negative Dialectics,* trans. E. B. Ashton (New York: Seabury Press, 1973).

16. Fish, "Fish v. Fiss," pp. 1332–39; Fish, "Working on the Chain Gang," p. 552. Unlike both Fiss and Dworkin, Fish is not so much concerned about objectivity in interpretation.

17. Fish, "Working on the Chain Gang," p. 562.

18. Ludwig Wittgenstein, *Zettel,* trans. G. E. M. Anscombe (Berkeley: University of California Press, 1967), para. 441, pp. 78e–79e (emphasis in original).

19. Wittgenstein, *Investigations,* para. 216, pp. 84e–85e.

20. Fish, "Working on the Chain Gang," p. 552.

21. Ibid., p. 553.

22. Fish, "Anti-Professionalism," p. 660.

23. Ibid., p. 664.

24. Ludwig Wittgenstein, *On Certainty,* ed. G. E. M. Anscombe and G. H. von Wright, trans. D. Paul and G. E. M. Anscombe (Oxford: Basil Blackwell, 1969), paras. 420–21, p. 54e.

25. Robert Gordon, "Critical Legal Histories," *Stanford Law Review,* vol. 36, no. 11 (1984).

26. Fish, "Anti-Professionalism," p. 660.

27. David Luban uses different terminology in his response to Fish, but he is making a similar point. Luban distinguishes between Fish's previous "interpretive community thesis" and his current "institution thesis." See David Luban, "Fish v. Fish or, Some Realism about Idealism," *Cardozo Law Review,* vol. 7 (1986).

28. Albrecht Wellmer, "On the Dialectic of the Modern and the Post-Modern," *Praxis International,* vol. 4, no. 337 (1985), pp. 352–53.

29. Wittgenstein, *Investigations,* para. 241, p. 88e.

30. Sabina Lovibond, *Realism and Imagination in Ethics* (Minneapolis: University of Minnesota Press, 1983), p. 124.

31. Wittgenstein, *Culture and Value,* p. 8e.

32. Wellmer, "On the Dialectic of the Modern and the Post-Modern," p. 351.

33. Lovibond, *Realism and Imagination,* pp. 163–64.

34. For a succinct summation of Derrida's own thinking on the subject, including why he uses the phrase "effects of subjectivity," see *Who Comes after the Subject?,* ed.

Eduardo Cadava, Peter Connor, and Jean-Luc Nancy (New York: Routledge, Chapman and Hall, 1991).

35. Fish, "Anti-Professionalism," p. 676.

36. Wittgenstein, *Culture and Value*, p. 56e.

37. Theodor Adorno, *Minima Moralia: Reflections from Damaged Life,* trans. E. F. N. Jephcott (London: New Left Books, 1974), p. 14.

2 Pragmatism, Recollective Imagination, and Transformative Legal Interpretation

1. Ronald Dworkin, *Law's Empire* (Cambridge, Mass.: The Belknap Press of Harvard University Press, 1986).

2. See David Kairys, "Law and Politics," *George Washington Law Review,* vol. 52 (1984), pp. 243–44, 247. ("The starting point of critical theory is that legal reasoning does not provide method or process that leads reasonable, competent, and fair-minded people to particular results in particular cases. . . . The ultimate basis for a decision is a social and political judgment incorporating a variety of factors, including the context of the case, the parties, and the substance of the issues. The decision is not based on, or determined by legal reasoning.")

3. As we saw in the last chapter, this conclusion does not follow from Wittgenstein's elaboration of how meaning is embedded in a form of life. Cf. chapter 1, " 'Convention' and Critique."

4. Charles S. Peirce, *The Collected Papers of Charles Sanders Peirce, 1931–1934,* ed. Charles Hartshorne and Paul Weiss (Cambridge, Mass.: The Belknap Press of the Harvard University Press, 1960), vol. 5, pp. 172–74.

5. Peirce, *Collected Papers,* vol. 1, pp. 161–70.

6. Ibid., vol. 8, p. 41.

7. Ibid., vol. 1, p. 18.

8. Ibid., p. 174.

9. Cf. chapter 1, " 'Convention' and Critique."

10. Peirce, *Collected Papers,* vol. 5, pp. 128–29.

11. Ibid., vol. 1, p. 255. For Peirce, the opening to the future results from his understanding of a sign or a proposition.

> The rational meaning of every proposition lies in the future. How so? The meaning of a proposition is itself a proposition. Indeed, it is no other than the very proposition of which it is the meaning: it is a translation of it. But of the myriads of forms into which a proposition may be translated, what is that one which is to be called its very meaning? It is, according to the pragmatist, that form in which the proposition becomes applicable to human conduct, not in these or those special circumstances, nor when one entertains this or that special design, but that form which is most directly applicable to self-control under every situation, and to every purpose. This is why he locates the meaning

in future time; for future conduct is the only conduct that is subject to self-control.

Ibid., vol. 5, p. 284.

12. Ibid., vol. 1, pp. 175–76.

13. Ibid., vol. 2, p. 134.

14. Ibid., vol. 5, pp. 312–13.

15. Ibid., p. 312.

16. Ibid., p. 330–31.

17. Ibid., p. 331.

18. See Dworkin, *Law's Empire*, p. 226.

19. Peirce, *Collected Papers*, vol. 5, pp. 330–31.

20. Ibid., p. 306.

21. Ibid., pp. 312–13.

22. Here we can give a different meaning to Derrida's insight that without the supplement there is no text. See Jacques Derrida, *Dissemination*, trans. Barbara Johnson (Chicago: University of Chicago Press, 1981), pp. 52–53, 63–64. In this very specific sense, infidelity to the past inheres in the very process of interpretation. Derrida shows us that there is an inevitable moment of fictionality or literarity in legal and political interpretation. As we have seen through the analysis of Peirce, this is because the other to thought and the otherness within thought itself disrupts the Hegelian recollection of the truth of the actual.

23. Perhaps there is no better example of the practice of recollective imagination than that offered to us in the writings of the "new" civic republicans and also in the work of the dialogic communitarians. It is also the self-conscious practice of recollective imagination that to some degree separates the two groups. In American law, we may owe more to Cass Sunstein than to anyone else for showing us that within the tradition given to us by the founders of the Constitution we can find "a republican" view of constitutional government, with its emphasis on public virtue and the creation of a moral community as the essential goal of legality. See Cass Sunstein, "Interest Groups in American Public Law," *Stanford Law Review*, vol. 38, no. 29 (1985), pp. 38–48. Although the republican ideal has not been the dominant trend within American constitutional law, Sunstein rightfully reminds us of what "might have been" if the legal community had emphasized a different aspect of our own tradition. Madison is undoubtedly the hero in Sunstein's work. Frank Michelman, on the other hand, in his foreword to the *Harvard Law Review*, has questioned whether we can truly pull out of Madison's writings all that Sunstein finds there. Frank Michelman, "Forward: Traces of Self-Government," *Harvard Law Review*, vol. 100, no. 4 (1986), pp. 17–24, 58–60. More importantly, he has wondered whether there may not be a serious political danger in the attempt to rely so heavily on an interpretation of Madison:

> The main conclusion Sunstein wishes to draw is that Madison's solution was emphatically *not* "to accept the interest group struggle as a desirable part of politics that would promote social welfare." Rather Madison kept

republican faith with the ideals of an objective public good and of the pursuit of this good through political deliberation. Having thus located in the Constitution this republican conception of politics—as a joint, good-faith deliberation about the public good—Sunstein urges that this conception both supports and suggests reform of the doctrine of judicial review of the "rationality" of statutes and of various aspects of administrative process.

. . . .

. . . Sustein's promise seems to reserve the ethically significant experience of self-government to the representatives; they are the ones who "have the virtue associated with classical republican citizens."

"Forward," pp. 59–60 (footnotes omitted).

For Michelman, there are contemporary problems and philosophical perspectives that were simply not present in Madison's time. Michelman is particularly concerned with Madison's rejection of the more radical vision of the republican tradition, which stresses the need for actual participation and self-government rather than the model of virtual representation ("Forword," pp. 58–59). Michelman finds in Sunstein's work the same tendency to play down the need to develop actual programs of participation consistent with a complex modern state and with the aspiration to individual freedom ("Forward," pp. 22–23). In like manner, Michelman has shown that an adequate civic-republican conception of property is still in the making, not something we can find in any way in the texts of the founding fathers ("Forward," pp. 55–57). When we recollect the conception of property in Madison, we are also asking ourselves what *should be* a civic-republican view of property that could meet modern expectations.

Although Michelman does not explain himself in these terms, I would argue that Michelman's critique of Sunstein's over-reliance on Madison expresses his concern that recollective imagination can all too easily slide into Dworkin's "pretending." To pretend that history offers us more than it does undermines the critique of the past, which must also be a part of legal and, more particularly in this case, constitutional reconstruction. In his remarks on Sunstein, Michelman implicitly worries about the dangers of recreating history ("Forward," pp. 57–58). We should not pretend that there is a better view of law and politics in the tradition than is actually operative under even the most generous interpretation. We must always be clear that we are bringing out the potential of the *might have been*. Within the group of the new civic republicans and dialogic communitarians, it is Bruce Ackerman who has forthrightly argued for the essential role of imagination in highlighting the potential of our tradition. What I offer here is a reading of the interpretive method he suggests. See Bruce Ackerman, *Social Justice in the Liberal State* (New Haven: Yale University Press, 1980). There, Ackerman spells out the conditions of dialogue he argues are inherent in an interpretation of the democratic constitutional tradition. Ackerman argues that what is most fundamental to our constitutional tradition is the legitimation of the demand for reasons in the face of the inequalities of life. For example, Ackerman says that "[t]he fundamental problem for liberal political theory is to determine what you could possibly say that might convince me of the legitimacy of your claim to power" (*Social Justice*, p. 327). The legitimation of power achieved through liberal theory's attempt to solve this "fundamental problem" implies the recognition that the citizens enjoy not only the right to respond but also the right to demand a justification. The state must, in other words, talk back and convince us with reasons, hence, the dialogic under-pinnings of constitutional government are established.

24. Roberto Mangabeira Unger, *The Critical Legal Studies Movement* (Cambridge, Mass.: Harvard University Press, 1986), pp. 60–75.

25. Ibid., p. 62.

26. See Georg W. F. Hegel's *Philosophy of Right,* trans. T. M. Knox (New York: Oxford University Press, 1952).

27. Unger, *The Critical Legal Studies Movement,* p. 73.

28. Ibid., p. 74.

29. I have examined Hegel's position on contract in an earlier article. See Drucilla Cornell, "Dialogic Reciprocity and the Critique of Employment at Will," *Cardozo Law Review,* vol. 10 (1989), p. 1575.

30. Ibid.

31. Unger, *The Critical Legal Studies Movement,* pp. 106–8.

32. Ibid., pp. 59–60.

33. Ibid., p. 24.

34. Ibid., p. 21.

35. Ibid., p. 60.

36. Ibid., pp. 58–60.

37. See Dworkin, *Law's Empire,* p. 88.

38. See Clare Dalton, "An Essay in the Deconstruction of Contract Doctrine," *Yale Law Journal,* vol. 94, no. 5 (1985), pp. 997, 1006 ("[T]he various guidelines proposed by liberal legalism lack the clarity on which the liberal order presents itself as depending"), and Mark Kellman, "Trashing," *Stanford Law Review,* vol. 36, no. 293 (1984), pp. 305–6 ("Mainstream" arguments are either "inevitably grounded in the emptiest generalities imaginable" or, in the case of economic theory, are "openly unempirical Utopian speculation about the nature of self-interest").

39. Dworkin, *Law's Empire,* p. 225 ("The adjudicative principle of integrity instructs judges to identify legal rights and duties so far as possible, on the assumption they were all created by a single author—the community personified—expressing a coherent conception of justice and fairness").

40. Jacques Derrida, "Des Tours de Babel," in *Difference in Translation,* ed. Joseph F. Graham (Ithaca: Cornell University Press, 1985), p. 191.

41. Peirce, *Collected Papers,* vol. 5, p. 281.

42. Ibid., vol. 8, p. 191.

43. Ibid., vol. 5, pp. 394–95.

44. See, generally, Jacques Derrida, "Signature Event Context," in *Limited Inc.,* trans. Samuel Weber and Jeffrey Mehlman (Evanston, Ill.: Northwestern University Press, 1988). First published in *Glyph,* vol. 1 (1977).

45. Ibid., pp. 179–80.

46. Ibid., pp. 180–85.

47. See, e.g., John Stick, "Can Nihilism Be Pragmatic?" *Harvard Law Review,* vol. 100, no. 332 (1986), pp. 387–89, 392–95.

48. There are moments, for example, when both Peller and Boyle are close to embracing the position that there is no institutionalized meaning that constrains the play of signifiers in a semiotic field. See James Boyle, "The Politics of Reason: Critical Legal Theory and Local Social Thought," *University of Pennsylvania Law Review,* vol. 133, no. 685 (1985), p. 721, and Gary Peller, "The Metaphysics of American Law," *California Law Review,* vol. 73 (1985), pp. 1151, 1167–70.

49. Emmanuel Levinas, *Otherwise than Being or Beyond Essence,* trans. Alphonso Lingis (The Hague: Martinus Nijhoff Publishers, 1981), p. 170.

50. See, e.g., Peirce, *Collected Papers,* vol. 5, p. 230 ("Doubt is an uneasy and dissatisfied state from which we struggle to free ourselves and pass into the state of belief . . .").

51. Ibid., vol. 1, pp. 331–32 (from the "Lowell Lectures of 1903").

52. Samuel Weber, *Institution and Interpretation* (Minneapolis: University of Minnesota Press, 1987), p. 14.

53. Immanuel Kant, *Critique of Practical Reason and Other Works on the Theory of Ethics,* trans. T. Abbot (6th ed. 1909), pp. 109–16. Reprinted in *Kant Selections,* ed. T. Greene (1929), pp. 289–95.

54. Cf. chapter 1, " 'Convention' and Critique."

55. Peirce, *Collected Papers,* vol. 1, p. 17 (from the "Lowell Lectures of 1903").

56. Weber, *Interpretation,* p. 15.

57. Theodor Adorno and Max Horkheimer, *Dialectic of Enlightenment,* trans. John Cumming (New York: Herder and Herder, 1972), pp. 43–80.

58. Robert Cover, "The Supreme Court, 1982 Term—Foreword: Nomos and Narrative," *Harvard Law Review,* vol. 97, no. 4 (1983), p. 68.

3 "Disastrologies"

1. Review and discussion of David Farrell Krell, *Postponements: Woman, Sensuality, and Death in Nietzsche* (Bloomington: Indiana University Press, 1986).

   I am borrowing the word "Disastrologies" from Jacques Derrida's book, *The Post Card: From Socrates to Freud and Beyond,* trans. Alan Bass (Chicago: University of Chicago Press, 1987). Originally published as *La Carte postale* (Paris: Flammarion, 1980). "Disastrologies—would be the title, do you like it? I think it suits us well. One day you were walking in front of me without knowing me, without looking at me. I fell on you?" (*The Post Card,* p. 115).

2. Friedrich W. Nietzsche, *Beyond Good and Evil,* ed. and trans. Walter Kaufmann (Princeton: Princeton University Press, 1967), p. 283.

3. Hélène Cixous, "Sorties: Out and Out: Attacks/Ways Out/Forays," in Hélène Cixous and Catherine Clément, *The Newly Born Woman,* trans. Betsy Wing (Minneapolis: University of Minnesota Press, 1986), p. 98. Originally published as *La jeune née* (Paris: Union Générale d'Editions, 1975).

4. Krell, *Postponements,* note 3, p. 87.

5. Cited by Krell from Nietzsche's notes, ibid., p. 82.

6. Krell, *Postponements*, note 3, p. 10.

7. Ibid., p. 29.

8. Ibid., p. 30.

9. Nietzsche, *Beyond Good and Evil*, number 269 (as cited in Krell, *Postponements*, note 3, p. 25).

10. Friedrich W. Nietzsche, *Thus Spoke Zarathustra*, trans. Walter Kaufmann, p. 447 (as cited in Krell, *Postponements*, p. 55).

11. Cited in Krell, *Postponements*, p. 57, from Nietzsche's notes on Pana.

12. Jacques Derrida, *Spurs: Nietzsche's Styles/Eperons: Les Styles de Nietzsche*, trans. Barbara Harlow (Chicago: University of Chicago Press, 1978), p. 57.

13. Jacques Lacan, *Ecrits: A Selection*, trans. Alan Sheridan (New York: W. W. Norton and Company, 1977), p. 877. Originally published as *Ecrits* (Paris: Editions du Seuil, 1966).

14. Jacques Derrida, *Glas*, trans. John P. Leavey, Jr. and Richard Rand (Lincoln: University of Nebraska Press, 1986), p. 65. Originally published as *Glas* (Paris: Editions Galilée, 1974).

15. Jacques Derrida, *Signéponge/Signsponge*, trans. Richard Rand (New York: Columbia University Press, 1984), p. 4.

16. Ibid., p. 5.

17. Derrida, *The Post Card*, p. 112.

18. Ibid., p. 115.

19. Ibid., p. 59.

20. Ibid., p. 141.

21. Ibid., p. 5.

22. Ibid.

23. Samuel Menache, "Promised Land," in *Collected Poems* (Orono, Me.: The National Poetry Foundation, University of Maine, 1986), p. 27.

4 The Doubly-Prized World: Myth, Allegory, and the Feminine

1. James Joyce, *Finnegans Wake* (New York: Penguin Books, 1939), p. 439.

2. Elizabeth V. Spelman, *Inessential Woman: Problems of Exclusion in Feminist Thought* (Boston: Beacon Press, 1988).

3. Trinh T. Minh-ha, *Woman, Native, Other: Writing PostColoniality and Feminism* (Bloomington: Indiana University Press, 1989).

4. Michèle Montrelay, "Inquiry into Femininity," in *French Feminist Thought: A Reader*, ed. Toril Moi (New York: Basil Blackwell, 1987), p. 227.

5. Julia Kristeva, "Woman Can Never Be Defined", in *New French Feminisms: An Anthology*, ed. Elaine Marks and Isabelle de Courtivron (New York: Schocken Books by arrangement with University of Massachusetts Press, 1980). Originally

published as "La Femme, ce n'est jamais ça," *Tel Quel* (Autumn 1974). Cf. Julia Kristeva, "Women's Time," in *Feminist Theory: A Critique of Ideology,* ed. Nannerl O. Keohane, Michele Z. Rosaldo, and Barbara C. Gelpi (Chicago: University of Chicago Press, 1982).

6. Robin West, "The Difference in Women's Hedonic Lives: A Phenomenological Critique of Feminist Legal Theory," *Wisconsin Women's Law Journal,* vol. 3, no. 81 (1987). Cf. Robin West, "Jurisprudence and Gender," *University of Chicago Law Review,* vol. 55, no. 1 (1988).

7. Robin West does not use the term "phenomenology" in the strict philosophical sense. West's meaning is best understood in her own words. See West, "Women's Hedonic Lives," pp. 81–97.

8. Ibid., p. 118 (emphasis in original).

9. Ibid., pp. 96–108.

10. Ibid., p. 82.

11. Ibid., note 4.

12. Ibid. In this and the preceding note these references are made generally because it is in this article that West sets out the positions and positions *herself* vis-à-vis the feminist and the feminine. To gain an understanding of her position, the piece should be seen as a whole.

13. West, "Jurisprudence and Gender," p. 70.

14. Ibid.

15. Ibid.

16. West, "Women's Hedonic Lives," p. 140.

17. Ibid.

18. Ibid.

19. West, "Jurisprudence and Gender," p. 71 (emphasis in original).

20. See West, "Women's Hedonic Lives."

21. Ibid.

22. I use the word "postmodern" reluctantly. The very idea that periods of history can be rigidly separated is one I reject. "Postmodern" has become a catchall term that defines very different philosophical positions as giving a similar message. As a result, I believe that using the term "postmodern" can lead to losing what is unique and, thus, most important from a philosophical perspective, in these different positionings.
    For a more thorough discussion of my position vis-à-vis the use of the word "postmodern," see Drucilla Cornell, "What Is Postmodernity Anyway?" the introduction to *The Philosophy of the Limit* (New York: Routledge, Chapman and Hall, 1992).

23. Jacques Derrida, "Form and Meaning: A Note on the Phenomenology of Language," in *Margins of Philosophy,* trans. Alan Bass (Chicago: University of Chicago Press, 1982). Originally published as *Marges de la philosophie* (Paris: Les Editions de Minuit, 1972).

24. Derrida is commenting principally on Husserl's *Logical Investigations.*

25. Derrida, *Margins of Philosophy,* pp. 158–66.

26. Ibid., p. 164.

27. Ibid., p. 169.

28. Ibid., p. 160.

29. Ibid., pp. 171–72 (emphasis in original).

30. See generally West, "Women's Hedonic Lives."

31. See notes 20 to 26 and accompanying text.

32. West, "Women's Hedonic Lives," p. 127. West is relying on Adrienne Rich's argument that one of women's problems is that they lie.

33. Jacques Derrida, "White Mythology: Metaphor in the Text of Philosophy," in *Margins of Philosophy,* p. 270.

34. Ibid., p. 249.

35. See generally West, "Women's Hedonic Lives."

36. Ibid., p. 65.

37. It is important to note that Derrida, in his "Choreographies," is very careful to make this distinction between the dream of a new choreography of sexual difference that has not been and cannot be wiped out in spite of the oppressiveness of our current system of gender representation, and the reality of the oppression of women. Derrida's "utopianism" in this interview is often interpreted to mean that he is not a "feminist." But this is a seriously mistaken reading. Of course, Derrida is for legal reforms that *would* alleviate the most aggravated abuses against women. But these reforms cannot ultimately touch the deeper underlying problem of sexual difference as it has become expressed in rigid gender identities. Feminism, if it is conceived as a struggle of women for political power, and this definition is, of course, only one definition of feminism—cannot reach the "underlying" problem of why sexual difference has taken the limited and oppressive form it has. For power is a limited, if necessary, step in the "liberation" of women from rigid gender identity. Feminism, by this definition, replicates the dichotomous structure of the logos, even if it also seeks to put women on top. Therefore, there must be a "beyond" to feminism if we are to realize the dream of a new choreography of sexual difference.

38. It is important to note a pronounced tension in Kristeva's work between her comments on mothering and her insistence that, on a deeper level, woman cannot be. I am emphasizing one strand in Kristeva's work, because it is in her comments on mothering that Kristeva attempts to draw the connection between Woman and actual empirical women. For a more detailed analysis of this tension, see Drucilla Cornell and Adam Thurschwell, "Feminism, Negativity, Intersubjectivity," in *Feminism as Critique: On the Politics of Gender,* ed. Seyla Benhabib and Drucilla Cornell (Minneapolis: University of Minnesota Press, 1987).

39. Jacques Lacan, *Ecrits: A Selection,* trans. Alan Sheridan (New York: W. W. Norton and Company, 1977). Originally published as *Ecrits* (Paris: Editions du Seuil, 1966).

40. Jane Gallop, *The Daughter's Seduction: Feminism and Psychoanalysis* (Ithaca: Cornell University Press, 1982), p. 12.

41. Kristeva, "Woman Can Never Be Defined," p. 137.

42. Lacan, Ecrits, p. 287.

43. Ibid., p. 647.

44. This assertion lies at the root of Lacan's psychoanalytic theory of gender.

45. Kristeva, "Women's Time," p. 20.

46. Ibid.

47. Ibid., p. 48.

48. West, "Women's Hedonic Lives."

49. Ibid.

50. West, "Jurisprudence and Gender," p. 51 (citing Duncan Kennedy, "The Structure of Blackstone's Commentaries," in the *Buffalo Law Review*, vol. 28, no. 209 (1979), pp. 211–13).

51. bell hooks, *Yearning: race, gender and cultural politics* (Boston: South End Press, 1990).

52. In his early writings, Lacan argues that the progress of analysis takes the subject from the imaginary autonomy of the ego to its true location in the domain of intersubjectivity. The autonomy of the ego is, in other words, an illusion. See, generally, Lacan, *Ecrits*.

53. Marguerite Duras, *India Song,* trans. Barbara Bray (New York: Grove Press, 1976), p. 65. Originally published as *India Song* (Paris: Editions Gallimard, 1973).

54. Marguerite Duras, *The Vice-Consul,* trans. Ellen Ellenbogn (New York: Grove Press, 1968). Originally published as *Le Vice-Consul* (Paris: Editions Gallimard, 1966).

55. Duras, *India Song.*

56. Ibid., p. 132.

57. Marguerite Duras, *The Ravishing of Lol Stein,* trans. Richard Seaver (New York: Pantheon Books, 1966), p. 38. Originally published as *Le ravissement de Lol V. Stein* (Paris: Editions Gallimard, 1964).

58. Marguerite Duras, *The Malady of Death,* trans. Barbara Bray (New York: Grove Press, 1986). Originally published as *La maladie de la morte* (Paris: Les Editions de Minuit, 1982).

59. Ibid., p. 54.

60. I am borrowing the phrase "unavowable community" from Blanchot's extraordinary work of the same title; see Maurice Blanchot, *The Unavowable Community,* trans. Pierre Joris (New York: Station Hill Press, 1983). Originally published as *La Communauté inavouable* (Paris: Les Editions de Minuit, 1983).

61. Luce Irigaray, *This Sex Which Is Not One,* trans. Catherine Porter (Ithaca: Cornell University Press, 1985). Cf. Hélène Cixous and Catherine Clément, *The Newly Born Woman,* trans. Betsy Wing (Minneapolis: University of Minnesota Press, 1986). Originally published as *La Jeune Née* (Paris: Union Générale d'Editions, 1975).

62. Hélène Cixous, "Sorties," in *The Newly Born Woman,* p. 93.

63. See generally Montrelay, "Inquiry into Femininity."

64. I am using intimacy in the sense Bataille gives to the word. Intimacy is the fluid relationship between the self and the world that Bataille envisions as "water on water." In intimacy we experience the profound immanence of all that is, the soulful mingling of self and others. Intimacy cannot be expressed discursively. To quote Bataille:

> The swelling to the breaking point, the malice that breaks out with clenched teeth and weeps; the sinking feeling that doesn't know where it comes from or what it's about; the fear that sings its head off in the dark, the white-eyed pillar, the sweet sadness, the rage and the vomiting . . . are so many evasions. What is intimate, in the strong sense, is what has the passage of an absence of individuality, the unperceptable sorority of a river, the empty limpidity of the sky. . . .

Georges Bataille, *Theory of Religion*, trans. Robert Hurley (New York: Zone Books, 1989), p. 50. Originally published as *Théorie de la religion* (Paris: Editions Gallimard, 1973).

65. Catharine A. MacKinnon, *Feminism Unmodified: Discourses on Life and Law* (Cambridge: Harvard University Press, 1987), pp. 38–39.

66. West, "Women's Hedonic Lives," p. 127 (footnotes omitted).

67. See, generally, Jean-François Lyotard, *The Differend: Phrases in Dispute*, trans. George Van Den Abbeele (Minneapolis: University of Minnesota Press, 1988). Originally published as *Le Différend* (Paris: Les Editions de Minuit, 1983).

> A differend, I say, and not a litigation. It is not that humans are mean, or that their interests or passions are antagonistic. On the same score as what is not human (animals, plants, gods, God and the angels, extraterrestrials, seasons, tides, rain and fair weather, plague and fire), they are situated in heterogeneous phrase regimens and are taken hold of by stakes tied to heterogeneous genres of discourse. The judgment which is passed over the nature of their social being can come into being only in accordance with one of these regimens, or at least in accordance with one of these genres of discourse. The tribunal thereby makes this regimen and/or this genre prevail over the others. By transcribing the heterogeneity of phrases, which is at play in the social and the commentary on the social, the tribunal also necessarily wrongs the other regimens and/or genres.

Lyotard, *The Differend*, p. 140.

68. Ibid., p. 13.

69. I put the word "discover" in quotation marks because once we understand the metaphorical dimension of feminine reality we can no longer completely separate discovery and invention. Our reality is in the process of being created in our very effort to "discover" its meaning for us. This point about feminine reality should be understood within the context of a shifting understanding of the nature of reality itself, once we understand that what "is" comes to us wrapped in language.

70. Lyotard, *The Differend*, p. 9.

71. Susan Estrich, *Real Rape* (Cambridge, Mass.: Harvard University Press, 1987), pp. 29–41.

72. Ibid., pp. 100–103.

73. As Karen Barrett explained in an article designed to increase women's awareness of the phenomenon of date rape, there is a "pervasive . . . notion of female responsibility in the face of boys-will-be-boys reality. A young man explains, 'It's like driving—a woman has to use her rear-view mirror, get out of the fast last if someone's coming up behind her. Otherwise, she's going to get into trouble.' " Karen Barrett, "Date Rape—A Campus Epidemic?" *Ms.*, Sept. 1982, pp. 48, 50. Barrett warned against the "temptation to see college-boy mashers merely as victims of horny adolescent confusion" (p. 130). Instead, she urged young women to realize that acquaintance rape is as serious, and often as premeditated and violent as other kinds of rape.

74. Regina Austin, "The Black Woman, Sisterhood, and the Difference/Deviance Divide," *New England Law Review,* vol. 26, no. 3 (Spring 1992), p. 877.

75. See, generally, Lacan, *Ecrits,* and Freud.

76. Ibid.

77. Jacques Derrida, *Glas,* trans. John P. Leavey, Jr. and Richard Rand (Lincoln: University of Nebraska Press, 1986). Originally published as *Glas* (Paris: Editions Galilée, 1974).

78. Jacques Derrida, *The Post Card: From Socrates to Freud and Beyond,* trans. Alan Bass (Chicago: University of Chicago Press, 1987). Originally published as *La Carte postale* (Paris: Flammarion, 1980).

79. Jacques Derrida, *Spurs: Nietzsche's Styles/Éperons: Les Styles de Nietzsche,* trans. Barbara Harlow (Chicago: University of Chicago Press, 1978).

80. Jacques Derrida and Christie V. McDonald, "Choreographies," *Diacritics,* vol. 12 (Summer 1982), reprinted in *The Ear of the Other: Otobiography, Transference, Translation,* ed. Christie V. McDonald, trans. Peggy Kamuf (Lincoln: University of Nebraska Press, 1985). Originally published as *L'Oreille de l'autre* (Montreal: V1B Editeur, 1982).

81. Derrida, *The Post Card,* pp. 441–42.

82. Derrida is primarily concerned here with Lacan's "Seminar" on *The Purloined Letter.* Alan Bass explains in his notes to *The Post Card* (see p. 421, notes 5 and 6) that the "Seminar" appears at the beginning of Lacan's *Ecrits.* As Derrida himself explains, the "Seminar" is concerned with *The Purloined Letter* as an example of the so-called fantastic literature which mobilizes and overflows *Das Unheimliche* (*The Post Card,* pp. 420–21).

83. Derrida, *The Post Card,* p. 426.

84. Jacques Derrida, "Deconstruction in America" (interview with James Creech, Peggy Kamuf, and Jane Todd), *Critical Exchange,* vol. 17 (1985), pp. 15–16.

85. Derrida, "Choreographies," p. 167.

86. Ibid., p. 169.

87. Derrida, *Spurs,* p. 59.

88. Ibid., p. 55.

89. Derrida, "Choreographies," pp. 170–71.

90. Ibid., pp. 174–75.

91. Ibid., p. 169.

92. Derrida, *Spurs*, p. 61.

93. Jane Gallop points out that "Lacan's contribution to Freudian theory of sexual difference is to articulate the castration complex around the phallus. . . . The phallus symbolizing unmediated, full *jouissance* must be lacking for any subject to enter . . . language. . . ." See Gallop, *The Daughter's Seduction*, pp. 95–96.

94. For a more detailed explanation of the Lacanian framework, see Cornell and Thurschwell, "Feminism, Negativity, Intersubjectivity," p. 145, note 2.

95. Derrida, *Glas*, p. 229.

96. Derrida, *Spurs*, p. 109.

97. Ibid., pp. 59–61.

98. Ibid., p. 61.

99. Derrida, "Choreographies," p. 183 (note omitted).

100. Ibid., pp. 181–82.

101. Ibid., p. 178.

102. Ibid., p. 175.

103. Ibid.

104. See, generally, James Joyce, *Finnegans Wake*.

105. See, generally, MacKinnon, *Feminism Unmodified*.

106. Ibid., p. 59 (emphasis added).

107. Ibid., p. 54 (emphasis in original).

108. Christa Wolf, *Cassandra: A Novel and Four Essays*, trans. Jan Van Heurck (New York: Farrar, Straus and Giroux, 1984).

109. "Anna Stessa Rising" is one of the titles of the Mamafesta in *Finnegans Wake*.

110. Andrea Dworkin, *Intercourse* (New York: The Free Press, 1987).

111. MacKinnon, *Feminism Unmodified*, p. 45.

112. Derrida, "Choreographies," p. 184.

113. In MacKinnon's view, which she elaborates upon in her writings, the world is divided into two groups: the "fuckors" and the "fuckees." Needless to say, MacKinnon considers women to constitute the latter group.

114. MacKinnon, *Feminism Unmodified*, p. 54.

115. See Bataille, *Theory of Religion*, pp. 50–52.

116. Ibid.

117. Ibid., p. 61.

118. Ibid.

119. *Jouissance* is feminine pleasure. The meaning, however, is not a simple one. See, generally, Irigaray, *This Sex Which Is Not One*, and Cixous, "Sorties," in Cixous and Clément, *The Newly Born Woman*.

120. Elizabeth Bishop's entire poem reads as follows:

> One Art
> The art of losing isn't hard to master;
> so many things seem filled with the intent
> to be lost that their loss is no disaster.
>
> Lose something every day. Accept the fluster
> of lost door keys, the hour badly spent.
> The art of losing isn't hard to master.
>
> Then practice losing farther, losing faster:
> places, and names, and where it was you meant
> to travel. None of these will bring disaster.
>
> I lost my mother's watch. And look! my last, or
> next-to-last, of three loved houses went.
> The art of losing isn't hard to master.
>
> I lost two cities, lovely ones. And, vaster,
> some realms I owned, two rivers, a continent.
> I miss them, but it wasn't a disaster.
>
> —Even losing you (the joking voice, a gesture
> I love) I shan't have lied. It's evident
> the art of losing's not too hard to master
> though it may look like (*Write* it!) like disaster.

Elizabeth Bishop, "One Art," in *The Complete Poems, 1927–1979* (New York: Farrar, Straus and Giroux, 1983), p. 178.

121. MacKinnon, *Feminism Unmodified*, p. 39 (note omitted).

122. Ibid., pp. 97–98.

123. Hélène Cixous, "Tancredi continues," in *Writing Differences: Readings from the Seminar of Hélène Cixous*, ed. Susan Sellers (New York: St. Martin's Press, 1988), p. 52.

124. Irigaray, *This Sex Which Is Not One*, p. 33.

125. Ibid., p. 213.

126. Ibid., p. 215.

127. MacKinnon, *Feminism Unmodified*, pp. 198–205.

128. Ibid., p. 77.

129. For an excellent discussion of the role of the collaborator against the feminist movement, see Susan Faludi, *Backlash: The Undeclared War against American Women* (New York: Crown Publishers, 1991).

130. Joyce, *Finnegans Wake*.

131. MacKinnon, *Feminism Unmodified*, pp. 1–17.

132. Roland Barthes, *Mythologies*, trans. Annette Lavers (New York: Noonday Press, 1972), p. 129.

133. Ibid., p. 135.

134. See, generally, Kristeva, "Women's Time." Cf. Julia Kristeva, *Powers of Horror* (New York: Columbia University Press, 1982).

135. See, generally, Bataille, *Theory of Religion.*

136. Hans Blumenburg, *Work on Myth,* trans. Robert M. Wallace (Cambridge, Mass.: The MIT Press, 1985), p. 2. Originally published as *Arbeit am Mythos* (Frankfurt am Main, FRG: Suhrkamp Verlag, 1979).

137. See, e.g., Cixous and Clément, *The Newly Born Woman.*

138. See generally, Lacan, *Ecrits.*

139. Carol J. Gilligan, "Feminist Discourse, Moral Values, and the Law—A Conversation," *Buffalo Law Review,* vol. 34 (1984) (transcript of discussion between Ellen C. DuBois, Mary C. Dunlap, Carol J. Gilligan, Catherine A. MacKinnon, and Carrie J. Menkel-Meadow held 19 October 1984 at the Law School of S.U.N.Y. Buffalo as part of the James McCormick Mitchell Lecture Series).

140. See, generally, Wolf, *Cassandra.*

141. Ibid., p. 157.

142. Gilligan, "Feminist Discourse," pp. 73–75. See also MacKinnon, *Feminism Unmodified,* pp. 38–39.

143. See, generally, Carol Gilligan, *In a Different Voice: Psychological Theory and Women's Development* (Cambridge, Mass.: Harvard University Press, 1982).

144. Ibid., p. 30.

145. Gilligan, "Feminist Discourse," p. 74.

146. Ibid.

5 Sexual Difference, The Feminine, and Equivalency

1. Catharine A. MacKinnon, *Toward a Feminist Theory of the State* (Cambridge, Mass.: Harvard University Press, 1989). Hereinafter *Feminist Theory.*

2. See Catharine A. MacKinnon, *Sexual Harassment and the Working Woman: A Case of Working Women* (New Haven: Yale University Press, 1979), hereinafter *Sexual Harassment;* see also Meritor Savings Bank, FSB v. Vinson, 477 U.S. 57 (1986) (argued by Catharine MacKinnon).

3. Other writers have voiced similar concerns and have noted the way in which MacKinnon not only disparages women's sexuality but also how she portrays it in such a way as to increase the very problem of sexual abuse that she so desperately seeks to correct. See, e.g., Jeanne Schroeder, "Feminism Historicized: Medieval Misogynist Stereotypes in Contemporary Feminist Jurisprudence," *Iowa Law Review,* vol. 75 (1990), p. 1135. Cf. Jeanne Schroeder, "Abduction from the Seraglio: Feminist Methodologies and the Logic of Imagination," *Texas Law Review* (1991).

4. I first developed this concept of equivalent rights in "Sex Discrimination Law and Equivalent Rights," published in *Dissent,* vol. ___ and as "Gender, Sex and Equivalent Rights," in *Feminists Theorize the Political,* ed. Judith Butler and Joan W. Scott (New York: Routledge, Chapman and Hall, 1991).

5. While affirmative action is inadequate to address the inequalities that a program

of equivalent rights, as I will argue, can remedy, it nevertheless remains an important means to address broad notions of inequality. For a comprehensive discussion of affirmative-action programs as they relate to women's issues, see Michel Rosenfeld, *Affirmative Action and Justice* (New Haven: Yale University Press, 1991), pp. 197–204.

6. Catharine A. MacKinnon, *Feminism Unmodified: Discourses on Life and Law* (Cambridge, Mass.: Harvard University Press, 1987), chapters 5 and 6, p. 127, n. 2. Hereinafter *Feminism Unmodified*.

7. The term *feminine* is normally used in a pejorative sense in feminist circles to refer to societally constructed notions of the ideal woman. Here, I use it to indicate the feminine imaginary irreducible to any conception or empirical designation of the characteristics of actual women. In this sense, the feminine is separated from both sociological knowledge of women as objects of study and from conventional, popular notions of what the "feminine woman" should be.

8. Because MacKinnon conflates sex, sexuality, and gender identity, she can speak of a simple division between men and women and the masculine and the feminine in a way that I do not accept. Because this conflation is an impossibility for me, I would not speak so simply of the "us" and the "them" as MacKinnon does. This does not mean that I deny the specificity of feminine sexual difference—far from it. But I do argue against the us/them dichotomy as a material unshakable reality. See, generally, Drucilla Cornell, *Beyond Accommodation: Ethical Feminism, Deconstruction, and the Law* (New York: Routledge, Chapman and Hall, 1991). Cf. Drucilla Cornell and Adam Thurschwell, "Feminism, Negativity, Intersubjectivity," in *Feminism as Critique: On the Politics of Gender*, ed. Seyla Benhabib and Drucilla Cornell (Minneapolis: University of Minnesota Press, 1987), p. 143.

9. For an analysis of sexual shame in women, see Eleanor Galenson and Herman Roiphe, "The Impact of Early Sexual Discovery on Mood, Defensive Organization, and Symbolization," *The Psychoanalytic Study of the Child*, vol. 26 (1972), p. 195.

10. See chapter 3, "Disastrologies."

11. Luce Irigaray, *Speculum of the Other Woman*, trans. Gillian Gill (Ithaca: Cornell University Press, 1985), pp. 11–129.

12. Amartya Sen, "Inequality Reexamined: Capability and Well-Being," paper delivered at the Conference on the Quality of Life, organized by the World Institute of Economics Research (Wider) and held at Helsinki Finland, July 1988 (on file with author), pp. 5–6.

13. Ibid., p. 5.

14. *Feminist Theory*, p. 127.

15. Ibid., p. 128.

16. Ibid.

17. Ibid., p. 129.

18. Ibid., p. 111 (citations omitted).

19. Ibid., p. 129.

20. MacKinnon, *Feminism Unmodified*, pp. 127, 129.

21. "Congress shall make no law . . . abridging the freedom of speech. . . ." U.S. Const. Amend. I.

22. MacKinnon, *Feminist Theory*, p. 138 (note omitted).

23. Ibid., pp. 161–62 (note omitted).

24. Ibid., p. 115.

25. MacKinnon first developed this Marxist critique in a two-part essay published as Catharine A. MacKinnon, "Feminism, Marxism, Method, and the State: An Agenda for Theory," *Signs*, vol. 7 (1982), and Catharine A. MacKinnon, "Feminism, Marxism, Method, and the State: Toward Feminist Jurisprudence," *Signs*, vol. 8 (1983), p. 635.

26. MacKinnon, *Feminist Theory*, p. 162 (note omitted).

27. Ibid., p. 163.

28. Ibid., p. 219.

29. Ibid., p. 249.

30. 488 U.S. 905 (1988).

31. MacKinnon, *Feminist Theory*, p. 164.

32. Ibid., p. 164.

33. Ibid., pp. 164–65.

34. MacKinnon, *Feminist Unmodified*, p. 219.

35. See, generally, Bruce Ackerman, *Social Justice in the Liberal State* (New Haven: Yale University Press, 1980); Ronald Dworkin, *Law's Empire* (Cambridge, Mass.: The Belknap Press of Harvard University Press, 1986); Thomas Nagel, *Partiality and Equality* (Princeton: Princeton University Press, 1991); John Rawls, *A Theory of Justice* (Cambridge, Mass.: Belknap Press, 1971); Steven Shiffrin, *The First Amendment, Democracy, and Romance* (Cambridge, Mass.: Harvard University Press, 1990); C. Edwin Baker, "Neutrality, Process, and Rationality: Flawed Interpretations of Equal Protection," *Texas Law Review*, vol. 58 (1980), p. 1029; Sylvia Law, "Rethinking Sex and the Constitution," *University of Pennsylvania Law Review*, vol. 132 (1984), p. 955; Wendy Williams, "Equality's Riddle: Pregnancy and the Equal Treatment-Special Treatment Debate," *New York University Law Review*, vol. 14 (1985), p. 325.

36. See Robert Bork, "Neutral Principles and Some First Amendment Problems," *Indiana Law Journal*, vol. 47 (1971), p. 1; Herbert Wechsler, "Toward Neutral Principles of Constitutional Law," *Harvard Law Review*, vol 73 (1959), p. 1.

37. Rae Langton, "Whose Right? Ronald Dworkin, Women, and Pornographers," *Philosophy and Public Affairs*, vol. 19 (1990), p. 311.

38. Ronald Dworkin, *A Master of Principle* (Cambridge, Mass.: Harvard University Press, 1985).

39. Nagel argues that

    the argument for a liberal solution, which gives the second answer, has to depend on the judgment that it is terrible to have one's desired form of sexual expression restricted by others who find it repellent, as part of their own strong sexual feelings. The suppression of homosexuality is so much worse for the homosexual than is the relaxation of ambient taboos and restrictions for the sexual puritan, that even the puritan should decide in favor of freedom unless he is prepared to claim that no legitimate state need consider the potential objections of homosexuals because homosexuality is wicked and worthy of suppression for its own sake. This, however, is not a position that no one could reasonably reject, and the puritan is simply mistaken if he thinks it is.

Thomas Nagel, *Partiality and Equality* (Princeton: Princeton University Press, 1991), p. 200.

40. In the case of the homosexual, Nagel argues that [t]he freedom to act on these desires is therefore a leading candidate for protection as a right." Ibid., pp. 200–01. On the other hand, in the case of pornography, he states, "This does not exclude prohibitions against acute and direct offense to the equally deep sensibilities of others; but it does mean that personal and private activities (including the consumption of pornography) should be protected from political control." Ibid., p. 201.

41. Cass Sunstein, *Neutrality and Constitutionality with Special Reference to Pornography, Abortion, and Surrogacy* (1991) (unpublished manuscript on file with author).

42. Ibid., p. 22–23 (notes omitted).

43. As Luce Irigaray puts it,

> How can the double demand—for both equality and difference—be articulated? Certainly not by acceptance of a choice between "class struggle" and "sexual warfare," an alternative that aims once again to minimize the question of the exploitation of women through a definition of power of the masculine type. More precisely, it implies putting off to an indefinite later date a women's "politics," a politics that would be modeled rather too simplistically on men's struggles.

Luce Irigaray, *This Sex Which Is Not One*, trans. Catherine Porter (Ithaca: Cornell University Press, 1985), pp. 81–82. Originally published as *Ce sexe qui n'est pas un* (Paris: Les Éditions de Minuit, 1977).

44. See Richard Rorty, *Philosophy and the Mirror of Nature* (Princeton: Princeton University Press, 1979), pp. 357–94.

45. Judith Butler, *Gender Trouble: Feminism and the Subversion of Identity* (New York: Routledge, Chapman and Hall, 1990).

46. This basic Hegelian insight has been the basis of what are now called either pragmatic or postmodern critiques of scientism. See Georg W. F. Hegel, *Phenomenology of Mind*, trans. J. Baillie (New York: MacMillan, 1931), pp. 147–213.

47. Ernesto Laclau and Chautal Mouffe, "Hegemony and Socialist Strategy" (London: Verso, 1985), p. 108.

48. See, e.g., Jean-François Lyotard, *The Differend: Phrases in Dispute*, trans. George Van Den Abbeele (Minneapolis: University of Minnesota Press, 1988). Originally published as *Le Différend* (Paris: Les Editions de Minuit (1983).

49. See, e.g., Karen Barrett, "Date Rape—A Campus Epidemic?" *Ms.*, Sept. 1982, pp. 48, 50.

50. MacKinnon explains that "[a]lmost half of all women . . . are raped or victims of attempted rape at least once in their lives. Almost 40 percent are victims of sexual abuse in childhood" (*Feminist Theory*, p. 176).

51. Ibid., p. 219.

52. Ibid., pp. 113–14 (note omitted).

53. Audre Lorde, *Sister Outsider* (Trumansburg, N.Y.: The Crossing Press, 1984), p. 116.

54. **bell hooks,** *Yearning: race, gender, and cultural politics* (Boston: South End Press, 1990), p. 57.

55. Ibid., p. 58.

56. Cornell, "The Feminist Alliance with Deconstruction," in *Beyond Accommodation.*

57. Jacques Derrida has demonstrated that, as the repressed Other, the feminine is irreducible to that which it supposedly is designated to be, the lack that signifies woman within the Symbolic. This irreducibility of the feminine also results from what Derrida calls the "logic of parergonality," by which he argues that the very frame that designates social reality always implies "more" because our reality is necessarily enframed. See Jacques Derrida, *The Truth in Painting*, trans. Geoffrey Bennington and Ian McLeod (Chicago: University of Chicago Press, 1987).

58. MacKinnon, *Feminist Theory*, p. 129.

59. Drucilla Cornell, "What Is Postmodernity Anyway? in *The Philosophy of the Limit* (New York: Routledge, Chapman and Hall, 1992).

60. See Cornell, *Beyond Accommodation.*

61. Ricoeur argues that we must treat the verb "to be" as a metaphor itself and recognize in "being as" the correlate of "seeing as." Paul Ricoeur, *Time and Narrative*, vol. 3 (1984), p. 155.

62. Derrida suspects that through Woman's remetaphorization we will once again capture women in a new concept, one in which the very process of metaphorization will itself be erased. See generally Jacques Derrida and Christie V. McDonald, "Choreographies," *Diacritics,* vol. 12 (Summer 1982), reprinted in *The Ear of the Other: Otobiography, Transference, Translation,* ed. Christie V. McDonald, trans. Peggy Kamuf (Lincoln: University of Nebraska Press, 1985). Originally published as *L'Oreille de l'autre* (Montreal: V1B Editeur, 1982).

63. *Jouissance* is a term which, as used by Lacan, lacks direct translation. In contemporary philosophical and psychoanalytic discourse, it is often taken to refer to women's specifically feminine, total sexual pleasure. For a more detailed and nuanced explication of this aspect, see Hélène Cixous and Catherine Clément, *The Newly Born Woman,* trans. Betsy Wing (Minneapolis: University of Minnesota Press, 1986), pp. 88–89. Originally published as *La jeune née* (Paris: Union Générale d'Éditions, 1975).

64. See MacKinnon, *Feminism Unmodified,* pp. 60–61.

65. In "The Herethics of Carnality," in Cornell, *Beyond Accommodation,* I present a

comprehensive treatment of these authors and their efforts to write of feminine desire and pleasure differently, in a way that refuses to repudiate the feminine while it insists on believing in the woman writer and, thus, in woman's new beginning.

66. MacKinnon, *Feminist Theory*, pp. 153–54 (quoting Ti-Grace Atkinson, "Why I'm against S/M Liberation," in *Against Sadomasochism: A Radical Feminist Analysis*, ed. E. Linden, D. Pagano, D. Russel, and S. Star (Palo Alto, California: Frog in the Well, 1982), p. 91).

67. See, generally, R. Schott, *Cognition and Eros: A Critique of the Kantian Paradigm* (1988).

68. I am indebted to A. Collin Biddle for suggesting the word "desolation" which, to my mind, so effectively describes women's experience of having to make this kind of "choice" about their "sex" and sexuality.

69. Luce Irigaray offers us a beautiful and poetic description of this kissing:

> Kiss me. Two lips kissing two lips: openness is ours again. Our "world." And the passage from the inside out, from the outside in, the passage between us, is limitless. Without end. No knot or loop, no mouth ever stops our exchanges. Between us the house has no wall, the clearing no enclosure, language no circularity. When you kiss me, the world grows so large that the horizon itself disappears. Are we unsatisfied? Yes, if that means we are never finished. If our pleasure consists in moving, being moved, endlessly. Always in motion: openness is never spent nor sated.

Irigaray, *This Sex Which Is Not One*, p. 210.

70. Ibid., p. 213.

71. Monique Wittig, *The Lesbian Body*, trans. David Le Vay (Boston: Beacon Press, 1975). Originally published as *Le Corps Lesbien* (Paris: Les Editions de Minuit, 1973).

72. See, generally, Andrea Dworkin, *Intercourse* (New York: The Free Press, 1987).

73. Irigaray, *This Sex Which Is Not One*, p. 88 (quoting Jacques Lacan, *Encore, Le Séminaire XX* (Paris: Éditions du Seuil, 1975)).

74. For insight into Lacan's basic theories of feminine sexuality, see, generally, Jacques Lacan, *Feminine Sexuality: Jacques Lacan and the école freudienne*, ed. Juliet Mitchell and Jacqueline Rose, trans. Jacqueline Rose (New York: W. W. Norton and Company, 1985) (questioning any certainty or authority in conceptions of psychic and sexual life). For a detailed explanation of the Lacanian framework, see Cornell and Thurschwell, "Feminism, Negativity, Intersubjectivity," pp. 145–46. For Derrida's intervention into Lacan's psychoanalytic theories, see, generally, Derrida, *The Ear of the Other*.

75. See, e.g., Galenson and Roiphe.

76. Graciela Abelin-Sas has convincingly argued that the fear that a woman will be "found out" is connected to the definition of Woman as not having the phallus. The phallus is projected out as the property of the Other to whom she must bow down due to her own inadequacy. Any claim that she too has "it" is feared because of the retaliation it will bring down on her head, which is why Abelin-Sas entitles

her paper " 'Headless Woman': Scheherazade's Sorrows" (unpublished manuscript on file with author). The complex I just described Abelin-Sas has named as the Scheherazade Syndrome. For Abelin-Sas, the only solution is to deconstruct the penis-phallus conflation and to resignify the phallus.

77. Samuel Beckett, *Happy Days* (New York: Grove Press, 1961), p. 60 (emphasis in original; stage directions omitted).

78. For a more thorough examination of the concept of innovative capability, see chapter 3, "Disastrologies."

79. MacKinnon, p. 138 (note omitted).

80. For examples of the refiguration and remetaphorization of feminine figures, see, generally, Hélène Cixous and Catherine Clément, *The Newly Born Woman;* Irigaray, *This Sex Which Is Not One* (developing the concept of "writing" the feminine body); Julia Kristeva, *The Kristeva Reader,* ed. Toril Moi (New York: Columbia University Press, 1986). For my analysis, see Cornell, "Feminine Writing, Metaphor and Myth," in *Beyond Accommodation.*

81. MacKinnon, *Feminist Theory,* pp. 215–34.

82. Irigaray, *How to Define Sexuate Rights?* (date unknown) (unpublished manuscript on file with author).

83. See Cornell, *Beyond Accommodation.*

84. Louise Kaplan has brilliantly argued that pornography reflects the infantile view of rigid gender identity. Pornography for Kaplan is always in the service of the perverse strategy which attempts to live out the infantile conception of gender as truth. See generally Louise Kaplan, *Female Perversions* (New York: Anchor Books, Doubleday, 1991), pp. 321–61.

85. 109 S. Ct. 3040 (1989).

86. Blackmun stated: "I fear for the future. I fear for the liberty and equality of millions of women who have lived and come of age in the 16 years since *Roe* was decided. I fear for the integrity of, and public esteem for, this Court. I dissent." Ibid. at 3067 (Blackmun, J., dissenting). See also Cruzan v. Director, Mo. Dep't of Health, 110 S. Ct. 2841, 2851 (1990) (affirming constitutionally protected liberty interest in refusing unwanted medical treatment).

87. Torborg Nedreaas, *Nothing Grows by Moonlight,* trans. Bibbi Lee (Lincoln: University of Nebraska Press, 1987), pp. 189–90. Originally published as *Av Maneskinn Gror Det Ingenting* (1947; W. Nyaard: H. Aschehoug and Co., 1975).

88. Graciela Abellin-Sas, "To Mother or Not to Mother: Abortion and Its Challenges" (1992) (unpublished manuscript on file with author).

89. Ibid.

6 Sex-Discrimination Law and Equivalent Rights

1. I say "conventionally interpreted," because there are dissident circuits and judges who not only do not make this mistake, but who also strive to expose the dangers inherent in the imposition of these kinds of stereotypes in the area of sex-discrimination law.

2. 42 U.S.C.A. Sections 2000e–2000e–17. Title VII prohibits the use of discriminatory employment practices on the part of an employer. The statute states, in relevant part, that:

> (a) It shall be an unlawful employment practice for an employer—
> (1) to fail or refuse to hire or to discharge any individual, or otherwise to discriminate against any individual with respect to his compensation, terms, conditions, or privileges of employment, because of such individual's race, color, religion, sex, or national origin; or
>
> (2) to limit, segregate, or classify his employees or applicants for employment in any way which would deprive or tend to deprive any individual of employment opportunities or otherwise adversely affect his status as an employee, because of such individual's race, color, religion, sex, or national origin.

   42 U.S.C.A. Section 2000e–2.

3. It should be noted that this question is crucial not only in cases of sex discrimination, but also in the area of reproductive rights, whether it be a matter of pregnancy leave or the right of abortion.

4. *Bowers v. Hardwick*, 478 U.S. 186 (1986).

5. *Griswold v. Connecticut*, 381 U.S. 479 (1965).

6. *Roe v. Wade*, 410 U.S. 113 (1973).

7. *Carey v. Population Services International*, 431 U.S. 678 (1977).

8. *Bowers v. Hardwick*, 478 U.S. 186 (1986), pp. 190–91.

9. Ibid., p. 189. The Ninth Amendment reads: "The enumeration in the Constitution, of certain rights, shall not be construed to deny or disparage others retained by the people." U.S. Const. Amend. IX.

   The Due Process Clause of the Fourteenth Amendment provides that "[n]o State shall make or enforce any law which shall abridge the privileges or immunities of citizens of the United States; nor shall any State deprive any person of life, liberty, or property, without due process of law." U.S. Const. Amend. XIV, cl. 1.

10. *Bowers v. Hardwick*, 478 U.S. 186 (1986), pp. 190–91.

11. See ibid., p. 199 (Blackmun, J., dissenting).

12. See ibid. Blackmun reminds us that "[i]t is revolting to have no better reason for a rule of law than that so it was laid down in the time of Henry IV. It is still more revolting if the grounds upon which it was laid down have vanished long since, and the rule simply persists from blind imitation of the past." (quoting Oliver W. Holmes, "The Path of the Law," *Harvard Law Review*, vol. 10 (1897), p. 469).

13. See, generally, Jacques Lacan, *Feminine Sexuality: Jacques Lacan and the école freudienne*, ed. Juliet Mitchell and Jacqueline Rose, trans. Jacqueline Rose (New York: W. W. Norton and Company, 1985). For insight into Lacan's basic theories, see Jacques Lacan, *Ecrits: A Selection*, trans. Alan Sheridan (New York: W. W. Norton and Company, 1977). Originally published as *Ecrits* (Paris: Editions du Seuil, 1966). In addition, for a detailed explanation of the Lacanian framework, see Drucilla Cornell and Adam Thurschwell, "Feminism, Negativity, Intersubjectivity," in *Feminism as Critique: On the Politics of Gender*, ed. Seyla Benhabib and

Drucilla Cornell (Minneapolis: University of Minnesota Press, 1987), pp. 144–145, note 2.

For Derrida's intervention into Lacan's psychoanalytic theories, see, generally, Jacques Derrida and Christie V. McDonald, "Choreographies," *Diacritics,* vol. 12 (Summer 1982), reprinted in *The Ear of the Other: Otobiography, Transference, Translation,* ed. Christie V. McDonald, trans. Peggy Kamuf (Lincoln: University of Nebraska Press, 1985). Originally published as *L'oreille de l'autre* (Montreal: V1B Editeur, 1982), Jacques Derrida, *Spurs: Nietzsche's Style/Éperons: Les Styles de Nietzsche,* trans. Barbara Harlow (Chicago: University of Chicago Press, 1978).

14. Throughout his work, Lacan uses the term *significance* to refer to that "movement in language against, or away from, the positions of coherence which language simultaneously constructs." Jacqueline Rose, "Introduction II," in *Feminine Sexuality,* pp. 51–52. As Jacqueline Rose goes on to explain, "[t]he concept of *jouissance* (what escapes in sexuality) and the concept of *significance* (what shifts in language) are inseparable" (p. 52).

15. This was the project of some earlier feminist Freudians and post-Freudians who wanted to salvage the truth of femininity so as to understand our unique identity.

16. In a recent article in *Dissent,* Seyla Benhabib argued that the alliance between feminism and so-called postmodern philosophy is, at best, uneasy. Her worry— and it is a worry frequently articulated in feminist political critiques of deconstruction and postmodern philosophy more generally—is that Jacques Derrida's deconstruction of gender identity reinstates the patriarchal view of Woman as the mysterious Other, without a knowable essence, substance, or identity. Feminists, on the other hand, have militantly rejected the so-called nonidentity of Woman as one more mystification that justifies the subordination of actual women. Derrida is accused of the restoration of feminine stereotypes through his very deconstruction of gender identity and, more particularly, of a graspable female identity which could provide us with a basis for a specifically feminist politics. Ultimately, however, this reading misunderstands the ethical and political significance of Derrida's deconstruction of the structures of gender identity.

17. Wilhelm Reich, *Reich Speaks of Freud: Conversations with Kurt Eissler,* ed. Mary Higgins and C. M. Raphael (New York: Farrar, Straus and Giroux, 1967), pp. 42–43.

18. It should be noted that this purpose is consistent with Title VII's intervention into a world of rigid race and sex stereotypes.

19. The term "mommy track" refers to an arrangement whereby women who need a flexible schedule to meet the needs of their families are given the "opportunity" to work part-time. Unfortunately, in terms of career goals, this accommodation serves only to relegate these women to positions where they have no hope of reaching senior management positions or achieving partnership. Some women have taken the position that corporations ought to recognize two different groups of women managers: those who put career first and those who need a flexible schedule for personal reasons. See, e.g., Felice Schwartz, "Management Women and the New Facts of Life," *Harvard Business Review,* January–February 1989, p. 65. Others take a stronger stance, demanding equal pay and an equal sense of entitlement for women. See, e.g., Judy Mann, "The Demeaning 'Mommy Track': Separate and Unequal," *Washington Post,* 15 March 1989, p. C3. See also Jennifer A. Kingson,

"Women in the Law Say Path Is Limited by 'Mommy Track,'" *New York Times,* 8 August 1988, p. A1 (discussing how, in the legal profession in particular, even though the "mommy track" allows for flexible working hours, child care, and lenient maternity leave, it nevertheless fosters unequal standards when it comes to decisions regarding partnership, choice assignments, and stature).

20. The economist Amartya Sen is the leading proponent of the concept of the vision of equality referred to in the economics literature as the equality of welfare. See, e.g., Amartya Sen, *Resources, Values and Development* (Cambridge, Mass.: Harvard University Press, 1984); Amartya Sen, *Choice, Welfare and Measurement* (Cambridge, Mass.: The MIT Press, 1982).

21. Amartya Sen, "Inequality Reexamined: Capability and Well-being," a paper delivered at Conference on the Quality of Life, organized by the World Institute of Development Economics Research (WIDER) and held at Helsinki, Finland, July 1988, p. 5.

7 Gender Hierarchy, Equality, and the Possibility of Democracy

1. Hannah Arendt, *The Human Condition* (Chicago and London: University of Chicago Press, 1958), pp. 194–95.

2. Ibid., pp. 197–98.

3. Ibid., p. 198.

4. See, generally, Andrew Arato and Jean Cohen, *Civil Society and Political Theory,* ed. Thomas McCarthy (Boston: Institute of Technology Press, 1992).

5. Aristotle, *Politics,* 1328b35.

6. See Jacques Derrida, "The Politics of Friendship," *Journal of Philosophy,* vol. 80, no. 2 (1988), pp. 632–45.

7. Ibid.

8. Arendt, *The Human Condition,* pp. 205–6.

9. Hannah Arendt, "What Is Authority?" in *Between Past and Future: Eight Exercises in Political Thought* (New York: Penguin Books, 1977), p. 117.

10. Ibid., pp. 117–118.

11. Ibid., p. 116.

12. Ibid., p. 117.

13. Arendt, *The Human Condition,* p. 33.

14. Jacques Derrida, *Spurs: Nietzsche's Styles/Éperons: Les Styles de Nietzsche,* trans. Barbara Harlow (Chicago: University of Chicago Press, 1978).

15. Jacques Derrida, *Glas,* trans. John P. Leavey, Jr. and Richard Rand (Lincoln: University of Nebraska Press, 1986). Originally published as *Glas* (Paris: Editions Galilée, 1974).

16. Derrida, *Spurs: Nietzsche's Styles/Éperons: Les Styles de Nietzsche,* p. 61.

17. Arendt, *The Human Condition,* p. 194.

18. Idib., p. 237.

19. Thomas McCarthy, "The Politics of the Ineffable: Derrida's Deconstructionism," *Philosophical Forum,* vol. 21 (Fall–Winter 1989–90).

20. The mechanism here is apparently similar to the one proposed by Freud as the heart of fetishism: an incapacity to bear the significance of a creature without a male genital and a concomitant conviction that, regardless of appearances, it is still, and always really there.

21. See, e.g., Jacques Derrida and Christie V. McDonald, "Choreographies," *Diacritics,* vol. 12 (Summer 1982), reprinted in *The Ear of the Other: Otobiography, Transference, Translation,* ed. Christie V. McDonald, trans. Peggy Kamuf (Lincoln: University of Nebraska Press, 1985). Originally published as *L'Oreille de l'autre* (Montreal: V1B Editeur, 1982).

22. Jacques Lacan, "Some Reflections on the Ego," *International Journal of Psychoanalysis,* vol. 34, no. 1, p. 12.

23. Jacques Derrida, *Glas,* p. 65.

8 What Takes Place in the Dark

1. Clifford Geertz, "The Uses of Diversity," *Michigan Quarterly Review* (Ann Arbor: University of Michigan, 1986).

2. Ludwig Wittgenstein, *Culture and Value,* trans. Peter Winch (Chicago: University of Chicago Press, 1984), p. 74e.

3. Gananath Obeyesekere, *The Work of Culture: Symbolic Transformation in Psychoanalysis and Anthropology* (Chicago and London: University of Chicago Press, 1990).

4. For Obeyesekere's own definition of logocentrism, see ibid., p. 277.

5. See ibid., pp. 278–79.

6. Richard Rorty, "On Ethnocentrism: A Reply to Clifford Geertz," *Objectivity, Relativism, and Truth: Philosophical Papers,* vol. 1 (Cambridge: Cambridge University Press, 1991).

7. Ibid., p. 204.

8. The expression "wet" liberalism is interesting in itself given all the endless discussions in feminist literature about the association of the female body with fluids (cf. Drucilla Cornell, *Beyond Accommodation: Ethical Feminism, Deconstruction, and the Law* (New York: Routledge, Chapman and Hall, 1991) and the corresponding disparagement of fluidity and wetness. Psychoanalysis has certainly helped us explain why we use certain words disparagingly in both our "public" and our "private" discourse. We will come back to this discussion when I turn to how the economies of desire within North American culture are "colored."

9. Rorty, "On Ethnocentrism," p. 203.

10. Geertz, "The Uses of Diversity," p. 112.

11. Ibid.

12. Ibid., p. 115.

13. Ibid., p. 118.

14. Ibid., p. 123.

15. Ludwig Wittgenstein, *Remarks on Frazer's "Golden Bough,"* ed. Rush Rhees, trans. A. C. Miles (Atlantic Highlands, N.J.: Humanities Press, 1979), p. 5e.

16. Obeyesekere, *The Work of Culture*, p. 90.

17. Like Obeyeskere himself, I am using this expression advisedly, but it will become important to my discussion of Jacques Lacan's specific contribution to the critique of logocentrism.

18. Sigmund Freud, *The Interpretation of Dreams*, Standard Edition, vol. 4 (1900; London: The Hogarth Press, 1981).

19. Obeyesekere, *The Work of Culture*, p. 55 (emphasis in original).

20. Ibid., p. 281 (emphasis in original) (citations omitted).

21. See, generally, Paul Ricoeur, *Freud and Philosophy: An Essay on Interpretation* (New Haven: Yale University Press, 1977).

22. See, generally, Ferdinand de Saussure, *Course in General Linguistics* (London: Fontana, 1974).

23. Jacques Lacan, *Ecrits: A Selection,* trans. Alan Sheridan (New York: W. W. Norton and Company, 1977), p. 161. Originally published as *Ecrits* (Paris: Editions du Seuil, 1966).

24. For an excellent discussion of the relationship of Saussure's structural linguistics to Lacan's theory of the unconscious, see Samuel Weber, *Return to Freud: Jacques Lacan's Dislocation of Psychoanalysis,* trans. Michael Levine (Cambridge, Mass.: Cambridge University Press, 1991), pp. 25–40. Originally published as *Rückkehr zu Freud: Jacques Lacan Enstellung du Psychoanalyse* (Berlin: Verlag Ullstein GmbH, 1978).

25. Lacan, *Ecrits,* p. 147.

26. Ibid., p. 126.

27. Ibid., p. 150.

28. We will return to why this correction of Obeyesekere's tendency to ontologize the unconscious because of his own desire to develop a nonlogocentric approach to culture can have important political implications.

29. Obeyesekere, *The Work of Culture,* p. 282 (emphasis in the original).

30. Ibid., p. 288.

31. The "inessential woman" is a phrase coined by Elizabeth Spelman in the title of her book. Elizabeth V. Spelman, *Inesssential Woman: Problems of Exclusion in Feminist Thought* (Boston: Beacon Press, 1988).

32. Nancy Fraser and Linda J. Nicholson, "Social Criticism without Philosophy: An Encounter between Feminism and Postmodernism," in *Feminism/Postmodernism,* ed. Linda J. Nicholson (New York: Routledge, Chapman and Hall, 1990), p. 31.

33. For a brilliant analysis of how black masculinity is symbolized, see bell hooks, "Representations: Feminism and Black Masculinity," in *Yearing: race, gender, and cultural politics* (Boston: South End Press, 1990), pp. 65–77.

34. Jacquelyn Dowd Hall, " 'The Mind That Burns in Each Body': Women, Rape, and Racial Violence," in *Powers of Desire: The Politics of Sexuality,* ed. Ann Snitow,

Christine Stansell, and Sharon Thompson (New York: Monthly Review, 1983), p. 332.

35. Ibid., p. 333.

36. Obeyesekere, *The Work of Culture,* p. 288.

Bibliography

Ackerman, Bruce. *Social Justice in the Liberal State* (New Haven: Yale University Press, 1980).

Adorno, Theodor. *Negative Dialectics*, trans. E.B. Ashton (New York: Seabury Press, 1973).

———. and Max Horkheimer. *Dialectic of Enlightenment*, trans. John Cumming (New York: Herder and Herder, 1972).

———. *Minima Moralia: Reflections from Damaged Life*, trans. E.F.N. Jephcott (London: New Left Books, 1974).

Arato, Andrew and Jean Cohen. *Civil Society and Political Theory*, ed. Thomas McCarthy (Cambridge, Mass.: The MIT Press, 1992).

Arendt, Hannah. *The Human Condition* (Chicago: University of Chicago Press, 1958).

———. "What is Authority?" in *Between Past and Future: Eight Exercises in Political Thought* (New York: Penguin Books, 1977).

Austin, Regina. "The Black Women, Sisterhood, and the Difference/Deviance Divide," *New England Law Review*, vol. 26 (Spring 1992), p. 877.

Baker, C. Edwin. "Neutrality, Process, and Rationality: Flawed Interpretations of Equal Protection," *Texas Law Review*, vol. 58 (1980), p. 1029.

Barrett, Karen. "Date Rape—A Campus Epidemic?," *Ms.*, Sept. 1982, p. 48.

Barthes, Roland. *Mythologies*, trans. Annette Lavers (New York: Noonday Press, 1972).

Bataille, Georges. *Theory of Religion*, trans. Robert Hurley (New York: Zone Books, 1989). Originally published as *Theorie de la Religion* (Paris: Éditions Gallimard, 1973).

Beckett, Samuel. *Happy Days* (New York: Grove Press, 1961).

Bishop, Elizabeth. "One Art," in *The Complete Poems 1927–1979* (New York: Farrar, Straus and Giroux, 1983).

Blanchot, Maurice. *The Unavowable Community*, trans. Pierre Joris (New York: Station Hill Press, 1983). Originally published as *La Communauté Inavouable* (Paris: Les Éditions de Minuit, 1983).

Blumenburg, Hans. *Work on Myth*, trans. Robert M. Wallace (Cambridge, Mass.: The MIT Press, 1985). Originally published as *Arbeit am Mythos* (Frankfurt am Main FRG: Suhrkamp Verlag, 1979).

Bork, Robert. "Neutral Principles and Some First Amendment Problems," *Indiana Law Journal*, vol. 47 (1971), p. 1.

Boyle, James. "The Politics of Reason: Critical Legal Theory and Local Social Thought," *University of Pennsylvania Law Review*, vol. 133 (1985), p. 721.

Butler, Judith. *Gender Trouble: Feminism and the Subversion of Identity* (New York: Routledge, Chapman and Hall, Inc., 1990).

Cixous, Hélène. "Sorties: Out and Out: Attacks/Ways Out/Forays," in Hélène Cixous and Catherine Clément, *The Newly Born Woman*, trans. Betsy Wing (Minneapolis: University of Minnesota Press, 1986). Originally published as *La jeune née* (Paris: Union Générale d'Éditions, 1975).

———. "Tancredi continues," in *Writing Differences: Readings from the seminar of Hélène Cixous*, ed. Susan Sellers (New York: St. Martin's Press, 1988).

Clément, Catherine and Hélène Cixous. *The Newly Born Woman*, trans. Betsy Wing (Minneapolis: University of Minnesota Press, 1986). Originally published as *La jeune née* (Paris: Union Générale d'Éditions, 1975).

Cohen, Jean and Andrew Arato. *Civil Society and Political Theory*, ed. Thomas McCarthy (Cambridge, Mass.: The MIT Press, 1992).

Cornell, Drucilla. *Beyond Accommodation: Ethical Feminism, Deconstruction, and the Law* (New York: Routledge, Chapman and Hall, Inc., 1991).

———. "Dialogic Reciprocity and the Critique of Employment at Will," *Cardozo Law Review*, Vol. 10 (1989), p. 1575.

———. and Adam Thurschwell. "Feminism, Negativity, Intersubjectivity," in *Feminism as Critique: On the Politics of Gender*, ed. Seyla Benhabib and Drucilla Cornell (Minneapolis: University of Minnesota Press, 1987).

———. "Feminist Legal Reform, Systems Theory and the Philosophy of the Limit," in *Deconstruction and the Possibility of Justice*. (New York: Routledge, Chapman and Hall, Inc., 1992).

———. "Gender, Sex and Equivalent Rights," in *Feminists Theorize the Political*, eds. Judith Butler and Joan W. Scott (New York: Routledge, Chapman and Hall, Inc., 1991).

———. *The Philosophy of the Limit*, (New York: Routledge, Chapman and Hall, Inc., 1992).

———. "Sex Discrimination Law and Equivalent Rights," *Dissent*, vol. 38 (1991), p. 400.

Cover, Robert. "The Supreme Court, 1982 Term—Foreword: Nomos and Narrative," *Harvard Law Review*, vol. 97 (1983), p. 68.

Dalton, Clare. "An Essay in the Deconstruction of Contract Doctrine," *Yale Law Journal*, vol. 94 (1985), p. 997.

Derrida, Jacques. "Des Tours de Babel," in *Difference in Translation*, ed. and trans. Joseph F. Graham, (Ithaca: Cornell University Press, 1985).

———. and Christie V. McDonald. "Choreographies," *Diacritics*, vol. 12 (summer, 1982), reprinted in *The Ear of the Other: Otobiography, Transference, Translation*, ed. Christie V. McDonald, trans. Peggy Kamuf (Lincoln: University of Nebraska Press, 1985). Originally published as *L'oreille de l'autre* (Montreal: V1B Editeur, 1982).

————. "Deconstruction in America" (interview with James Creech, Peggy Kamuf, and Jane Todd), *Critical Exchange*, vol. 17 (1985), p. 15.

————. *Dissemination*, trans. Barbara Johnson (Chicago: University of Chicago Press, 1981).

————. *Glas*, trans. John P. Leavey, Jr. and Richard Rand (Lincoln: University of Nebraska Press, 1986). Originally published as *Glas* (Paris: Éditions Galilée, 1974).

————. "Form and Meaning: A Note on the Phenomenology of Language," in *Margins of Philosophy*, trans. Alan Bass (Chicago: University of Chicago Press, 1982). Originally published as *Marges de la philosophie* (Paris: Les Éditions de Minuit, 1972).

————. *Positions*, trans. Alan Bass (Chicago: University of Chicago Press, 1981).

————. "The Politics of Friendship," in *Journal of Philosophy*, vol. 80, no. 2 (1988), p. 632.

————. *The Post Card: From Socrates to Freud and Beyond*, trans. Alan Bass (Chicago: University of Chicago Press, 1987). Originally published as *La Carte Postale* (Paris: Flammarion, 1980).

————. "Signature Event Context," in *Limited Inc.*, trans. Samuel Weber and Jeffrey Mehlman (Evanston, Ill.: Northwestern University Press, 1988). First published in *Glyph*, Vol. I (1977).

————. *Signéponge/Signéponge*, trans. Richard Rand (New York: Columbia University Press, 1984).

————. *Spurs: Nietzsche's Styles/Éperons: Les Styles de Nietzsche*, trans. Barbara Harlow (Chicago: University of Chicago Press, 1978).

————. *The Truth in Painting*, trans. Geoffrey Bennington and Ian McLeod (Chicago: University of Chicago Press, 1987).

————. "White Mythology: Metaphor in the Text of Philosophy," in *Margins of Philosophy*, trans. Alan Bass (Chicago: University of Chicago Press, 1982). Originally published as *Marges de la philosophie* (Paris: Les Éditions de Minuit, 1972).

————. *Who Comes After the Subject?*, eds. Eduardo Cadava, Peter Connor, Jean-Luc Nancy (New York: Routledge, Chapman and Hall, Inc., 1991).

Duras, Marguerite. *India Song*, trans. Barbara Bray (New York: Grove Press, 1976). Originally published as *India Song* (Paris: Éditions Gallimard, 1973).

————. *The Malady of Death*, trans. Barbara Bray (New York: Grove Press, 1986). Originally published as *La maladie de la morte* (Paris: Les Éditions de Minuit, 1982).

————. *The Ravishing of Lol Stein*, trans. Richard Seaver (New York: Pantheon Books, 1966). Originally published as *Le ravissement de Lol V. Stein* (Paris: Éditions Gallimard, 1964).

————. *The Vice-Consul*, trans. Ellen Ellenbogn (New York: Grove Press, 1968). Originally published as *Le Vice-Consul* (Paris: Éditions Gallimard, 1966).

Dworkin, Andrea. *Intercourse* (New York: The Free Press, 1987).

Dworkin, Ronald. "Law as Interpretation," *Texas Law Review*, vol. 60 (1986).

————. *Law's Empire* (Cambridge, Mass.: The Belknap Press of Harvard University Press, 1986).

————. *A Matter of Principle* (Cambridge, Mass.: Harvard University Press, 1985).

———. "My Reply to Stanley Fish (and Walter Benn Michaels): Please Don't Talk About Objectivity Any More," in *The Politics of Interpretation*, ed. W.J.T. Mitchell (Chicago: University of Chicago Press, 1983).

Estrich, Susan. *Real Rape* (Cambridge, Mass.: Harvard University Press, 1987).

Faludi, Susan. *Backlash: The Undeclared War Against American Women* (New York: Crown Publishers, 1991).

Fish, Stanley. "Anti-Professionalism," *Cardozo Law Review*, vol. 7 (1986), p. 645.

———. "Fish v. Fiss," *Stanford Law Review*, vol. 36 (1984).

———. "Working on the Chain Gang: Interpretation in Law and Literature," *Texas Law Review*, vol. 60 (1982).

Fiss, Owen. "Objectivity and Interpretation," *Stanford Law Review*, vol. 34 (1982).

Fraser, Nancy and Linda J. Nicholson. "Social Criticism Without Philosophy: An Encounter Between Feminism and Postmodernism," in *Feminism/Postmodernism*, ed. Linda J. Nicholson (New York: Routledge, Chapman and Hall, Inc., 1990).

Freud, Sigmund. *The Interpretation of Dreams (1900)*, Standard Edition (S.E.), vol. 4 (London: The Hogarth Press, 1981).

Galenson, Eleanor and Herman Roiphe. "The Impact of Early Sexual Discovery on Mood, Defensive Organization, and Symbolization," *The Psychoanalytic Study of the Child*, vol. 26 (1972), p. 195.

Gallop, Jane. *The Daughter's Seduction: Feminism and Psychoanalysis* (Ithaca: Cornell University Press, 1982).

Geertz, Clifford. "The Uses of Diversity," *Michigan Quarterly Review* (Ann Arbor: University of Michigan, 1986).

Gilligan, Carol J. *In A Different Voice: Psychological Theory and Women's Development* (Cambridge, Mass.: Harvard University Press, 1982).

———. "Feminist Discourse, Moral Values, and the Law—A Conversation," *Buffalo Law Review*, vol. 34 (1984) (transcript of discussion between Ellen C. DuBois, Mary C. Dunlap, Carol J. Gilligan, Catharine A. MacKinnon and Carrie J. Menkel-Meadow held 19 October 1984 at the Law School of S.U.N.Y. Buffalo as part of the James McCormick Mitchell Lecture Series).

Gordon, Robert. "Critical Legal Histories," *Stanford Law Review*, vol. 36 (1984).

Hall, Jacquelyn Dowd. "'The Mind that Burns in Each Body': Women, Rape, and Racial Violence," in *Powers of Desire: The Politics of Sexuality*, ed. Ann Snitow, Christine Stansell, and Sharon Thompson (New York: Monthly Review, 1983).

Hegel, Georg W. F. *Phenomenology of Mind*, trans. J. Baillie (New York: MacMillan, 1931).

———. *Philosophy of Right*, trans. T. M. Knox (New York: Oxford University Press, 1952).

Horkheimer, Max and Theodor Adorno. *Dialectic of Enlightenment*, trans. John Cumming (New York: Herder and Herder, 1972).

hooks, bell. *Yearning: race, gender and cultural politics* (Boston: South End Press, 1990).

Irigaray, Luce. *This Sex Which Is Not One*, trans. Catherine Porter (Ithaca: Cornell

University Press, 1985). Originally published as *Ce sexe qui n'est pas un* (Paris: Les Éditions de Minuit, 1977).

———. *Speculum of the Other Woman*, trans. Gillian Gill (Ithaca: Cornell University Press, 1985).

Joyce, James. *Finnegan's Wake* (New York: Penguin Books, 1939).

Kairys, David. "Law and Politics," *George Washington Law Review*, vol. 52 (1984), p. 243.

Kant, Immanuel. *Critique of Practical Reason and Other Works On the Theory of Ethics*, trans. T. Abbot (6th ed. 1909). Reprinted in *Kant Selections*, ed. T. Greene (1929).

Kaplan, Louise. *Female Perversions* (New York: Anchor Books, Doubleday, 1991).

Kellman, Mark. "Trashing," *Stanford Law Review*, vol. 36 (1984), p. 305.

Kennedy, Duncan. "The Structure of Blackstone's Commentaries," *Buffalo Law Review*, vol. 28 (1979), p. 211.

Kingson, Jennifer A. "Women in the Law Say Path is Limited by 'Mommy Track,'" *The New York Times*, August 8, 1988, p. A1.

Krell, David Farrell. *Postponements: Woman, Sensuality and Death in Nietzsche* (Bloomington: Indiana University Press, 1986).

Kristeva, Julia. *The Kristeva Reader*, ed. Toril Moi (New York: Columbia University Press, 1986).

———. *Powers of Horror* (New York: Columbia University Press, 1982).

———. "Woman Can Never Be Defined," in *New French Feminisms: An Anthology*, ed. Elaine Marks and Isabelle de Courtivron (New York: Schocken Books by arrangement with University of Massachusetts Press, 1980). Originally published as "La femme, ce n'est jamais ça," *Tel Quel* (Autumn 1974).

———. "Women's Time," in *Feminist Theory: A Critique of Ideology*, eds. Nannerl O. Keohane, Michelle Z. Rosaldo and Barbara C. Gelpi (Chicago: University of Chicago Press, 1982).

Lacan, Jacques. *Écrits: A Selection*, trans. Alan Sheridan (New York: W.W. Norton and Company, 1977). Originally published as *Écrits* (Paris: Éditions du Seuil, 1966).

———. *Feminine Sexuality: Jacques Lacan and the École Freudienne*, eds. Juliet Mitchell and Jacqueline Rose, trans. Jacqueline Rose, (New York: W. W. Norton and Company, 1985).

———. "Some Reflections on the Ego," *International Journal of Psychoanalysis*, vol. 34, no. 1, p. 12.

Laclau, Ernesto and Chantal Mouffe. *Hegemony and Socialist Strategy* (London: Verso, 1985).

Langton, Rae. "Whose Right? Ronald Dworkin, Women, and Pornographers," *Philosophy and Public Affairs*, vol. 19 (1990), p. 311.

Law, Sylvia. "Rethinking Sex and the Constitution," *University of Pennsylvania Law Review*, vol. 132 (1984), p. 955.

Levinas, Emmanuel. *Otherwise Than Being or Beyond Essence*, trans. Alphonso Lingis (The Hague: Martinus Nijhoff Publishers, 1981).

Lorde, Audre. *Sister Outsider* (Trumansburg, New York: The Crossing Press, 1984).

Lovibond, Sabina. *Realism and Imagination in Ethics* (Minneapolis: University of Minnesota Press, 1983).

Luban, David. "Fish v. Fish or, Some Realism About Idealism," *Cardozo Law Review*, vol. 7 (1986).

Lyotard, Jean-Francois. *The Differend: Phrases in Dispute*, trans. George Van Den Abbeele (Minneapolis: University of Minnesota Press, 1988). Originally published as *Le Différend* (Paris: Les Éditions de Minuit, 1983).

MacKinnon, Catharine A. *Feminism Unmodified: Discourses on Life and Law* (Cambridge, Mass.: Harvard University Press, 1987).

———. "Feminism, Marxism, Method, and the State: An Agenda for Theory," *Signs*, vol. 7 (1982)

———. "Feminism, Marxism, Method, and the State: Toward Feminist Jurisprudence," *Signs*, vol. 8 (1983).

———. *Sexual Harassment and the Working Woman: A Case of Working Women* (New Haven: Yale University Press, 1979).

———. *Toward a Feminist Theory of the State* (Cambridge, Mass.: Harvard University Press, 1989).

Mann, Judy. "The Demeaning 'Mommy Track': Separate and Unequal," *The Washington Post*, March 15, 1989, p. C3.

McCarthy, Thomas. "The Politics of the Ineffable: Derrida's Deconstructionism," *Philosophical Forum*, vol. 21, nos. 1–2, (Fall-Winter 1989–90).

McDonald, Christie V. and Jacques Derrida. "Choreographies," *Diacritics*, vol. 12 (summer, 1982), reprinted in *The Ear of the Other: Otobiography, Transference, Translation*, ed. Christie V. McDonald, trans. Peggy Kamuf (Lincoln: University of Nebraska Press, 1985). Originally published as *L'oreille de l'autre* (Montreal: V1B Editeur, 1982).

Menache, Samuel. "Promised Land," in *Collected Poems* (Maine: The National Poetry Foundation, University of Maine, 1986).

Michelman, Frank. "Forward: Traces of Self-Government," *Harvard Law Review*, vol. 100 (1986), p. 17.

Minh-ha, Trinh T. *Woman, Native, Other: Writing PostColoniality and Feminism* (Bloomington: Indiana University Press, 1989).

Montrelay, Michèle. "Inquiry Into Femininity," in *French Feminist Thought: A Reader*, ed. Toril Moi (New York: Basil Blackwell, 1987).

Mouffe, Chantal and Ernesto Laclau. *Hegemony and Socialist Strategy* (London: Verso, 1985).

Nagel, Thomas. *Partiality and Equality* (Princeton: Princeton University Press, 1991).

Nedreaas, Torborg. *Nothing Grows by Moonlight*, trans. Bibbi Lee (Lincoln: University of Nebraska Press, 1987). Originally published as Av Maneskinn Gror Det Ingenting (1947; W. Nyaard: H. Aschehoug & Co., 1975).

Nicholson, Linda J. and Nancy Fraser. "Social Criticism Without Philosophy: An Encounter Between Feminism and Postmodernism," in *Feminism/Postmodernism*, ed. Linda J. Nicholson (New York: Routledge, Chapman and Hall, Inc., 1990).

Nietzsche, Friedrich W. *Beyond Good and Evil*, ed. and trans. Walter Kaufmann (Princeton: Princeton University Press, 1967).

Obeyesekere, Gananath. *The Work of Culture: Symbolic Transformation in Psychoanalysis and Anthropology* (Chicago and London: University of Chicago Press, 1990).

Peirce, Charles S. *The Collected Papers of Charles Sanders Peirce, 1931–1934*, eds. Charles Hartshorne and Paul Weiss (Cambridge, Mass.: The Belknap Press of the Harvard University Press, 1960).

Peller, Gary. "The Metaphysics of American Law," *California Law Review*, vol. 73 (1985), p. 1151.

Rawls, John. *A Theory of Justice* (Cambridge: The Belknap Press, 1971).

Reich, Wilhelm. *Reich Speaks of Freud: Conversations with Kurt Eissler*, eds. Mary Higgins and C.M. Raphael (New York: Farrar, Strauss & Giroux, 1967).

Ricoeur, Paul. *Freud and Philosophy: An Essay on Interpretation* (New Haven: Yale University Press, 1977).

———. *Time and Narrative*, vol. 3 (1984), p. 155.

Roiphe, Herman and Eleanor Galenson. "The Impact of Early Sexual Discovery on Mood, Defensive Organization, and Symbolization," *The Psychoanalytic Study of the Child*, vol. 26 (1972), p. 195.

Rorty, Richard. "On Ethnocentrism: A Reply to Clifford Geertz," *Objectivity, relativism, and truth, Philosophical Papers*, vol. I (Cambridge: Cambridge University Press, 1991).

———. "Feminism and Pragmatism," *Michigan Quarterly Review*, (Ann Arbor: University of Michigan, Winter, 1991), p. 231.

———. *Philosophy and the Mirror of Nature* (Princeton: Princeton University Press, 1979).

Rose, Jacqueline. "Introduction II," in *Feminine Sexuality*, p. 51.

Rosenfeld, Michel. *Affirmative Action and Justice* (New Haven: Yale University Press, 1991).

Sandel, Michael J. *Liberalism and the Limits of Justice* (Cambridge, Mass.: Harvard University Press, 1982).

de Saussure, Ferdinand. *Course in General Linguistics* (London: Fontana, 1974).

Schroeder, Jeanne. "Abduction from the Seraglio: Feminist Methodologies and the Logic of Imagination," *Texas Law Review*, Vol. 70 (1991), p. 109.

———. "Feminism Historicized: Medieval Misogynist Stereotypes in Contemporary Feminist Jurisprudence," *Iowa Law Review*, vol. 75 (1990), p. 1135.

Schwartz, Felice. "Management Women and the New Facts of Life," *Harvard Business Review*, January–February 1989, p. 65.

Sen, Amartya. *Choice, Welfare and Measurement*, (Cambridge, Mass.: The MIT Press, 1982).

——. *Resources, Values and Development*, (Cambridge, Mass.: Harvard University Press, 1984).

Shiffrin, Steven. *The First Amendment, Democracy, and Romance* (Cambridge, Mass.: Harvard University Press, 1990).

Spelman, Elizabeth V. *Inessential Woman: Problems of Exclusion in Feminist Thought* (Boston: Beacon Press, 1988).

Stick, John. "Can Nihilism be Pragmatic?," *Harvard Law Review*, vol. 100 (1986), p. 387.

Sunstein, Cass. "Interest Groups in American Public Law," *Stanford Law Review*, vol. 38 (1985), p. 38.

Thurschwell, Adam and Drucilla Cornell. "Feminism, Negativity, Intersubjectivity," in *Feminism as Critique: On the Politics of Gender*, ed. Seyla Benhabib and Drucilla Cornell (Minneapolis: University of Minnesota Press, 1987).

Unger, Robert Mangabeira. *The Critical Legal Studies Movement* (Cambridge, Mass.: Harvard University Press, 1986).

Weber, Samuel. *Institution and Interpretation* (Minneapolis: University of Minnesota Press, 1987).

——. *Return to Freud: Jacques Lacan's Dislocation of Psychoanalysis*, trans. Michael Levine (Cambridge: Cambridge University Press, 1991). Originally published as *Rückkehr zu Freud: Jacques Lacan Enstellung du Psychoanalyse* (Berlin: Verlag Ullstein GmbH, 1978).

Wechsler, Herbert. "Toward Neutral Principles of Constitutional Law," *Harvard Law Review*, vol. 73 (1959), p. 1.

Wellmer, Albrecht. "On the Dialectic of the Modern and the Post-Modern," *Praxis International*, vol. 4, no. 337 (1985).

West, Robin. "The Difference in Women's Hedonic Lives: A Phenomenological Critique of Feminist Legal Theory," *Wisconsin Women's Law Journal*, vol. 3 (1987).

——. "Jurisprudence and Gender," *University of Chicago Law Review*, vol. 55 (1988), p. 1.

Williams, Wendy. "Equality's Riddle: Pregnancy and the Equal Treatment-Special Treatment Debate," *New York University Law Review*, vol. 14 (1985), p. 325.

Wittgenstein, Ludwig. *Culture and Value*, ed. G.H. von Wright, trans. Peter Winch (Oxford: Basil Blackwell, 1980).

——. *On Certainty*, eds. G.E.M. Anscombe and G.H. von Wright, trans. D. Paul and G.E.M Anscombe (Oxford: Basil Blackwell, 1969).

——. *Philosophical Investigations*, trans. G.E.M. Anscombe (Oxford: Basil Blackwell, 1968).

——. *Remarks on Frazer's "Golden Bough,"* ed. Rush Rhees, trans. A.C. Miles (Atlantic Highlands, New Jersey: Humanities Press, 1979).

——. *Tractatus Logico-Philosophicus*, trans. D.F. Pears & B.F. McGuinness (New York: Routledge, Chapman and Hall, Inc., 1971).

————. *Zettel*, trans. G.E.M. Anscombe (Berkeley: University of California Press, 1967).

Wittig, Monique. *The Lesbian Body*, trans. David Le Vay (Boston: Beacon Press, 1975). Originally published as *Le Corps Lesbien* (Paris: Les Éditions de Minuit, 1973).

Wolf, Christa. *Cassandra: A Novel and Four Essays*, trans. Jan Van Heurck (New York: Farrar, Straus and Giroux, 1984).

Index

Abelin-Sas, Graciela, 145, 217–218
    n.76
Abortion, 143–145
Ackerman, Bruce, 123, 201 n.23,
    214 n.35
Adorno, Theodor, 14, 22, 26, 51,
    198 n.15, 199 n.37, 203 n.57
Allegory and myth, 57–59, 73, 80,
    86, 90, 99, 104, 107–108
Arato, Andrew, 158–159, 221 n.4
Arendt, Hannah, 8–9, 156–162,
    164, 166–168, 221 nn. 1,9
    polis, 8, 156–161
    homo faber, 161, 164
    viva activia, 162, 166–167
Aristotle, 158–160, 221 n.5
Austin, Regina, 209 n.74
AZT, 147

Baker, C. Edwin, 123, 214 n.35
Barrett, Karen, 209 n.73, 216 n.49
Barthes, Roland, 107, 211 n.132
Bataille, Georges, 103, 108, 208
    n.64
Beckett, Samuel, 138–139, 218
    n.77
Biddle, A. Collin, 217 n.168
Bishop, Elizabeth, 104, 211 n.120
Blackmun, Justice, 144, 149, 153,
    218 n.86, 219 n.12
Blanchot, Maurice, 207 n.60
Blumenburg, Hans, 108, 212 n.136
Bork, Robert, 123, 214 n.36
Bowers v. Hardwick, 148–149,
    153, 219 n.4
Boyle, James, 203 n.48
Butler, Judith, 4, 195 n.6, 215 n.45

Capability, 7
Carey v. Population Services Interna-
    tional, 148, 219 n.7
Castration, 131, 137
Chodorow, Nancy, 189
Civic friendship, 8
Cixous, Hélène, 46, 56, 80–81,
    105, 109, 134, 203 n.3, 207
    n.62, 210 n.119, 211 n.123,
    212 n.137, 216 n.63
Cleaver, Eldridge, 78
Clément, Catherine, 207 n.61, 212
    n.137, 216 n.63
Cohen, Jean, 158–159, 221 n.4
Columbus, Christopher, 30
Communitarian, 2–3
    new, 2–3
Community, 3–4
Convention, 1–3, 5, 12–13, 18
Cornell, Drucilla, 41, 195 n.11, 196
    n.18, 202 n.29, 205 n.22, 206
    n.38, 210 n.94, 212 n.4, 213
    n.8, 216 n.59, 218 n.83, 219–
    220 n.13, 222 n.8
Cover, Robert, 44, 203 n.58
Critical Legal Studies, 23–24, 28,
    31, 35
Critique, 1–3, 5, 9, 13–21

Dalton, Clare, 202 n.38
Date Rape, 209 n.73
Death, *see mourning*
Deconstruction, 4–5, 66, 71, 97,
    152
Délaissement, 150, 155
Deleuze, Giles, 48, 50
Democracy, 8–10

participatory, 4, 8–10
Derrida, Jacques, 6, 8, 10–11, 14–
    15, 21, 38–39, 44, 50, 52–56,
    64–69, 86–97, 101, 133, 140,
    150–153, 156, 159, 165–168,
    195 n.13, 196 n.20, 198 n.14,
    200 n.22, 202 n.40, 204 n.15,
    205 n.23, 206 n.25, 209 n.77,
    210 n.99, 216 n.57, 217 n.74,
    220 n.13, 221 n.14, 222 n.21
  Derridian hymen, 6, 95–96
  invagination, 95
Deviationist Doctrine, 31–34
Difference, 1, 7, 10
  class, 6
  of lesbians and gay men, 7
  sexual, 5–7, 11
  women, 6
Differend, 82–83, 109
Disastrologies, 49
Discrimination
  sexual orientation discrimination,
    148
  sex discrimination, 6, 147–155
Duras, Marguerite, 79–81, 88, 207
    n.53
Dworkin, Andrea, 100–101, 210
    n.110, 217 n.72
Dworkin, Ronald, 13–14, 16, 23–
    24, 28, 30, 33, 35–36, 38, 40,
    123–124, 136, 197 n.7, 199
    n.1, 200 n.18, 202 n.37, 214
    n.35

Equality, 7–9
  capability and well-being, 7
  economic, 5
  women's, 8–9
Equivalency, 7
Equivalent rights, 6–8, 147, 153–
    155
Essentialism, 6
  inessentialism, 58
Estrich, Susan, 84, 209 n.71

Faludi, Susan, 211 n.129
Feminine Sexual Difference, 5–6,
    57–59, 70–73, 78–79, 80, 84,
    106–108

Feminine, 4–8, 11, 45–54, 57–60,
    74–76, 78–87, 91, 98, 101,
    108–110, 213 n.7
Femininity, 5–8, 11, 45–46, 51
Feminism, 1, 5–6, 11, 46
First Amendment, 118, 122, 127,
    214 n.21
Fish, Stanley, 1–4, 12–22, 27, 197
    n.5, 198 n.10, 199 n.35
  anti-professionalism, 3, 12–13,
    16–17
  internal realism, 27
  social systems, 1
Fiss, Owen, 13–14, 197 n.8
Fraser, Nancy, 178, 189–190, 223
    n.32
Freud, Sigmund, 85, 164, 179,
    181–182, 184, 189, 223 n.18
Fuckee, 134, 210 n.113
Fuckor, 134, 210 n.113
Fucking, see Penis

Galenson, Eleanor, 137–138, 143,
    213 n.9
Gallop, Jane, 210 n.93
Geertz, Clifford, 170–177, 182,
    187, 190, 194, 222 n.1
Gender, 5, 9–10
Gilligan, Carol J., 59, 109–110,
    212 n.139
Gordon, Robert, 17, 198 n.25
Griswold v. Connecticut, 148, 219
    n.5

Hall, Jacquelyn Dowd, 191, 223
    n.34
Hegel, Georg W. F., 20, 25–27,
    30–32, 34–35, 51, 54, 202
    n.26, 215 n.46
Heterosexuality, 5, 7, 46, 50, 148–
    152
Homosexuality, 50, 148–153
Horkheimer, Max, 51, 203 n. 57
hooks, bell, 101, 130–131, 216
    n.54, 223 n.33
Husserl, Edmund, 63–67, 69–70

Identity, 1–2, 6, 10
Indeterminacy thesis, 24–25, 34, 40

Irigaray, Luce, 80–81, 96, 106,
    115, 134–135, 140–142, 207
    n.61, 210 n.119, 211 n.124,
    213 n.11, 215 n.43, 217 n.69,
    218 n.82

Johnson, Barbara, 73
Jouissance, 47–51, 104, 210 n.119,
    216 n.63
Joyce, James, 57, 97, 107, 204 n.1,
    210 n.104, 211 n.130,
    fici-fact, 97

Kairys, David, 199 n.2
Kant, Immanuel, 2–3, 42, 203 n.53
    noumenal self, 1–3
Kaplan, Louise, 218 n.84
Kellman, Mark, 202 n.38
Kennedy, Duncan, 17, 77
Kingson, Jennifer A., 220 n.19
Krell, David F., 45–50, 52, 56, 203
    n.1, 204 n.5
    postponements, 45–47, 50
Kristeva, Julia, 60, 73–77, 80–81,
    85, 108, 204 n.5, 207 n.41,
    212 n.134, 218 n.80

Lacan, Jacques, 7–10, 50–54, 57,
    60, 74–75, 85–87, 89–93, 102,
    109, 136–137, 143–144, 150–
    153, 156, 163–165, 167–168,
    171, 181–184, 186–187, 196
    n.17, 204 n.6, 206 n.39, 207
    n.42, 209 n.75, 212 n.138, 217
    n.74, 219 n.13, 222 n.22, 223
    n.23
    the Imaginary, 163–165
    the Symbolic, 164
Laclau, Ernesto, 128, 215 n.47
Langton, Rae, 124, 214 n.37
Law, Sylvia, 123, 214 n.35
Lesbianism, 5, 7
Levinas, Emmanuel, 40, 203 n.49
Lorde, Audre, 130, 216 n.53
Love, 48–56
Lovelace, Linda, 118
Lovibond, Sabina, 198 n.30
Luban, David, 198 n.27

Lyotard, Jean-François, 82–83, 208
    n.67, 215 n.48

MacKinnon, Catharine A., 5–7, 71,
    81, 97–107, 110, 112–123,
    126, 128–136, 138–142, 146,
    208 n.65, 210 n.111, 211
    n.121, 212 n.1, 213 n.6, 214
    n.22, 216 n.50, 217 n.66, 218
    n.79
Mamet, David, 78
Mann, Judy, 220 n.19
Marx, Karl, 161
Masculine, 4, 8
McCarthy, Thomas, 167, 222 n.19
McDonald, Christie V., 91, 209
    n.80, 216 n.62, 220 n.13, 222
    n.21
Menache, Samuel, 56, 204 n.23
Metaphor, 182–186
Metonymy
    metonymic displacement, 6
Michelman, Frank, 200 n.23
Minh-ha, Trinh T., 59, 204 n.3
Mommy Track, 154–155, 220 n.18
Montrelay, Michèle, 60, 204 n.4,
    208 n.63
Mouffe, Chautal, 128, 215 n.47
Mourning, 53–56,

Nagel, Thomas, 123–128, 214 n.39
Natality, 41
    birthed, 41
Naturalism, 6
Nedreaas, Torborg, 144, 218 n.87
Nicholson, Linda J., 189–190, 223
    n.32
Nietzsche, Friedrich W., 7, 45–52,
    56, 203 n.2, 204 n.9
    death and pestilence, 45–46, 49–
    50, 52, 54–55
    sensuality, 45–46
Nomos, 36, 40, 44
Normative reality
    patriarchy, 5, 7–8

Obeyesekere, Gananath, 171, 178–
    181, 184–187, 189–190, 193,
    222 n.3, 223 n.16, 224 n.36

Oedipus complex, 163
Otherness, 174, 190

Peirce, Charles S., 3–4, 23–29, 32, 35–37, 40–44, 199 n.4, 200 n.19, 202 n.41, 203 n.50
  secondness, 26, 29–30
  thirdness, 26–27
Peller, Gary, 203 n.48
Phallic Mother, 51–52, 75, 101
Phallogocentricism, 14
Phallus, 10, 131, 137–140
  penis, 137–138
  transcendental signifier, 152
Poeisis, 156
Pornography, 113, 118, 122–128, 143
Positivism, 178
Postmodernism, 2, 4, 205 n.22
Pragmatism, 4
Psychoanalysis, 9–10

Race and Nationality
  african american, 188
  native american, 175–177
  whiteness, 9, 131, 188, 190–193
  blackness, 9, 131, 189–193
  culture, 186–187
Radical Feminist, 9
Rape, 113, 117–118, 128–129, 131
Rawls, John, 2, 123, 195 n.1, 214 n.35
Real, 5
Reason, 3
Recollective Imagination, 4, 23–24, 31–32, 38, 42–43
Reconstruction, 30, 38
Reich, Wilhelm, 220 n.17
Rich, Adrienne, 82
Ricoeur, Paul, 133, 181, 216 n.61, 223 n.21
Roe v. Wade, 148, 219 n.6
Roiphe, Herman, 213 n.9
Rorty, Richard, 4, 171–175, 177, 182, 186–187, 189, 194, 195 n.7, 215 n.44, 222 n.6
  anti-anti-ethnocentricism, 172
Rose, Jacqueline, 220 n.14
Rosenfeld, Michel, 213 n.5

Sameness
  sameness ideology, 140–143
  likeness, 141
de Saussure, Ferdinand, 181–184, 223 n.22
  parole, 181
  langue, 181, 189
Schott, Robin, 217 n.67
Schroeder, Jeanne, 212 n.3
Schwartz, Felice, 220 n.19
Sen, Amartya, 7, 116, 155, 195 n.15, 213 n.12, 221 n.21, capability, *see Capability*
Shiffrin, Steven, 123, 214 n.35
Sittlich, 12, 14–15, 20, 27, 32–33, 36
Sittlichkeit, 25–26, 32, 34, 40
Spelman, Elizabeth V., 204 n.2, 223 n.31
Stick, John, 203 n.47
Subject, 2–4
  I, 20–21
  autonomy, 2
Sunstein, Cass, 126–127, 200 n.23, 215 n.41
Synchronization, 35–36, 39

Temporality
  past, 23–31, 33, 38–39
  might have been, 30, 34, 200 n.23
  future, 24, 26–30, 33, 36, 38
Thurschwell, Adam, 206 n.38, 210 n.94, 213 n.8, 219 n.13
Title VII, 147–148, 150, 153–154, 219 n.2
Transformation, 1–4, 6–7, 9–10

Unconscious, 9–10, 171–172, 177–194
Unger, Roberto M., 31–34, 36, 202 n.31

Virginia v. American Bookseller Association, Inc., 122

Weber, Samuel, 41, 43, 203 n.52, 223 n.24

Webster v. Reproductive Health Services, 144
Wechsler, Herbert, 123, 214 n.36
Wellmer, Albrecht, 18–19, 198 n.28
West, Robin, 60–64, 67, 69–74,
    76–78, 80–82, 84–85, 205 n.6,
    206 n.30, 207 n.48, 208 n.66
  biology, 9, 62–63, 76, 88
  Aristotelian naturalism, 70
White, Justice, 148–149
Williams, Wendy, 213, 214
    n.35

Wittgenstein, Ludwig, 12–19, 21–
    22, 26, 170–171, 177–178,
    180, 187, 196 n.2, 197 n.4,
    198 n.24, 199 n.36, 222 n.2,
    223 n.15
  anti-essentialism, 196 n.3
  therapy, 14
Wittig, Monique, 134–136, 217
    n.71
Wolf, Christa, 109–111, 210 n.108,
    212 n.140
Woman, 5–6, 9–11